# Instant Advantage.com

*Steve Kirshoff · Stephen Mendonca*

Prentice Hall PTR
Upper Saddle River, New Jersey 07458
http://www.phptr.com

ISBN 0-13-017908-6

90000

9 780130 179081

Editorial/Production Supervision: *Kathleen M. Caren*
Acquisitions Editor: *Karen McLean*
Editorial Assistant: *Michael Fredette*
Manufacturing Manager: *Alexis R. Heydt*
Marketing Manager: *Bryan Gambrel*
Art Director: *Gail Cocker-Bogusz*
Interior Series Design: *Meg VanArsdale*
Cover Design Director: *Jerry Votta*
Cover Design: *Design Source*
Compositor: *April R. Messina*
Copyeditor: *Mary Loudin*

© 2000 Compaq Computer Corporation
Published by Prentice Hall PTR
Prentice-Hall, Inc.
Upper Saddle River, NJ 07458

The publisher offers discounts on this book when ordered in bulk quantities.
For more information, contact

Corporate Sales Department,
Prentice Hall PTR
One Lake Street
Upper Saddle River, NJ 07458
Phone: 800-382-3419; FAX: 201-236-7141
E-mail (Internet): corpsales@prenhall.com

Printed in the United States of America

10 9 8 7 6 5 4 3 2 1

ISBN 0-13-017908-6

Prentice-Hall International (UK) Limited, *London*
Prentice-Hall of Australia Pty. Limited, *Sydney*
Prentice-Hall Canada Inc., *Toronto*
Prentice-Hall Hispanoamericana, S.A., *Mexico*
Prentice-Hall of India Private Limited, *New Delhi*
Prentice-Hall of Japan, Inc., *Tokyo*
Pearson Education Asia Pte. Ltd.
Editora Prentice-Hall do Brasil, Ltda., *Rio de Janeiro*

# Contents

iii

# Introduction

## THE EMERGING DIGITAL ECONOMY

Over the past few years, the impact of the Internet has focused our attention on the new imperatives of innovation and speed. In ways that are still being defined, the Internet has unleashed new technologies and practices that are transforming our business environment. Not surprisingly, business and industry leaders are reacting swiftly, realizing that their companies must come to grips with the Internet if they want to succeed. They have found that there are no easy answers; there is no haven from the struggle; there is no turning back the clock.

From market capitalization to pricing to channel delivery, conventional business practices are undergoing radical change. Established business models are being redefined in the wake of technologies that remove the barriers between buyers and sellers, simplify collaboration and decision-making, and shorten time to market in every industry. What we have instead is a digital economy, emerging from the new possibilities opened up by e-commerce, global value chains, and e-communities. And it's booming before our very eyes:

- Business-to-business e-commerce surpassed $100 billion in 1999 and is forecasted to reach or exceed $1.3 trillion by 2003.
- Today, almost 200 million people are online worldwide; and in the next four years, that figure will have soared past 500 million.
- By the end of 1999, $1 billion in US venture capital funds was invested per week in e-commerce start-ups.

The 1999 holiday shopping season produced a threefold increase in online sale over the previous year. The growth trend continues to be explosive and relentless– across industries, global regions, and classes of users—and cannot be dismissed as bubble. Corporations and governments have begun focusing on the Internet's impli cations and opportunities in earnest.

Underlying the new economy is what can be called a quantum shift in the inde of economic value. According to classic economic theory, a company's value wa determined by its capital assets—its physical and monetary capital, plus the preser value of the income stream derived from those assets. The effectiveness of the com pany in managing its assets would eventually result in a market presence and a pel ceived market value. As rational as this may seem to us, we find ourselves wooed b a new and revolutionary model of economic value, exemplified by the many Interne startup companies whose market cap has soared beyond the wildest expectation. They represent a new breed of businesses that create value through services and tecl nology initiatives.

In this new environment, information—not physical assets—has become th new currency, the new gold standard. What increasingly determines a company's mal ket value today relates to the following considerations:

- How information is leveraged to enhance responsiveness to customers.
- How information is used to accelerate sound business decisions.
- How a company uses its online presence to differentiate itself in the mar- ketplace.
- How information is generated, stored, and applied to business purposes.

Information management is, in this sense, the key to building shareholder value, a leading companies are proving over and over again.

# COMPETITIVE PRESSURES

As a result of the new marketing paradigm, business executives everywhere are unde pressure to catch up with the market leaders that have established their presence in th new marketplace. Companies are finding it harder to win new contracts, largel because of competition from fast-moving, innovative players who embraced th Internet early in the game. Online buyers are known to make a snap judgment about company's worth in the course of a few mouse clicks. Companies must therefore fin ways to project their value to a customer through the initial experience of their wel site. An instant advantage has become the selling proposition of our times.

Easier said than done. For many, the hurdles seem insurmountable. Beleaguered by changing trends and global competition, business and IT executives are concerned about the skills and technological resources needed to provide customers with the services they demand. They are asking themselves, "What do we need to do to act quickly to meet customers' raised expectations? What kind of business model or paradigm must we adopt to seize new e-commerce opportunities? What do we need to do to be agile and fast moving? How can we expand our offerings and enter new markets with our current infrastructure and service providers?" They are in search of an approach that balances stability and risk, while keeping their IT investments aligned with their business goals and initiatives.

# NEED FOR EFFECTIVE ENTERPRISE STRATEGIES

Many business executives originally thought that being an Internet player only required them to develop a pretty storefront on the World Wide Web, and that would be that. However, the success of new e-business leaders like priceline.com and auto-bytel.com proved them wrong. A piecemeal approach to the massive changes associated with a digital economy falls far short of what is needed to achieve success and sustainable growth.

What is really needed is the realignment of business strategy with Information Technology (IT). While many have paid lip service to this alignment, companies operating successfully in the new Internet environment are living it. If one looks carefully at those companies, it becomes clear that the CIO not only reports directly to the CEO, but serves on the company's executive committee, working hand-in-hand with the CEO in the development of business and IT strategy. Not surprisingly, companies now are making the previously unprecedented decision to promote the CIO to the top spot in the company, as was recently the case at Compaq Computer Corporation.

We are now entering the second phase, or early maturation stage, of the Internet and the digital economy it spawned. The early winners are scrambling to protect their territory by developing comprehensive strategies for winning in a new environment. Companies that lost ground by being cut out of traditional supply chains—they have been "disintermediated"—are struggling to play catch-up any way they can. IT System Integrators are becoming IT/Business Strategy Integrators. Moreover, IT vendors are responding to customers by developing a 24/7 internal infrastructure that will be modular and accommodate explosive business growth. The IT industry is responding vigorously.

# INSTANTADVANTAGE.COM

This book is written for CEOs, CIOs, and other decision-makers in business and
who need to understand and embrace the new dynamics unleashed by the Internet.
will help them develop comprehensive strategies for adapting to the realities of t
digital economy. This book will also help those who have begun the journey to onli
success but are in need of a refresher, or those who are looking for confirmation a
additional guidance along the way.

Unlike most books that survey e-commerce trends, this book offers business a
IT managers the strategic pointers they need to begin their journey toward transfor
ing their companies into e-businesses. Our discussion of the issues will help lay t
foundation for a business and IT plan of attack that takes into account the lesso
learned by the e-commerce pioneers. Interspersed throughout the book are prov
approaches and best practices of some of the most successful e-businesses around t
world. The book offers specific guidelines for developing e-solutions, modeled af
the examples of the best-known online companies. In addition, we let you hear dire
ly from CEOs and others who talk about the lessons they learned in leading the
respective companies into the online era.

# GAINING INSTANT ADVANTAGE

We believe the transformational strategies and tactics presented here will enable y
to lay the groundwork for creating an online business in your enterprise. We carne
ly hope that, by absorbing and applying the concepts presented in this book, you wi

- Anticipate the impact of the emerging online ecosystem on your business.
- Discover ways to better service and retain your customers.
- Create and sustain competitive advantage through a 24/7 services model.
- Leverage IT through constant innovation in the face of continuing market
  disruptions.
- Establish a results-oriented plan with measurable ROI and benefits.
- Maximize the payback across the total enterprise value chain.

You will find that the success factors in the digital economy come down to thes

1. Understanding and embracing the dynamics of the new online marketplace.

2. Leveraging Internet technologies to engage customers, partners, and suppliers in the creation of value.

3. Building an e-culture in your company that rewards vision, innovation, and the entrepreneurial spirit.

# Acknowledgements

W hen it comes to writing a book, we live in the best of times and the worst of times. The new millennium has brought with it a rush of new perspectives, against the backdrop of a global marketplace that spins and churns with relentless energy. Much to write about. Yet, the rate of change is simply astonishing: what's innovative today quickly becomes standard practice somewhere or loses ground to the next leap forward. So, our hope is that this book will stand the test of time—for at least a few Internet years!

Fortunately, our focus has been on the enduring importance of staying relevant in the marketplace, while leveraging the power of the Internet and the dynamics of the digital economy. It is our hope that the principles, practices, and guidance offered here have lasting value for decision-makers tasked with transforming their business for success in the e-world taking shape around us.

The contents of this book reflect many months of experience with the evolving Internet marketplace. We have tried to represent best practices from a range of market firms, and have selected solution implementations that exemplify simplicity, resilience, agility, and the reduction of risk. Those values define the path to e-business success.

Certain market statistics and business viewpoints were drawn with permission from reports by the GartnerGroup, Forrester Research, Inc., International Data Corporation. and Market Data Group. In addition, we acknowledge and appreciate personal contributions and insights from Lee Sudan, Sam Kirchoff, Mike Krodel, Sean Gresh, Dan Wise, and Arlene Leggio who lent their talents and helped keep this project on course.

We also owe our appreciation to the many who shared their comments and sug
gestions; we certainly couldn't have gone the distance without the support and encour
agement of our colleagues at Compaq. In fact, it's fair to say that the entrepreneuria
spirit of this company was the inspiration and impetus behind the message of ou
book.

The Authors

# Part 1
## Turning Business Inside Out: Disruptions and Opportunities

# 1

# The Internet, Convergence, and a New Inflection Point

*Summary:* In this chapter, we discuss the Internet and how the convergence of technologies has enabled it to change the business landscape, consumer behavior, and society. More than any other technological development in the 20$^{th}$ century, the Internet's impact represents an inflection point that signals a new way of determining total economic value. We also discuss the emergence of new models—or paradigms—and the new rules of engagement for participating in an e-commerce business environment.

A full decade after its emergence, the Internet continues to astonish us with its power to bring sweeping change and create new vistas of opportunity. No one could have predicted the impact it has had on virtually every sector of industry and every walk of life. The early adopters and pioneers took bold risks and reaped unprecedented rewards. However, most leading corporations and industries face daunting challenges and steep learning curves. It's fair to say that the global business community was caught unaware.

Stories abound about new uses for Internet technology, new Internet companies, and how organizations old and new are becoming believers:

Hotmail, the first free e-mail service, was the brainchild of a twenty-something entrepreneur, Sabeer Bhatia. In revolutionizing the way people communicate online, Bhatia was rewarded with $400 million in Microsoft stock, which he received when he sold his company to Microsoft in 1998. Even so, Hotmail is a testament to bulldog tenacity. Bhatia was turned down by 19 venture-capital firms when he was trying to get Hotmail up and running in 1995. "Back when I started Hotmail," Bhatia explains, "people said the Internet was a fad. No one believed in it."

The financial world has changed since then. As of the year 2000, more than half of the US venture capital funding goes to Internet startups. Successful IPOs of companies like Amazon.com ($561 million) and eBay ($1.9 billion) have been replicated and surpassed by startups in a variety of industries. Stock markets around the world have smiled approvingly at such firms because they hold great promise of liquid and represent a dedicated focus on creating specific customer value.

If you track the more dramatic changes in business, using lines on a chart, y can mark them accurately with the use of inflection points. In his book, *Only* Paranoid Survive, Andrew Grove, Chairman of Intel Corporation, defines an infle tion point as "…a major change in the way business is done. These major chang might occur when there are shifts of 10X magnitude in the power, vigor, and comp tence of customers, suppliers, competition, new entrants, substitutes, and compleme tors. To succeed, you have to make major changes to the business model."

Of the many inflection points in technology during the last three decades, fe are more dramatic than the evolution of Information Technology (IT). Advances processor-design, high-speed networks, storage, and related technologies have shru development cycles and increased transaction processing rates. The resulting benef of speed, power, and flexibility have raised the stakes of market competiti Companies can be proactive in responding to customer needs, or even using chan itself as a strategic weapon (see Figure 1.1).

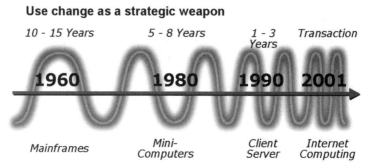

**Use change as a strategic weapon**

| 10 - 15 Years | 5 - 8 Years | 1 - 3 Years | Transaction |
|---|---|---|---|
| 1960 | 1980 | 1990 | 2001 |
| Mainframes | Mini-Computers | Client Server | Internet Computing |

**Figure 1.1**

Internet-Enabled Business Drivers

In the IT domain, the computing model has progressed from centralized p cessing to distributed computing to client/server computing. With the rise of brows based computing, we are seeing different versions of a client-to-services model.

It's important to note the key differences in these successive models. In client/server environment, users rely on applications running on a server, which in t may be supported by central repositories or utilities, resident in a mainframe compu This hierarchical system of processing places limitations on both client and server terms of access to network data, throughput, and flexibility. Users could also be impa ed by support issues like incompatible application protocols between client and serv

By contrast, Internet-driven computing provides browser-enabled access dire ly to resources on the Internet, which permits connectivity to unlimited nodes, rega less of physical location. Data resides at or near the source, allowing an almost continuous refreshing of data by the content provider. By enabling timely and prompt access to network data, the Internet-centric paradigm vastly expands the possibilities of individual computing, collaborative workflow, storage, and application integration across the enterprise.

The paradigm of Internet computing has triggered far-reaching changes in the business environment. Companies find they cannot be complacent with past successes. They must rethink and regroup, with an eye to new opportunities for securing customers faster and serving them in radically better ways.

The stage was set for the online economy in the 1980s with the development of a viable worldwide network connecting the world's largest research and development facilities. In the early 1990s, browser technology emerged. For the first time, it enabled a uniform method of communication and access of information and other repositories of data across different computer platforms.

Few, however, were prepared for the magnitude of the change that was created by the Internet. Rarely have changes in technological, personal, social, and business environments happened so quickly. The advent of the telephone, automobile, radio, semiconductors, and television all altered society—but nothing compares to the impact of the Internet.

An estimated 10 million new users sign on to the Internet every month. At this rate, the Internet community will increase from 140 million users in 1999 to more than 500 million over the next three years.

As a result of the Internet, we are seeing the rise of new companies, service provider communities, and rapidly-forming online industry exchanges for business-to-business commerce. Competition has emerged almost instantaneously. New wealth has been created. Not since the gold rush or the era of oil discovery have so many personal fortunes been made so quickly.

The Internet is transforming our world—the business landscape, consumer behavior, educational curricula, and the social worlds of people across the globe, as illustrated in Figure 1.2. Perhaps in the not-too-distant future, children will learn how to create Internet-ready, hyperlinked text just as they learn grammar today.

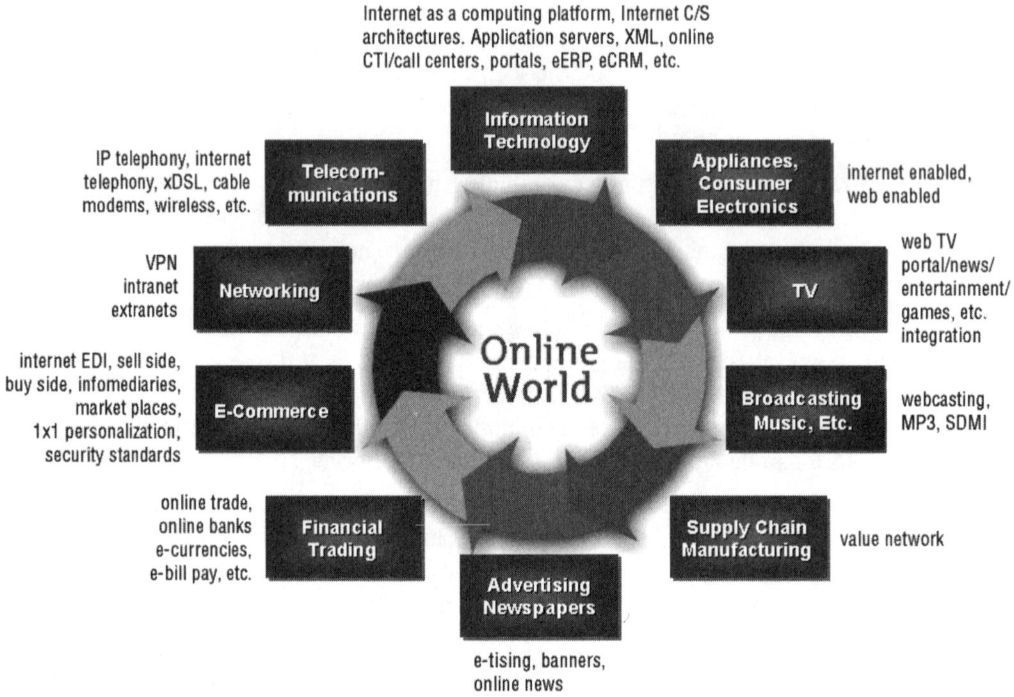

Internet as a computing platform, Internet C/S
architectures. Application servers, XML, online
CTI/call centers, portals, eERP, eCRM, etc.

IP telephony, internet
telephony, xDSL, cable
modems, wireless, etc.

**Information Technology**

**Telecommunications**

**Appliances, Consumer Electronics**

internet enabled,
web enabled

VPN
intranet
extranets

**Networking**

**TV**

web TV
portal/news/
entertainment/
games, etc.
integration

**Online World**

internet EDI, sell side,
buy side, infomediaries,
market places,
1x1 personalization,
security standards

**E-Commerce**

**Broadcasting Music, Etc.**

webcasting,
MP3, SDMI

online trade,
online banks
e-currencies,
e-bill pay, etc.

**Financial Trading**

**Supply Chain Manufacturing**

value network

**Advertising Newspapers**

e-tising, banners,
online news

**Figure 1.2**

The Impact of the Online World *Used with the permission of Market Data Group, LLC.*

# A NEW PARADIGM ......................

What has emerged is a global online economy that encompasses work, entertainme
research, purchasing, selling, and business. It is an economy with a new breed of cc
sumers, suppliers, vendors, competitors, and business processes. It has caused the
definition of such concepts as growth, assets, liabilities, commerce, and informati
technology blueprints.

People around the world now have access to the same information and the sa
media for conducting business. Some experts temper this whole notion by pointing
that only a certain percentage of the world is connected. However, even with just
10% of the world's population connected, the impact on business and economy wo
be enormous. To fully comprehend the impact this has had on business, it helps to ta
the perspective of Total Economic Value. Instead of looking at one piece of the p
zle at a time, the Total Economic Value analysis takes a complete end-to-end view
the internal and external change factors. This approach gives a clearer picture of w
it takes to participate in the emerging online world successfully.

# HE EMERGENCE OF A NEW
# ΓOTAL ECONOMIC VALUE" MODEL . . . . . . . . . . . . . .

The impact of the Internet is being felt in every corner of the enterprise. Recent market valuations of online enterprises, such as eToys, Yahoo!, Lycos, Amazon, eBay, e-Trade, and Charles Schwab, have given them the power to acquire and invest, putting their traditional brick-and-mortar competitors at a disadvantage. This fact has not gone unnoticed by the corporate giants and is now getting the full attention of management in many Fortune 500 companies that wish to become enterprise dot.coms. These companies, including GE, Allied Signal, Merrill Lynch, Toys 'R Us, Universal, and others in the music industry and the media, have now started to focus heavily on the online aspects of their businesses.

To get a true picture of Total Economic Value, an enterprise must assess the overall benefits not only to the company, but also to its partners and customers, and their ability to reshape the market ecosystems. Enterprises that create higher Total Economic Value for their virtual network of collaborators and suppliers will be in a better position to serve customers, attract new partners, and win in the emerging ecosystem.

Today, the Total Economic Value of the emerging online landscape is being shaped by an entirely new set of factors. For example, in this new world, information is more important than physical assets for increasing revenue, lowering costs, increasing profitability, and retaining customers.

A startling change reflected in the new model is that the traditional emphasis on percentage of gross margins may no longer be a significant factor. The asset and gross margin requirements for profitable online businesses are substantially different from traditional enterprise models. To get a true picture of Total Economic Value, you need to re-evaluate all prior economic assumptions.

Table 1.1 compares key differences between conventional and online economic values.

**Table 1.1**   Key Differences between Conventional and Online Economic Values

| Conventional Economic Value | New Economic Value |
| --- | --- |
| Driven by leveraging physical assets and associated financial business models | Driven by leveraging information assets and associated business models |
| Generally focused on optimizing internal factors that enhance the company's market value | Focused on the internal/external factors that enhance the total customer enterprise, as well as partner and supplier values |
| Differentiation based on benefits/attributes of product and solutions | Differentiation based on benefits/attributes of services throughout the buy-supply-service life cycle |
| Increase business by selling more products and solutions to many new customers | Value made higher by capturing larger share of customer wallet |
| Growth potential driven by expansion of physical presence in the world | Growth potential achieved by reaching the global customer and leveraging the Internet ecosystem |
| Cost and time-to-market goals achieved by minimizing the friction in enterprise supply chain transactions | Cost and time-to-market goals achieved by minimizing buffers with zero-latency supply chain transactions |
| Product design requirements based on historical data | Product designed on JIT infrastructure |
| Economic value increased by: <br> Operational excellence <br> Corporate relationships <br> Technology innovation | Value increased by: <br> Excellence in customer information <br> 1:1 relationships <br> Innovative services |
| Manufacturing/inventory management by field forecasts | Manufacturing/inventory management by orders |
| Cost reduction by focusing on internal process optimizations | Costs decreased by leveraging internal and external processes and capabilities |
| IT as a function supporting the computing requirements of the business | IT as an enabler for using change as a competitiv weapon |
| Economic value change, both increase and decrease, takes place in calendar years | Change in much faster time. Requires creation of new barriers/switching considerations |
| Enterprise valuation based on the potential of price-to-earnings ratios | Enterprise valuation based on the potential of business innovation |

# USTOMER-DRIVEN ECONOMIC VALUE . . . . . . . . . . .

The major reversal in the business equation caused by the advent of the Internet is that the buyer is now in control of the business transaction.

In the online world, the customer decides what is important and how he or she wants to buy. The customer is armed with more information than ever before, and that information is based on a much broader view in terms of time, competition, and comparative values. An enterprise that has information about customer needs and can present customers with relevant solutions, services, and information will motivate them to keep coming back and, in the process, will create more Total Economic Value.

The asset that will continue to deliver competitive advantage to an enterprise is in-depth information on the customer's demographics, psychographics, and online buying behaviors. In the past, the emphasis was on product innovation and excelling in operations. In the new environment, that same level of innovation and excellence needs to be applied to the methods, sources, and tools used to capture and leverage customer information.

Growth of the enterprise is no longer limited by its physical presence, but by its ability to tailor information to individual customer needs. An enterprise must take into consideration that it has an international audience—so choice of languages, color schemes, and graphics should have broad appeal.

The international arena means more competition. Even major companies like AOL can't get to the top spot in most European countries because local competitors are winning by customizing their offerings to suit local tastes.

In the new model, the cost reduction processes for purchasing, invoicing, marketing, selling, and support are also different. In the old economic value model, cost reduction is achieved by focusing on the optimization of internal processes. It is easier to link cost cutting to internal processes than to external ones. The emerging online solutions allow for group purchasing arrangements. Many companies such as Compaq, IBM, and GE are saving hundreds of millions of dollars by automating their procurement processes and using new trade exchanges and hubs.

Interactive customers now drive Total Economic Value, where information attributes are as valuable as product attributes. The ability to get the right content, information, services, and support in the fastest and most suitable manner creates higher value and satisfaction. Many companies have reduced their costs by millions of dollars by having customers help themselves. While the enterprise saves, customers win, by maximizing their time and effort in the buying cycle.

Once a customer places an online personalized order, the information is used to update the manufacturing/inventory systems, and JIT orders are sent to the suppliers. This process reduces inventory-holding costs and provides the opportunity for capturing customer information. In this "just-in-time" transaction cycle, the enterprise also creates the best value for partners by lowering transaction costs and increasing the understanding of the customer.

Viewed from an IT perspective, these JIT scenarios are similar to what tl Gartner Group has called "zero-latency." Zero-latency architectures and workflc reduce the time (and resource) buffers between sequential processes, requiring tl enterprise to respond in new ways. For example, there would be little point in trir ming transaction times between back-end processes and call centers if there wasn't way to provide a continuous real-time flow of information to those call centers. Th is what we call real-time or zero-latency operational data.

# IN-DEPTH UNDERSTANDING OF CUSTOMERS . . . . . .

To be successful, an enterprise must provide relevant information and services f product selections, configuration, comparison, financing, insurance, shipping, a tracking. The enterprise must also have an in-depth understanding of customer pu chasing scenarios. Moreover, partner enterprises must be engaged in the value n work for the best overall solution for the customer.

In the old model, sales professionals collected customer information. In this sc nario, customer information usually remained with the sales force, isolated in th heads, and never got back to the enterprise in a timely or useful fashion. The n online world gives companies the opportunity to capture customer data on an ente prise level, consistently and accurately.

The last point in the table about company valuation should be clear. Intern startups and dot.com companies have multiples based on their perceived future inr vation and online operational excellence, provided they have good business model

To succeed in the new model, enterprises will need to create strategies on he to jump to the higher Total Economic Value curve faster and more effectively than competition.

There are many examples of enterprises that did business the old way decades, but have now embraced the new value curve. One such company that breathing new life into a century-old business model is Bloemenveiling Aalsmeer.

# BLOEMENVEILING AALSMEER— HE NETHERLANDS . . . . . . . . . . . . . . . . . . . . . . .

Besides generating new breeds of businesses, the Internet has rocked the foundation of old-line companies and has brought about many refreshing outcomes. One example is Bloemenveiling Aalsmeer, a growers' cooperative in Aalsmeer, the Netherlands. It conducts the largest horticultural auction in the world.

The operation generates more than $1.4 billion (US) in annual revenue and sells more than 17 million flowers and 2 million plants each day. The Aalsmeer auction outsells all other flower markets by almost any measure—annual turnover, daily trading volume (50,000 transactions a day), and physical space. Bloemenveiling Aalsmeer's complex is the world's biggest indoor commercial facility.

Today, Bloemenveiling Aalsmeer is transforming its thriving, century-old business. Anticipating the opportunities and risks of global markets, the co-op has built an e-market exchange that expands the reach of growers and ensures faster delivery of flowers and plants.

Bloemenveiling Aalsmeer's new Web-based trading solution, FlowerAccess (floweraccess.com), is already helping the co-op to form strong bonds with overseas customers. FlowerAccess currently supports 500 worldwide retailers.

"We're bringing the business back to the players, the growers, and buyers," says Jean Paul Aubrun, Marketing and Sales Director of the EVA, the e-commerce business unit of the 7,000-grower co-op, which serves 1,700 registered buyers. "FlowerAccess is the first application of an enterprise-wide trading infrastructure that we are building based on Microsoft Windows NT software and Compaq servers."

The cooperative enlisted growers and buyers in devising an easy-to-use front end for the trading environment that works across countries, currencies, time zones, and cultures. FlowerAccess builds in the distribution expertise of the wholesalers that is an essential link in the e-commerce supply chain between the growers (who cut, sort, and pack their product) and the retailers.

"Our sales team is promoting this service throughout the United States," relates Hans Maarschalk, owner of the Florisina Group. "We expect to serve 5,000 retailers through FlowerAccess by the end of 1999. That's just five percent of the US market."

This customer-driven approach suits such fertile markets as the United States, a country that lags far behind Europe in per-capita flower consumption.

# THE ONLINE ECONOMY:
# THREAT OR OPPORTUNITY? . . . . . . . . . . . . . . . . .

An Internet-enabled online economy represents tremendous opportunity for those wil ing to change. For those resisting the changing economy, the Internet represents a threa

In a period of radical transformation of the business environment, many que tions need to be answered. How does one learn to navigate through treachero waters? To whom should one listen? Who are the leaders that will emerge as champ ons in the new economy? What is the role of Information Technology?

How do planning business strategies differ from the way they were done in pre-online economy? Do we prepare for this inflection point in the same way that v have done in the past? Or, does it require a new look at everything from custom behavior to business processes? In such a fast changing environment, how does o define a business strategy for creating competitive advantage? Specifically, how do one create a blueprint for the next generation of Information Technology to accelera the advantage faster than others? How does one quantify results and demonstrate tl return on IT investments?

In a pre-online economy, business planners and strategists would approach the questions and challenges by scanning the market landscape to determine user need Then they would define a strategy to create differentiation and cost advantages.

Accordingly, IT strategies were aligned with the business strategy and proces es to gain maximum value from supply chain automation. This created competiti advantage, improved productivity, reduced costs, and improved relations with cu tomers.

# NEW STRATEGIES FOR NEW TIMES . . . . . . . . . . . . .

Traditional strategies, however, do not work today. Things are happening too fa Markets change in a matter of months, and planning cycles have been shortened ev more. In his book, *Thought Leaders—Insights On the Future of Business*, Jol Chambers, CEO of Cisco, points out that Cisco is now planning in Internet yea rather than calendar years. It is a matter of necessity.

Traditional approaches do not work because of the changed role of distributi channels, the emergence of new intermediaries, and the new role of Informati Technology in the corporation. In anticipation of and in response to a new online eco omy, Amazon.com created a new paradigm that enlists the support of 200,000+ ass ciates who constantly funnel business to them. This model was implemented witho the additional heavy investment of money, organization, and time.

Because of the Internet, new paradigms are being developed that create opportunities for enterprises. Earlier models focused primarily on a company's need to achieve competitive advantage. Newer models center on creating new opportunities through the improvement of customer service, increased productivity, more efficient operations, cost reduction, and new order-to-cash business models.

Another reflection of imaginative new paradigms for doing business in the age of the Internet is the development of a new jargon that enshrines the values of enterprise differentiation and customer intimacy. *Immediacy, personalization 1:1, disintermediate, and agile* are some examples. These words refer to the ability of companies to create a new advantage in relationship building by personalizing content and serving it up in ways that keep customers coming back.

# HANGE OR DIE . . . . . . . . . . . . . . . . . . . . . . . . .

For an enterprise to succeed in the online economy, it needs to make fundamental changes in how its value proposition is created and delivered. Being first may have many advantages, but it does not guarantee continued success. History has shown that repeatedly. Prodigy and CompuServe were ahead in online business. Although AOL is the market leader today, the threat of competition looms on the horizon with the merger of MindSpring and Earthlink.

Risks are as great as rewards in the new online economy. According to a Gartner Group study completed in September 1999, 75% of all e-business projects will fail because of poor business planning and a lack of understanding of the technology.

Even amazon.com, the stock market's darling of the e-commerce world, is not immune to outside perceptions of poor business planning. In one business day, October 28,1999, Amazon's stock lost 10% of its value when analysts downgraded the company, including Prudential Security's cut from a "strong buy" to a "hold." The downgrades were based on analysts' growing impatience with Amazon's continued losses and their perception that Amazon did not have a clear business plan.

"It does seem the plan changes every quarter," reports Dalton Chandler, an analyst with Needham & Co. "We really want to see a road map. Just lay out the plan— say 'Here's how it works'."

To win in the new emerging environment, one must look at the fundamentals of change that have affected the business processes and peoples' values.

New techniques have to be devised, which can truly take advantage of the new capabilities of the technology. Best practices must be explored. Unless these steps are taken, even the most powerful technology will not make an impact.

## NEW RULES OF ENGAGEMENT . . . . . . . . . . . . . . .

As a result of our observations and work with hundreds of the leading online comp
nies in the world, we have seen common themes emerge that can be translated into t
new rules of engagement for an online economy. These rules of engagement embra
tactics, strategies, processes, and the quality of an enterprise's personnel to he
achieve the maximum Total Economic Value in the emerging online environment.

Here are five rules of engagement, which can help you buck conventional w
dom as you grapple with the challenges and opportunities in the new global onli
economy:

### Rule One: Address the Big Picture

Do not simply analyze selected trends in stovepipe markets based on previous hist
ry. In this emerging online economy, the boundaries of supply chain processes ha
shifted dramatically. To create a new value proposition and facilitate delivery of t
value proposition, the whole ecosystem has to be explored. Anticipate emerging tren
rather than react to current events.

### Rule Two: Be Guided by the Customer's Proposition

Think in terms of a customer proposition rather than your value proposition. That w
be more meaningful in the customer's decision-making process.

Immediately deploy Internet capabilities to make it easy for customers to
business with you. Do not wait to form a master plan, although you will certainly ne
one. Get started and then create the grand plan—a blueprint for building your Intern
presence, which is detailed below in rule 5.

### Rule Three: Reinvent Your Enterprise

Reinvent the way you work with your customers and do business. Change busine
models and processes to match the dynamics of the new global online econor
Create a best-in-class customer value procurement strategy rather than a value del
ery strategy. Use the online technologies to improve operations, relationships, a
innovation. Force fitting existing methods will get the job only half done and even c
ate confusion and disadvantage. A market that is hot today may not be a good be
few months later.

## Rule Four: Build an Enterprise.com

Create an enterprise culture that has fully embraced the Internet and IT to conduct business, service customers, develop strategy, collaborate with partners, and structure workflow. Today, IT is used as an enabler rather than as a business creator. In the new economy, information is key to success. Initiatives, such as knowledge management, customer relationship management, enterprise resource planning, business intelligence, and collaboration, have to be augmented with the new online capabilities; since customers are in control, the transformed enterprise is focused to make it easier to do business with them.

## Rule Five: Create an Infrastructure Blueprint

The infrastructure blueprint responds in Internet time, increases the ease of doing business, and creates new business opportunities faster than the competition. Without this, the efforts won't go anywhere. Your infrastructure should be secure, scalable, standards-based, manageable and, most important of all, enable a 24/7 service model.

A continuous commerce services infrastructure is critical for doing business in a business environment that operates 24 hours a day, around the world, and depends on inter-enterprise collaboration.

A realistic strategy needs a results-oriented framework that allows consistent execution of corporate, business, and departmental initiatives. Begin by defining overall goals and outcomes. These could be: personalizing relationships faster, converting page views to higher order rates, increasing customer satisfaction by making it easy for customers to do business, decreasing time to market, reducing costs, or selling more effectively. Be sure to give the highest priority to customer-facing processes. Develop a focused plan of applications that can deliver measurable value. Integrate with legacy systems. Create a results path with technology as a means to deliver it. Staff and fund adequately.

The framework in Figure 1.3 captures the essence of these five rules. The circle reflects the scope of the online challenge and the four axes address enterprise priorities (see Rules 2 through 5). Excellence is achieved by simultaneous progress along all axes.

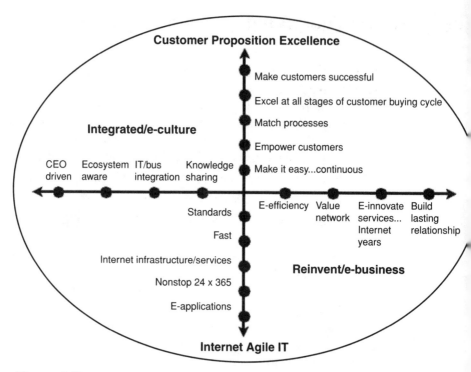

**Figure 1.3**

Global Online Ecosystem *Used with the permission of Market Data Group, LLC.*

# BEYOND RE-ENGINEERING ....................

Over the years, we have seen many instances where corporations that re-engineer core processes are now forced to redefine them all over again due to Internet-relat edicts from the top.

We have also seen cases where some of them created overarching IT framewor which do not meet their business needs in a timely fashion. In other cases, ad hoc bu ness needs have driven IT actions and created disparate islands of technology.

Our intent is to provide a framework of checks and balances for driving a cc sistent and measurable business and IT strategy, without slowing down the ability respond to change in Internet years.

The execution of these activities will vary from company to company, depen ing upon the needs and situation. Our focus is to provide planning tools, customer ca studies, and a discussion framework, which will help focus discussions and provi effective frameworks for the development of enterprise business/IT strategies.

# EGIN WITH QUESTIONS . . . . . . . . . . . . . . . . . . . . .

One of the best ways to get started is to reflect on your business and ask some fundamental questions:

- How does the Internet impact my business? What is the emerging customer proposition?
- Who is the best-in-class example of making it easy for customers to do business with them online—specifically in my business arena?
- How many of my critical business processes are being transformed—especially where they impact the customer or the value chain? Can we quantify the payoff?
- How many of my employees—and management in particular—have had first-hand experience with online business?
- How agile is my IT infrastructure and strategy in taking advantage of new business opportunities?

# 2

# Disruptive Changes and New Opportunities

....................

*S*ummary: *Change is difficult and often painful. It can also represent new and exciting opportunities. To respond to change, one must understand what is changing and why. In this chapter, we outline the major disruptive changes associated with the explosion and convergence of Internet technologies, and we discuss the new opportunities accompanying them. Chapter highlights include the following:*

- Changes in consumer and customer dynamics
- Total Economic Value and its impact on global online business
- A power shift toward customers; the role and importance of Internet-driven standards
- The creation of new IT deployment strategies
- The development of new services and processes

## DISRUPTIONS CREATE OPPORTUNITIES . . . . . . . . . . . .

The rapid-fire introduction of new technologies associated with the Internet is causing disruptive change in all markets. Before we discuss the new paradigms and rules of engagement for doing business in an online economy, it is important to consider the major disruptions and how they are affecting the new environment. Keep in mind that as each disruption is forcing major changes, each is also presenting new opportunities. We give them a twin label—disruptions and opportunities.

## Disruption #1:  New Financial Dynamics

New online companies are going against the grain and defying traditional principle of success. The traditional Wall Street stock price principles, for example, have bee shattered as some of these new companies have achieved higher valuations than th top Fortune 100 companies.

The valuation of many of these companies has allowed them to acquire larg amounts of capital, which is reinvested in the form of mergers, acquisitions, ar developments. Their valuations represent commonly shared perceptions that are base on new criteria not considered in the valuation of traditional companies—the impo tance of information, the positioning of a company, and the public's belief in a com pany's potential for growth in the coming years. Consider these examples:

- AOL's purchase of Netscape for $6 billion
- Amazon.com's investments in several companies that range from exchange.com for specialty rare books to drugstore.com
- Lycos's purchase of Peapod
- Yahoo!'s $3 billion acquisition of GeoCities to gain access to its millions of users and communities
- eBay's $250 million purchase of Kruse International, an auction house, and Billpoint, Inc.

In each case, the necessary capital for these acquisitions was created in the stoc market from investors' perceptions of immediate value and their belief in each com pany's potential for future earnings.

## Disruption #2:  Power Shifts from Sellers
## to Buyers

One of the most important dynamics driving the expansion of the global online env ronment is the shift of power in the business relationship from seller to buyer. All bus ness relationships now must assume a customer who is informed about all competitiv offerings, and who will insist that business be done the way the customer wants i where the customer wants it, and when the customer wants it. That means that key co porate systems will be exposed to customers, that "24/7" (continuous taken literall will be the standard, that one customized unit will be a standard batch, and that cu tomers can buy goods and services from anywhere, at anytime.

In a related development, customers are working together to increase their bu ing power. For example, groups of hospitals are working together to create a buyir hub for their needs. According to Forrester Inc., consumer groups like AARP ar AAA will use Internet communities to pool the buying power of geographically di persed constituents and match them with cooperative merchants. Corporate buyers will participate in auctions and bid for commodities like energy, newsprint, microchips, and other large volume items, seeking basic service at minimum prices.

## Disruption #3:  Self-Help Drives New Business Models

The business models of many companies such as Charles Schwab, DLJ, and Fidelity Investments have changed to accommodate the onslaught of online investing and trading by people who would rather help themselves than go through brokers. Some brokerage houses are expecting in excess of 50% of their trading business to be online in the next couple of years. Charles Schwab, which embraced the Internet early on, took the bold and unusual step of cannibalizing its own conventional broker business model rather than losing it to competition. New companies, such as E-trade and Ameritrade and other online brokers, have become players in this well-established market by making it easy for anyone to become his or her own stockbroker.

# HE CHANGING DYNAMICS OF UYING AND SELLING . . . . . . . . . . . . . . . . . . . . . . . .

The buying and selling cycle was, prior to the Internet, quite consistent. More often than not, the direct sales force enabled the outcome by matching the bid to the customer value proposition. Figure 2.1 outlines a typical buyer-seller exchange:

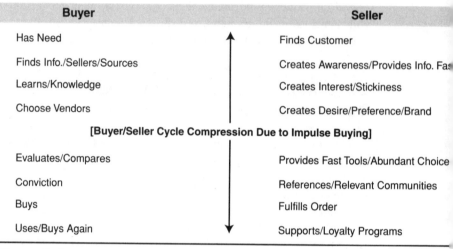

**Figure 2.1**
Buyer-Seller Exchange

The Internet has altered this exchange. New online brand names like Yahoo AltaVista, and Lycos, for example, can now influence where the customer starts the buy ing cycle. Impulse buying compresses the cycle and the customer may end up buyin things quickly, but in the brick-and-mortar world they would have taken longer to ma a decision. The element of personal contact is still necessary, but in a different contex

## Disruption #4:  Shifting Supply Chain Boundaries

The old static supply chain is taking the form of a dynamic Value Network. A dynam ic network of value acquires new components based on the need to customize offe ings. Now, instead of static relationships between suppliers and manufacturer dynamic relationships are being established with sources that deliver the best valu based on orders and configurations that are demanded by customers.

The supply chain concept, where the manufacturer sits in the middle and creat value for customers by assembling different suppliers' content, is no longer vali Today the customer occupies the center, responding to the manufacturer's offerings the light of relationships and value strategies.

Today online customers and suppliers have gained a higher level of intelligen in all aspects of the value chain. All the fundamental concepts of reducing the time el ment, minimizing handoffs, reducing the friction, and lowering transaction costs in t traditional supply chain have a new bar to scale. Customers want products faster, a lower cost, with more efficiency, and with a greater level of customer service.

Much of this also has to do with real time, ease of connectivity, changing process boundaries, and the ease of information sharing. Information must be made available to any department and organization. Since everyone is more aware of what is going on, the general expectation of quality and satisfaction is much higher.

The Internet has driven changes in the supply chain in a number of ways. In the past, one aspect of the supply chain depended on Electronic Data Interchange (EDI). Orders were keyed in, sent, received, and then keyed in again. Both the supplier and the customer had to be EDI-enabled. The whole process was slow and expensive. Today the Internet is changing all that. Software can be downloaded off the Internet, invoices can go directly to the manufacturing floor, customers can query the delivery times themselves—and all of this is possible at a much lower cost. In a sense, the Internet functions as a type of middleware, eliminating layers within the distribution chain.

## Disruption #5: New Paradigms of Value

In a traditional business transaction, the offer of products and services was based on many attributes, ranging from performance, choice, and quality to price, availability, and other tangibles. That scheme has given way to a newer framework of value creation, one based on the quality of the relationship between buyer and seller.

In the online economy, the website or portal becomes the medium for projecting a company's identity and will, therefore, play a crucial role in defining the limits of relationship with customers and prospects. The better the website, the higher the odds of the customer building a positive bonding experience, and the greater the probability of repeat visits. The relationship forms the basis for predicting how customers will respond to offers, promotions, and services.

One illustration of such relationship building via the Internet is *Compaq ActiveAnswers®*, an expert website from Compaq that enables the configuring, ordering, and support of infrastructure solutions. Resellers, integrators, and customers use *ActiveAnswers* to obtain online sizers, configurators, and other resources that accelerate the deployment of e-business solutions. A satisfied customer is very likely to return to this website for further exploration.

## Disruption #6: Diminished Advantage of Mass Production

At one time, the ability to churn out products in mass quantities and reduce costs was the key to success. Slowly, the phenomenon of mass customization developed. For many customer segments, mass customization may carry more weight than lower cost advantages from mass production. Now enterprises have the ability to get their customers' preferences online and create customization to meet their needs. Companies like Gap and Levi Strauss are offering customized merchandise.

Leading companies are using customer information to custom-design their off
ings. The information must be gathered with the knowledge and permission of cu
tomers. Corporations like Compaq are creating an instant advantage in the mark
place by responding to online requests and fine-tuning their offerings to better me
customer needs. Best-known among these approaches is the configure-to-order, whi
leading computer manufacturers like Compaq are using to provide a basis for "cu
tomer choice."

In short, companies used to fine-tune their production operations to meet mark
demands; the new standard of excellence is mass customization.

## Disruption #7:  New Measure of Time

Before the online era, time was measured in calendar years. Now, business process
are described in Internet years. Internet speed dominates the business culture, impa
ing investment decisions, growth assumptions, response times, and product develo
ment. Companies in many industries are now re-examining their overall busine
plans every quarter and are able to make major changes quickly, to adapt to rap
developments in the online marketplace.

In the e-business framework, speedier access to information becomes a diff
entiator. In fact, perhaps the best-known value of a well-architected network is th
information flows freely between a company's employees, its suppliers, vendors, a
partners. Under the Internet computing paradigm, real-time information is possib
through zero-latency operational data services.

According to The Gartner Group, zero-latency is a strategy that pushes the g
of information timeliness to its furthest limits. When applied to e-business, this com
to mean real-time customer data and knowledge management, enabling a rap
response from all appropriate points along the enterprise value chain.

## Disruption #8:  An End to Global Boundaries

An online business environment does not respect conventional trading boundari
geographic or political. Today, worldwide markets exist for every e-busines
Therefore, plans must be in place to address opportunities and issues that spring fro
the transformation of finite geographic markets to markets with no geographic lim
This consideration alone can make the difference between success and failure when
comes to website traffic and customer support.

## Disruption #9:  Changing IT Deployment Strategies

The old way of IT deployment was plan, execute, check, fix, and improve. The new mantra is execute, check, fix, plan, and improve. You cannot wait for long-term planning. Moreover, the assumptions you made in the planning process may no longer be valid by the time you actually implement them. The best way to begin is to begin; your ultimate plans will ultimately unfold. In the process, you will learn from the experience. We are not suggesting reckless behavior or thoughtlessness, but we are suggesting decisive action once a plan has been rationalized.

## Disruption #10:  New Inflection Points in Computing

The rapid evolution of industry-standard computing is the major force behind these cataclysmic disruptions in the emerging online business environment. This evolution has impacted all aspects of the enterprise and has changed the economics of IT. Industry-standard servers have dramatically lowered the total cost of ownership, while software solutions built to such standards take advantage of cross-platform compatibility, modularity of design, and a variety of benefits related to ease-of-deployment.

Coming on the heels of distributed computing and industry standards, the Internet and browser-based technologies have changed the face of computing forever. In the past, simply creating a network capable of connecting a few hundred people could take months. Once installed, users on one network could not communicate with users on another network. Alternatives from value added networks were available, but the connectivity supported only tens of thousands of people versus the hundreds of millions in the online world.

The Internet has impacted almost all aspects of computing. Not only has it provided connectivity, but it has also provided interactivity, interoperability, a uniform interface, multimedia content and much more. These in turn have led to the most important consequence—namely, giving enterprises the capability to build relationships in virtually every area related to business, personal, and social interactions.

# THREE MAJOR INTERNET TRENDS . . . . . . . . . . . . . . . .

The disruptions described above have led to enormous opportunities for enterprises virtually every sphere of industry. These opportunities make up three major Intern trends, or paradigm shifts:

1. The Internet brings us closer to the "nirvana" of computing more than anything in the history of computing.
2. Internet-driven standards play a significant role in emerging computing architectures.
3. The Internet is the new platform for innovating services.

## The "Nirvana" of Computing

The "nirvana" of computing is the ability to connect with, access information, condu business or deliver services to anyone—from anywhere—anytime—using almost a device—securely—easily—cost effectively—and with a single click.

Nirvana may be an overstatement, but the Internet has brought us closer to t ultimate IT solutions and services definition and given us the ability to establish rel tionships easier, faster, better, and more cost-effectively than with any other techno ogy in history. The capabilities of the Internet, the World Wide Web, and browse including universal connectivity, extensive interactivity, the uniform interfac increased interoperability, and powerful multimedia content, have led to this nirva that all have been trying to achieve since the dawn of computing. Appendix . "Internet Technology and Standards," details some of the major capabilities that a making this nirvana possible.

## Internet-Driven Standards

The Internet is driving massive change in standards. The move toward standards in t world of Information Technology and the shift toward Internet-driven client-to-servic computing are transforming business methods. The move is characterized by a growi need for enterprises to collaborate, and for making it easy and secure for customers do business over the Internet. barnesandnoble.com is one of many companies that h gained much from standards-based IT. The barnesandnoble.com website zoomed fro the No. 31 e-commerce site in 1997 to the No. 4 shopping site in December 1998. I October 1999, barnesandnoble.com claimed 2.9 million customers.

A new marketplace has emerged for online booksellers that are already exten ing their reach through the creation of related markets.

"For the new marketplace to work, it will require participants to be standards-based, very reliable and very scalable," says Gary King, CIO at barnesandnoble.com.

Explains King, "We would define the next-generation marketplace as a seamless integration of user platforms back to the repositories of information. So, whether that platform is a browser-enabled device or something else, we see it connected into remote sources of information that can provide for either a shopping transaction or just a browsing transaction."

For barnesandnoble.com, the next-generation marketplace will be a virtual private network that connects end users, publishers, distributors, and other supply-chain members to stores of information. That way, says Alan Bourassa, Director of Distribution Systems, "You'll have a network that functions as a continuous, moving supply chain. Publishers, for example, might be able to just log onto this virtual network and access the data for orders we'll be placing with them."

None of the paradigm shifts and technologies had a pronounced impact on standardization until the Internet and the World Wide Web arrived. Their global popularity made the Web browser interface the most common user interface in the world.

Global networking is now driven by Internet Protocol, while only three years ago many alternatives, such as IBM SNA, Digital's DECnet, Novell's IPX, and International Standards Organization's OSI, were being used. Some of these are still in use for specific environments.

Three of the most perplexing issues of computing—universal connectivity, interoperability, and common user interface—would still be unresolved were it not for the flexibility and modularity made possible by industry standards.

The Internet is also impacting many other standards in middleware, database, applications, document management, security, and manageability.

## The Internet as the New Platform for Services Innovation

The third area where the Internet is driving major changes is online services-based solutions. The huge growth in this category will trigger an avalanche of new business solutions in the coming years.

Some new services might include, for example, one that automatically finds and links a few people whose combined knowledge is needed to respond to a particularly complex customer inquiry. Customers would then be presented with a consistent and accurate answer.

In contrast, the early online model proved to be less than optimal, making it difficult for users to find and access the best sources of information that they can use to make informed decisions.

Today we already see some embryonic service capabilities being offered to he customers facilitate their work in the online world. Software agents and capabiliti such as Jango, Junglee, MySimon, and others provide services to find the right pro ucts, based on what the user needs. Other forms of services include the ability to cor pare and recommend the most suitable products from a selection of different offering Infomediaries will provide information services.

Most of these are the result of a single service. When a user requires the cap bilities of more than one service, different services will be created that provide bas building blocks to meet the needs of users or enterprises. These services buildi blocks may include access services, discovery services, mediation, brokerage, prese tation, and management-type capabilities. Developers or enterprises can build or cu tomize these so they do not have to build them from scratch.

There is already a move toward standards in traditional information access a computing requirements. It will be some time before these new common sets of se vices are properly defined and standards are fully developed. Once they are, they w cause another wave of capabilities where users can simply ask for what they want a the services will oblige them. An example of these new capabilities might invol users conducting a search for the best mix of health services options from a variety medical, dental, and alternative medicine providers in a particular region.

# THE FUTURE IS HERE:
# THE INTERNET'S IMPACT .............................

The Internet has created a new business process capability, shifted business proce boundaries, obliterated old IT and networking paradigms, and created a new enviro ment—a global online economy.

It is growing so rapidly and differently that one cannot use conventional wisdc in making decisions. One cannot assume the same competition, market growth rate barriers to entry, differentiators, or even the same supply-chain fundamentals. Succe in the online economy requires new strategies, new partnerships, and new ways doing business.

The emerging Total Economic Value paradigm is very different from its predece sors. The global online economy has a new set of challenges. It is not following the ne mal market dynamics, the change patterns, and the traditional factors of segmentatio

The following examples demonstrate the incredible power of the Internet effect change in the way business is conducted on a global scale:

- Amazon.com is one of the outstanding examples of how the Internet impacts the creation of new business in an online economy. In 1997, amazon.com increased its annual sales by nearly 600%, with sales of six and a half million books.

- A Zona Research report showed that 79% of companies surveyed use the Internet for marketing purposes. Currently, only 10% use it for Internet sales, but the report predicts that 44% are likely to experience Internet sales within two years.

- The online economy has had a major impact on advertising. By 2002, advertising on the Net is expected to exceed $7.7 billion, compared to 1997's $940 million, according to Jupiter Communications, Inc.

- By some estimates, 1/3 of home mortgages and nearly 1/2 of all auto loans will be conducted over the Internet by 2005.

- In a year's time, Internet airline ticket sales nearly tripled; sales are expected to grow six-fold—to $5 billion a year—by 2000.

- Most major banks have Internet-based banking programs online or in development.

- According to Network Wizards, currently over 30 million computers are connected to the network. Internet usage grew more than 50% during the first six months of 1999.

- According to Forrester Research Inc., the worldwide online economy will approach $3.2 trillion by the year 2003. See Figure 2.2.

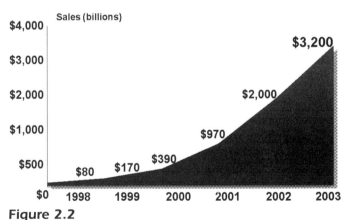

**Figure 2.2**

Worldwide Internet Economy *Used with the permission of Forrester Research, Inc.*

- The GartnerGroup is even more optimistic in their projections. They expect the volume of non-financial goods and services sold through business-to-business e-commerce alone to reach $7.29 trillion in 2004, which is 7% of the total global economy ($105 trillion) that is forecast for that year.

# 3

# The Online Economy: New Rules, Players and Growth Areas

..........................

*Summary: Whether your enterprise is an established company or an Internet start-up, it can be wildly successful if you and your colleagues are willing to change and adapt to today's dynamic—and often unpredictable—environment. In this chapter, we discuss how enterprises—old, new, large, or small—have collaborated in new ways to seize opportunities. We show how the introduction of new Internet technologies and applications has spawned new rules and expectations for participating in the online economy. Our focus is on how the Internet enables businesses to lower costs, increase operational efficiencies, and promote business development in four critical growth areas—business to business, business to and from consumers, consumers to consumers, and e-mediaries. Finally, we discuss the impact of creating a dynamic Internet infrastructure within the organizational structure, and the increasing demands on Information Technology systems to support 24/7 business. Chapter highlights include the following areas:*

- New players or marketmediaries who bring buyers and sellers together
- Building one-on-one relationships with customers
- Leading companies—old and new, large and small
- Challenges to going online
- Internet standards
- Scalability and availability requirements
- Growth of online services

# UNUSUAL ALLIANCES ARE SUCCEEDING . . . . . . . . . .

The online economy is driving different collaborations in almost all aspects of busines Chase Manhattan, for example, works with Edify Corporation and Entrust Technologi for business-to-business and business-to-consumer e-commerce applications.

Other examples of crossing conventional boundaries include the following:

- Intel's $1 billion investment in 200 companies, including CyberCash, Inc., a developer of Internet payment services, and VeriSign, Inc., a company involved in the digital certificates business.
- The strategic marketing partnership between Compaq and the Japanese firm, SESAMi, to support Asia's first dynamic e-commerce portal. The portal, SESAMi.NET, links buyers and suppliers to a global trading web of online marketplaces.
- Microsoft, again on the cutting edge of technology, recently paid $60 million for a 7% stake in Lernout & Hauspie, the international developer of speech translation software. Lernout & Hauspie is betting its future on the premise that keyboards soon will become obsolete. Some people at Microsoft believe they may be right.

New players are emerging in other fields. News and information, once the excl sive realm of ABC, NBC, CBS, BBC, and other broadcasting giants, is today at t epicenter of the war for dominance of the information content and dissemination fiel with such upstarts as C-Net, Yahoo!, AltaVista, AOL, and others.

Small towns are creating alliances to try to stay competitive with their big sist cities. A recent article in *Time* magazine about the impact of technology and t Internet on towns in the US told the story of a graphics designer who moved ba home, only to discover that the lack of high-speed telecommunications in his sm town put him at a distinct disadvantage. He found himself traveling two hours ea way every time he wanted to do business in the city. He was about to give up and mo back to the city when he learned that his small town had recently invested in sever technological advances that served his needs. Many small towns are now rapidly tr ing to stay abreast of the high bandwidth trend to provide residents with online se vices to stabilize their own population and environment.

# 'IRTUALLY INTEGRATED ALLIANCES . . . . . . . . . . . . . . .

To succeed in the global online economy, companies are forging new kinds of alliances. Virtual enterprises are sharing internal strategies that were once highly confidential. Partners are becoming part of the enterprise as e-processes are shared. Unlike *vertically* integrated mega-corporations of the second half of the 20th century, the new environment consists of corporate allies whose products, services, and processes are *virtually* integrated across organizational boundaries. The goal is to provide the optimal product and service offering to a customer who has unlimited choices, and is well-informed about those choices.

For instance, amazon.com has created a community of over 200,000 associates. This operation is one of a growing number of online storefronts that would have been unimaginable a few years ago. These associates may well create their own environments. As these online enterprises grow, the financial and delivery mechanisms change. Customer expectations escalate. In meeting those expectations, a company soon has millions of satisfied customers and access to the most valuable asset of this emerging environment—namely, comprehensive customer information.

Different technologies are being used to compete for the same opportunity, which is online business. Today telephone companies, media companies, software, hardware, entertainment, banking, and networking companies are finding ways to get a share of the customer's wallet. New partnerships and alliances are evolving, which benefit from the synergy of e-business. Consider Microsoft's recent investments in cable companies, including Comcast Corporation, the acquisition of WebTV, recent news of a $5 billion investment in AT&T, talks of investments in cable and wireless, and MSNBC's partnership with its parent company, Microsoft, NBC, and Disney.

Microsoft Corporation, which leads the software economy, has taken decisive steps to capture the huge online market spawned by the Internet. Similarly, shopping.com, which is owned by Compaq, sells brand-name consumer products at deep discounts and is integrated with the search engine AltaVista. These capabilities are being integrated to compete with gateway portals such as Yahoo! to reach further into the consumer world.

## SMALL AND LARGE ENTERPRISES COMPETE IN THE SAME MARKETS . . . . . . . . . . . . . . . . . . .

The emerging new environment has leveled the playing field in a number of way
What used to take dozens of years now can be accomplished in a fraction of the tim
While it may be true that many of the evolving companies have not yet turned pro
itable, they carry enough market value to acquire the technical expertise, marketi
know-how and loyal customer base that can outstrip even the most well establish
brick-and-mortar companies.

Most people in business have grown up with some fundamental concepts of ma
keting, finance, and business investments. The concepts still apply in this enviro
ment, but the rules have changed. Comparing gross margins between online and tr
ditional models doesn't make sense. Online models can have a higher bottom li
impact with much lower gross margins, due to differences in asset structures. W
could have guessed that eTrade, established in 1996, would have a market valuati
of around $10 billion (*Bloomberg News*, 4/99)? Compare that with the $6.2 billion v.
uation of Paine Webber, which has been in business since 1879.

Did Sotheby's ever imagine that a startup company like eBay would be valu
at $22 billion, compared to their own valuation of $1.9 billion? eBay was founded
1995; its venerable competitor has been around since 1778! It comes as no surpri
that Sotheby's has decided to go online. This should increase its access to people w
do not find it convenient to travel to Sotheby's auction rooms. Harrods of London
another example of an old-line retail institution that has gone online to attract sho
pers who surf the Web for convenience—and the list gets longer everyday.

## THE RISE OF E-MEDIARIES . . . . . . . . . . . . . . . . . . . .

A new category of value-added function is evolving—the e-mediary. Several class
of e-mediaries will emerge, ranging from those who provide information, to those w
provide online exchanges that link buyers and sellers by efficiently distributing ma
ket information. It is projected that within three years approximately half of all onli
business-to-business traffic will flow through such exchanges.

In their book, *Net Worth*, John Hagel III and Marc Singer describe the rap
emergence and growing importance of the infomediary. With the phenomenal grow
of the Internet, specific information will become increasingly difficult to find, for bo
consumers and vendors. Hagel and Singer present the argument that the infomedia
will become the vital link between buyer and seller.

For vendors, the promise of establishing 1:1 relationships and getting more of a share of the consumer's wallet is real only if they have accurate information about consumers.

At the same time, consumers are becoming increasingly wary of providing information. They believe that Internet information-gatherers are invading customers' privacy. Over time, Internet information-gatherers may not be able to capture the kind of meaningful information that enterprises need in order to sell successfully.

From the consumer perspective, the less time spent finding what he or she needs translates into a faster decision. Users may be willing to compensate infomediaries in return for having their privacy protected or for services that make it easier for them to find the right suppliers, manage their transactions, or negotiate deals.

# THE INTERNET INCREASES EFFICIENCIES AND LOWERS COSTS . . . . . . . . . . . . . . . . . . . . . . . .

Beyond leveling the playing field, the Internet has created new ways to increase operational efficiencies by making it easy to eliminate some of the manual processes in areas such as customer support. The Internet also reduces the time it takes to perform such functions as order entry. Similarly, it improves forecasting and inventory functions by gathering usage trends in real time.

New online solutions from Ariba Technologies, Inc., help companies manage purchasing costs by funneling purchases to authorized vendors. Online bill payment systems, such as CheckFree Corporation, also reduce expenses. MCI Worldcom, Inc., will save $1 a month per customer paying online. IBM is reducing its purchasing costs from 2% to 1% annually on a $40 billion volume. These cost reductions add up to hundreds of millions of dollars. Reducing the need for intermediaries in such functions as purchasing, selling, and support will make a significant difference in operating costs and efficiencies.

# BUSINESS OPPORTUNITIES ACROSS INDUSTRIES . . . . .

The Internet will fuel the creation of new kinds of opportunities that were not viable in a more traditional environment. These opportunities will come from shifts and overlaps in business processes across industries, technology, and geographic boundaries.

For example, the impact of consumers' online access to financial products has hastened the blurring of the lines of the banking, insurance and financial services industries. Each sees the other's markets as being ripe for exploitation. New hybrid

companies have emerged that specialize in online mortgages. Online shopping ve
dors provide linkages to financial institutions for instant credit. Online brokerages li
DLJdirect and Fidelity Investments now provide many of the same kinds of financ
services that banks have traditionally offered. Enterprises such as Intuit, I
(Quicken) and Microsoft (Money) started challenging the role played by financ
institutions some time ago. As these services have been honed, consumers have grov
increasingly comfortable with online banking.

Insurance companies are fighting hard to maintain their footing. At a time wh
payment protection plans—insurance programs offered by banks, credit card comp
nies, and financial services institutions—are standard add-ons, the insurance indus
has sunk millions of dollars into Internet marketing to level the playing field.

Third party insurance information providers, like Quicken's insuremarket.cc
and InsWeb at insweb.com, provide comparative quotes from participating insurar
companies. While giving consumers an apparently objective analysis of insurar
rates, they do not disclose their sources of income.

Forrester Research predicts that the online sale of auto, home and life insura
will hit $4.1 billion by 2003. While this is a drop in the bucket for a $200 billion ind
try, Forrester Research believes that as tech-savvy Gen-Xers start buying insuran
the revenue from online buying will soar.

# TURNING AN OLD INDUSTRY
# ON ITS HEAD  . . . . . . . . . . . . . . . . . . . . . . . . . .

Change is the byword in the world of automotive retail sales. Autobytel a
Microsoft's Car Point are just two of the hundreds of companies scrambling for a t
hold or shouldering their way to the top of the lucrative automotive resale mark
Ford Motor Company is testing schemes that will allow customers to choose fror
wide array of available cars, complete all the financial information, and place an or
via the Internet. Ford locates the nearest dealer and delivers the car within 48 hou

It would seem that Ford and other car manufacturers would have the muscle
dominate the automobile resale market on the Internet. They have the product, de
ers, marketing, maintenance, distribution, and unlimited financial resources. Howev
in the online economy, the fast can eat the big. David can still slay Goliath.

One of the hottest IPOs to come out of the Stanford Business School incuba
this year is BestOffer.com, an online used car site that combines some elements
eBay's auction concept with a 1990s used car megacenter. Jeff Reed and Pra
Mukherjee developed the business plan for BestOffer as an entry in an entreprene
ship contest at Stanford. When they reached the semifinals, Reed and Mukher
pulled out of the contest to develop their idea in earnest.

Their first step was to find backing. With $2 million from Draper Fisher Jurvetson, a California venture capital firm, the two entrepreneurs set up shop and set a killer timetable to be online in October 1999. It's not as easy as it sounds. Of the 10,000 business plans Draper Fisher Jurvetson looks at each year, it actually funds only 15.

Chrome Data Corporation is one of many ancillary businesses organized to support automobile sales. Chrome Data has developed a large database of information for the lease and application process. It links consumers, banks, and automotive network members. One of the objectives is to stop disintermediation by the emerging portals of banks in the leasing area. Using portals, leasing agreements are handled by dealers that have specific agreements with exclusive banks. With Chrome Data, dealers and banks pay a fee to Chrome Data for membership. Banks that link to Chrome Data can offer a quote and close a deal online right at the dealership.

# CROSSING GLOBAL BOUNDARIES . . . . . . . . . . . . . . . . .

The online economy crosses global boundaries and has provided businesses with opportunities to expand their markets in countries and regions they were previously unable to penetrate.

E-commerce has also created issues between the EU and US, due to differences in privacy requirements and commerce laws, as well as many other cultural and social issues. As the online economy expands and differences are resolved, there will be even bigger opportunities for global e-commerce.

While most of the current activity is in North America, many European countries—as well as Japan, Australia, and others—will catch up in a matter of a few years. However, there will continue to be barriers, due to sub-optimal telecommunications infrastructures and limited e-commerce. According to the IDC's reports, by 2003 the distribution of Internet users will be one-third in North America, one-third in Europe, and one-third in the rest of the world.

# HOT GROWTH AREAS IN A $3 TRILLION INDUSTRY . . . . . . . . . . . . . . . . . . . . . . . . . . .

The Internet-driven online economy will exceed three trillion dollars by 2003, accor
ing to IDC published reports. Much of the innovation and growth of the global onli
economy will be fundamentally in the following three major categories:

- business-to-business
- business-to-consumer
- consumer-to-consumer

## 1. Business-to-Business

Commerce involving business-to-business interchanges is the largest growth segment
the global economy. This is where businesses are selling, buying, collaborating or wor
ing in the virtual enterprise mode. In this segment are three predominant ways busine
is being conducted: the sell side, the buy side, and business forum marketplaces.

**The sell side:** The sell side involves businesses selling their solutions to busine
es or consumers. This is where most of the activity is today. Vendors like IBM, Comp.
Sun, HP, and others are offering many Internet-based e-commerce solutions. Microso
Open Market, Oracle, and Netscape are supplying e-commerce solutions softwa
Vendors like Siebel offer applications suitable for increasing the effectiveness of targ
ing, selling, supporting, and increasing customer satisfaction. Oracle and other key v
dors provide solutions that make up a Value Network—namely, solutions that integra
end-to-end, the sales and marketing process. Many newcomers like i2 Technologi
Clarify, Pivotal Software, and Vantive also are providing e-commerce solutions.

**The buy side:** The buy side involves corporations using the Internet to make
easy for employees to make purchases and adhere to company policies. Many co
panies like Ariba offer such solutions.

**Business forum marketplaces:** These marketplaces provide a forum for sel
and buyers who may have mutually beneficial interests. They are brought togethe
an online forum. Online sites like Fastparts and ONSALE let buyers and sellers m
to negotiate prices.

One of the obstacles limiting the growth of e-commerce is the desire of m:
customers to have face-to-face negotiations when purchasing goods and servic
especially in large production quantities. In addition, many companies already h:
EDI. Some of those companies are beginning to migrate from EDI to the Inter
especially since security and ease-of-use issues are being resolved.

One company that is using the Internet in business-to-business transactions is Avnet. Avnet has set up a special extranet with major suppliers such as AMD, Intel, and Motorola. The extranet allows these partners to look at each other's inventory on a real-time basis. This adds value to supply-chain operations, because what results is a higher level of integration across each company's supply chain. That is what Avnet is currently focused on—achieving integration between its customer and vendor systems to avoid problems like dual entry and logistical snags.

The business-to-business boom is exceeding everybody's projections. One reason is that much of its activity is being fueled by somewhat hidden engines called infomediaries. The model at work here is quite different from the well-known "direct" model of the leading e-commerce vendors (see Table 3.1). Infomediaries operate like commercial hubs within a given industry (telecommunications) or sub industry (equity loans or patio furniture). By aggregating demand and/or supply, they expand market volume and lower the cost of transactions.

Unlike their business-to-consumer equivalents, the business-to-business e-hubs create value for buyers as well as sellers, with huge economies of scale. E-hubs lower costs and time related to information search and transfer by using standard processes and selecting from global vendors. The benefits increase exponentially as the network of buyers and sellers expands.

Hubs or infomediaries are major drivers of value in the new economy, and companies cannot afford to ignore these elements in their go-to-market strategies. Likewise, Internet sites should be configured to accommodate the policy and legal requirements of hubs.

**Table 3.1**   Traditional E-Commerce Versus New E-Business

| Characteristics | EDI | Web-Driven Commerce |
|---|---|---|
| Use | Business-to-business | Business-to-business<br>Consumer-to-business<br>Business-to-consumer<br>Consume-to-consumer<br>Marketmediaries, brokers |
| Impact on enterprise | Only financial, speed of doing business | More than just financial; impact on distribution, relationship building, allows comparison shopping; information dissemination, self help and many others |
| Types of sales | Sell side; buy side but not as extensive and automated | Sell side<br>Buy side |
| Technology standards | EDI and VAN, ANSI 12 | Internet EDI, OBI, SET, JEPI, Wallet, Digi Cash |
| Business transactions | Predefined, predetermined arrangements/relationships; it takes place over existing value added networks | Online transactions with as many as possible from anywhere |
| Implementation and costs | Difficult and expensive; most second and third tier suppliers and partners usually cannot afford the costs and business process structures | Relatively inexpensive; anyone can be linked |
| Trust relationship | High | Getting higher with new standards |
| Frequency of use | Low, but much higher amount | Much higher |
| Flexibility | Low: to make changes in adding products, process, policies changes, etc. | Very flexible |

## 2. Business-to-Consumer

Business-to-consumer is the second largest opportunity. Estimates range from $25-$75 billion for this segment of the market, which now includes more than 200,000 sites worldwide and is increasing exponentially every year. Business-to-consumer activities range from one-person enterprises to the largest of enterprises in industries such as retail, office, travel, healthcare, and entertainment. Noteworthy sites are gap.com, levi.com, eTops.com, barnesandnoble.com, priceline.com, amazon.com, travelocity.com, autobytel.com, carpoint.com, 1800Flowers.com, compaq.com, cisco.com, ibm.com, and others.

Consumers are benefiting from new Web services that enable home delivery of goods and products. One example is deliverynet.com that can deliver products within a 30-minute window with the help of a dynamic scheduling system. American Grocer Inc. is another example of a high-tech web delivery service that is making use of dynamic scheduling, routing, and wireless communication technology. Companies trying to compete in the Web-driven consumer marketplace should prepare for the impact of the new digital wallet trend. Also called the e-wallet, this online service stores a shopper's personal profile (including shipping and financial data) in a central repository. This simplifies the shopping scenario since the data in the store invoice is automatically filled out while the customer supplies the incidental details of size, color, or unique feature. Many credit card companies and banks are already promoting this service, which is software-enabled by a host of companies like Cybercash, Microsoft, Qpass, and others.

The adoption of e-wallets by consumers will depend on their security, reliability, and convenience. The emergence of a common standard—the Electronic Commerce Modeling Language—is driving acceptance among merchants. The trend will undoubtedly spark new interest from aggregators, infomediaries, and vendors who specialize in consumer loyalty programs. This in turn will lead to alliances among service providers to offer seamless service to consumers.

## 3. Consumer-to-Consumer

The third fast-growing area of e-commerce in the online economy is consumer-to-consumer. Perhaps the most famous e-commerce site is ebay.com, where auctions are bringing millions of people together to sell and buy. eBay's success is spawning imitators who are experiencing similar successes. One example is amazon.com, the online bookseller now involved heavily in online auctions.

Many software developers like OpenSite; Technologies, Inc.; and Eye Media give enterprises the ability to handle bids and auctions on their own site.

Marketmediaries are creating sites for interactive bidding for contracts. Companies like VerticalNet, Inc., plan to host industrial auctions. W.R Hambrecht &

Co. is an example of the number of enterprising investment bankers that offer th
services online by allowing companies to make individual bids for new compan
planning to go public.

# THE ONLINE ECONOMY IMPACTS
# ORGANIZATIONAL STRUCTURE .............

The online economy is affecting the organizational structure of enterprises. So
companies are radically changing their organizations to conform to e-commerce
the Internet, while others are making only minor changes in key areas. The subject
changing the enterprise's culture and the overall organization structure is one of
most important issues of the emerging online economy. Here are three differ
approaches being used today:

1.  One approach is to make online business-related activities a separate func-
    tion and have that function managed by a senior executive or, in some
    cases, a CEO. This gives it complete accountability for results, and man-
    agement can measure the impact directly. Compaq.com was created in the
    beginning of 1999 to pull together a cohesive effort to make it easier for
    customers, suppliers, and partners to work with Compaq. Its organization-
    al structure began immediately to improve the internal effectiveness of al
    functions. The manager of compaq.com reports directly to Compaq's
    CEO. In another example, staples.com was spun off as a separate business
    unit in December 1998.

2.  The second approach involves a broader organization, since online solu
    tions encompass all corporate functions, including sales, marketing, and
    IT. Some companies have set up cross-function committees to address the
    integration of online solutions. While this approach can be effective, it too
    often takes a longer time to achieve results. Working in a networked world
    a forceful leader—one who is not tied down with cumbersome commit
    tees—is needed to get things moving quickly. Moreover, the hallmark o
    e-commerce is speed.

3.  The third approach is to realign the whole company with the online busi-
    ness strategy and make sure it is everybody's responsibility, rather than tha
    of a separate group. Newer companies like amazon.com employ such a
    integrated approach. Other companies, like Dell and Cisco, are getting clos
    er to this model as their percentage of online business increases every yea

# NCREASING DEMANDS ON IT SYSTEMS . . . . . . . . . .

The online economy will introduce new IT architecture requirements and is already impacting the fundamentals of scalability, availability, security, data integrity, and manageability. Already the norms of acceptable response specify a waiting period of no more than eight seconds, and an assumed standard of "no user-visible downtime." This is the foundation of the 24/7 computing framework established by Compaq to enable continuous business operations for its customers.

Early on, even the best planned IT systems crashed during critical business hours. To stay up and running at fail-safe levels, companies are learning that the old rules of planning and the old requirements for availability do not work. Consumers across the Internet have very high expectations, and 100 percent availability and reliability are two of them. If a company operating online suffers downtime—even for a matter of minutes—it risks losing substantial sums of money and thousands of customers to other, better-prepared online companies.

Charles Schwab is an example of a company building success by making a commitment to online trading and then putting the pieces in place to insure continuous operations. The company's commitment paid off. Schwab now receives 61% of its trades electronically.

Even Charles Schwab suffered growing pains in the early stages of its online development. In early 1999, for example, Schwab's system buckled when trade orders backed up on its mainframes. Similarly, during its startup period, Discover Brokerage Direct, Inc., a unit of Morgan Stanley Dean Witter, experienced a disruption of service when it failed to take orders for 30 minutes.

In the beginning, many online brokerage companies thought they were prepared for traffic peaks at three to four times the daily average. Now, with more experience—and many of the bugs in their systems eliminated—these companies handle at least 10 times their earlier expectations. The rules of planning assumptions have changed, and the results for many online brokers are impressive.

Online consumers are watching with heightened expectations. During the holiday season of 1998, online companies failed to meet customer expectations. Four out of 10 online consumers reported that poor Web performance over the holidays caused them to give up on certain e-commerce sites, according to a survey by Jupiter Communications. Consumers want accurate and fast service—and they will get it, or they will go elsewhere.

Steps are being taken to help enterprises handle overloads in their online business. Two steps include capacity planning and rewriting programs to distribute loads across networks. Some organizations are turning to a growing number of service options to ease website congestion, and they are employing tools that get them a better reading of site performance.

InterNAP Network Services, an Internet service provider (ISP), has an advanc
routing technology to better handle a company's traffic by directing users to W
servers closest to its geographic location. Concentric Network Corp, an ISP and W
hosting company, provides Web servers and bandwidth on an emergency basis. The
services usually rely on caching technology to replicate a company's Web pages
their own servers so that backup information is ready to help at the drop of a hat (
the drop of a link). eBay is a customer of InterNAP.

# THE ONLINE ECONOMY:
# MORE THAN PRETTY WEBSITES . . . . . . . . . . . . . . . . . . .

Along with the benefits of the online economy, there are reasons to be cautious wh
proceeding with new projects. Most projects require the modification of end-to-e
processes in order to benefit consumers online. It is not simply an issue of creatin;
front-end website. Interactive websites for e-commerce take time and effort, not
mention a significant capital investment. According to Forrester, the costs of an int
active website range anywhere from $300,000+ for medium-sized companies to m
than $2 million for large corporations.

In its simplest form, the purpose of going online may be to provide additio
information to visitors who already know who you are. In this case, the challenges
mostly about scalability, availability, download speed, and security. Beyond the
challenges, the major issue is keeping the content current. Obsolete information (
do major damage in customer satisfaction and lost sales. If a company decides to
online, it must commit to doing it right if it wants to keep its customers.

If you are online to create awareness, then the biggest challenge is to make s
that people know about your company and can access related links at popular sites.
you build it, they will come" is an Internet myth. Ways to create awareness are c
ered in later sections on e-marketing.

Generally, for startup and other companies that are narrowly focused, the onl
entry price can be quite modest. For smaller companies, there are options of doing
commerce with shopping malls on AOL and several other ISPs and portals. Fleet B
is one of several larger enterprises that has created shopping malls where the risk:
going online and doing secure transactions are reduced, because of the services p
vided by outsource providers who charge reasonable monthly fees.

However, if you are developing e-commerce for your medium to large en
prise, it's essential to integrate end-to-end processes with the legacy systems. T
involves major changes in connectivity, access, security, supplier, customer, part
and application server areas. In addition, changes to existing EDI mechanisms nee
be made. Another critical area, where major resources are needed, is getting c

sumers to come to your site. The marketing investment can be considerable. Sometimes marketing investments may equal or exceed your technology investments.

"Going online is all you need to do great volumes of business" is another Internet myth. For many years to come, traditional and online strategies will complement each other. Although 1:1 marketing will be key, mass marketing and advertising through traditional channels will help drive people to online sites. The role of brands will become even more important because you want people to feel confident that they are buying quality products.

Disintermediation will take the shape of new types of intermediation. Some low-value added functions like information aggregation and fast delivery may be eliminated, but services, support, and many other functions may get reintermediated by those who are being disintermediated.

There are other equally important factors to consider. One factor involves asset deployment. Some companies resist spending money to build facilities for distribution centers and warehouses that are required by their growth and increased sales. If you do not handle organizational issues well and disintermediate your proven partners, your efforts will come back to haunt you. You run the risk of having your partners become your new competitors who will steal loyal customers from you.

What makes your company different from any other company will remain a key issue in this online economy. Cultural issues, unless handled immediately, will continue to slow down your transition to an online business environment. Front office and back office cultures may keep fighting, because people want to control data and organize it to serve their needs—and not the needs of customers. Whatever efforts your enterprise takes to engage in online commerce, it must see the whole picture.

**Summary of Challenges:** Some of the major challenges you will face in developing a comprehensive approach to becoming a player in the online economy include:

### Business

- Marketing investments, ongoing
- Web investments
- Other associated investments in training
- Information capture, knowledge-sharing

### Organization/People

- Cultural change
- Effects of intermediation
- Skills deployment
- Stovepiped IT vs. business conflicts, policies, and procedures

**Process**

- Integration of front-end and legacy systems
- Integration of ERP, CRM, and the Internet
- Integration across functions, departments

**Technology**

- Integration/interoperability with legacy systems
- Scalability, reliability, performance, and manageability
- Bandwidth, download times
- Security, deployment of cost-effective mechanisms
- Centralized vs. distributed sites

Other challenges include privacy, taxation, international business policies, a
fraud prevention.

# Part 2

# Strategies for Instant Advantage in the Online Economy

# 4

# The Agile Enterprise

*S*ummary: *How do you gain instant advantage in the online economy? The key is to get your enterprise thinking and acting differently. In this chapter, we introduce five strategies for adapting to the emerging online economy. These strategies address business directions, technology, processes, and issues of society and culture. You'll learn why it's important to work within a Value Network that accommodates the business processes of everyone in the online economy—including your customers and business partners. We'll also discuss how to go beyond traditional business boundaries by incorporating complementary initiatives into your strategic plan.*

Winners and losers. That's what the online economy will produce. The question is: What does it take to be a winner? How should you look at today's realities and tomorrow's possibilities and merge them into a plan of action that you and your organization can follow today? Waiting until every committee and every layer of management have bought into the new paradigm for doing business in the online economy may be too late. The time to act is now. In this chapter, we present five steps that can get your organization started on the path to change.

Early winners have already emerged in the first phase of the global online economy. These are household names by now: Amazon, 1-800-Flowers, drugstore.com, eBay, Yahoo!, priceline.com, and others. All of these companies share some common characteristics. They all entered the game early. They all operated in corporate cultures that recognized the urgency of the opportunity. And they all were intensely focused on the customer.

Other companies, including Compaq Computer Corporation, Cisco, Charles Schwab, and Dell, adapted quickly to the Internet and have earned millions of dollars in incremental revenue.

By contrast, there are hundreds of stories of companies that rose fast and fell faster. What are the factors that make the difference? What sets the winners apart from the losers? What are the lessons that companies like Cullinet, PanAm, Eastern Airlines, Zayre, Levitz, and others failed to learn in time?

They allowed their market advantage to collapse by ignoring the signs and fai
ing to maintain a compelling value proposition. In today's market, the secret revolv
around the creation of value via the technologies of the Web.

# FIVE STRATEGIES FOR GAINING
# INSTANT ADVANTAGE . . . . . . . . . . . . . . . . . . . . . .

1. Seize market opportunities.
2. Become your customer's advocate.
3. Reinvent your enterprise.
4. Integrate business and IT strategies.
5. Create a blueprint for action.

How do these strategies differ from conventional approaches? See Table 4.1.

**Table 4.1**  *Comparison of Strategies*

| New Approach for Online Economy | Conventional Approach |
| --- | --- |
| Online economy's focus: Checks for shifting process boundaries, new business dynamics, linkages, collaborations, and for virtual enterprise value added. Decide your role in the online economy. Focus on new type of decision-makers. | Stovepipe market focus: Analysis of the existing and traditional markets. Value proposition and delivery based on stovepipe views of the enterprise and the market. Focus on traditional decision-makers. |
| Customer proposition: Takes the view that the customer is informed and is in charge. Customer buying process is an integral part of the proposition. Looks at it from the standpoint of what customers will propose, accept, and buy. | Value proposition: Generally based on internal view of enterprise strengths to match market segment requirements. Created from what will sell. Leaves buying proposition out of the equation as it is part of delivery. |
| Turns service discontinuity to continuity: A major issue today, especially in the emerging online economy, is establishment of dynamic relationships with several collaborators. This requires the capability to make connections, broker services on the fly, as customers are online, and keep | Emphasis is on using the Internet and making existing processes work better and faster.<br><br>Less consideration of emerging online dynamic transactions and collaborations. Focus is on the static |

| New Approach for Online Economy | Conventional Approach |
|---|---|
| the continuity of services, especially when the problem is out of the realm of normal processes. | supply chain with Internet providing extensions to customers, suppliers and partners. |
| Reinvent your enterprise: Focuses on the existing and emerging decision-maker and buying process. Defines business models required for customers to best procure value from your enterprise. Addresses the Dynamic Value Network rather than the static supply-chain model. | The Internet is applied to tweak existing processes and support existing business models. The supply chain is optimized by delivering value and not by how customers receive value. Many times the end-to-end process view is not taken, which creates discontinuities in the process. |
| A new strategy based on online culture and complete integration of business and IT. | Online is an add-on opportunity. |
| Creation of an infrastructure blueprint to work in online collaborative modes for low-cost and agility. | Focus on aligning IT strategies with business needs. Online functions. Piecemeal extensions of existing IT architectures to use the Internet. |

# FRAMEWORK FOR ASSESSING ONLINE ADVANTAGE—ACHIEVING EXCELLENCE . . . . . . . . . . .

An enterprise can measure its effectiveness by connecting different points along the axis, based on its status and plans (see Figure 4.1). The inner oval shows an enterprise lacking in e-culture/enterprise transformation. It has a less-than-desirable IT blueprint because it has not attained the goal of 24/7 operations. Instead, it is mostly focused on its operations. The enterprise has not attempted to build relationships, focus on customer-buying processes, or innovate with online solutions.

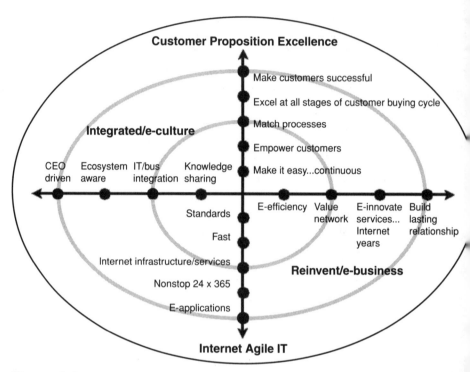

**Figure 4.1**

Global Online Ecosystem *Used with the permission of Market Data Group, LLC.*

The result is that its Total Economic Value may fall short when compared wi
competitors who have established better relationships, higher value solutions, a
more profitability.

The first strategy for gaining instant advantage is discussed in this chapter. T
remaining four are described in succeeding chapters.

## STRATEGY #1: SEIZE MARKET OPPORTUNITIES . . . . .

In the "old" days—a year or two ago—it wasn't necessary to have a complete und
standing of the environment in order to be successful. But, in the online economy, y
not only have to understand the market dynamics, you have to anticipate marl
changes and define the role that you will play in this market.

Business analysis traditionally was based on individual market segments: c
tomers, competition, suppliers, new entrants, and new solutions. These criteria are fi
when operating in a stable market. However, the emerging online economy is resu

ing from the merger of business processes, the melding of technologies, the development of new Value Networks, and the emergence of new players with deep pockets who are redefining the rules of business. In this case, it is difficult to define the next playing field and understand the new business rules unless you look at the big picture.

AT&T, Microsoft, Compaq, and AOL have made investments in fields that were out of their primary business model only a year or two ago. Intel has invested hundreds of millions of dollars in several companies that deliver everything from e-commerce solutions to telephony solutions.

The following three guidelines can help you know what to expect from the online economy, no matter what your business. Additional analysis of the specifics of the industry and associated processes is needed to complete these general guidelines.

Look beyond your traditional business, market, and technology boundaries:

1. Look at the whole economy.
2. Monitor key online change indicators.
3. Define your role and relevance in the new online economy.

# GUIDELINE 1: LOOK AT THE WHOLE ECONOMY . . . . .

Enterprises have been developing one-year, three-year and five-year plans by evaluating market trends, emerging customer needs, technology directions, and the impact of environmental, global, economic, and regulatory standards on the business.

In the next few pages, we address present and future core competency requirements for businesses, as well as the changing roles of suppliers and competitors. We will also look at a host of factors influencing success, including the choice of alternative markets, buyers and partners, barriers to entry, and switching costs.

Strategies that result from an examination of these factors will have an impact on industry leadership in product innovation, cost advantages due to operational excellence, the pursuit of after-niche markets, and alignment with customer strategies.

For these strategic considerations to have relevance, it is necessary to keep the global online economy in mind because in the online economy all business is global, which requires that your strategic plan include global tactical and strategic dimensions necessary to succeed.

## Automobiles and Auctions

If you are in the automotive business, you can no longer afford to limit your mark
view just to the automotive segment, its dealers and customers. Now you have to s
what else you can offer your customers—including such services as financial altern
tives that are available to customers from other online competition.

You also have to determine the companies with which you will collaborate ar
which dynamic online links will pull in your customers. Who are the e-mediarie
What other related complementary businesses can help make it easier for custome
to do business with you in the future? How will customers' buying processes chang
Who else may enter your business arena?

Autobytel.com is a good example of the changing car sales business in the di
ital economy. It has quickly become one of the Web's highest-profile electronic cor
merce sites, generating sales for its North American network of over 3,000 new ar
used car dealers. Visitors to the site browse through listings of available new and us
cars, look up information on specific models, then submit a purchase request to lea
or buy a vehicle from a local Autobytel.com Accredited Dealer, and even apply f
financing and insurance. The dealer contacts the customer within 24 hours with a fir
competitive price. Autobytel.com also offers an online service and maintenance are
an automotive superstore, and new and used car auction.

Autobytel.com is the market leader in online car sales. The company has gene
ated more than 4 million purchase requests since inception, and, in the first three qua
ters of 1999, processed over one and a half million vehicle purchase reques
Currently, Autobytel.com generates more than 1.2 billion dollars a month in car sal
through its Accredited Dealer Network, with an average of 50,000 cars sold a mont

Or look at the age-old example of auctioning and flea markets. From a trac
tional perspective, you might look at the competition, the historical growth rate
wealth index, and availability of antiques. Flea markets would be a different segme
with its own analysis. If anyone considered the role of IT, it might have been for kee
ing accounting and financial records and market data.

Then there's eBay. eBay is the online version of the flea market and the aucti
house. It emerges as a new way of doing business. Millions of people from all ov
the world trade through eBay and, in the process, establish new rules for financ
transactions.

If eBay's founders had a limited and traditional view of auctioning or flea ma
kets, they might not have scanned beyond traditional business practices and proce
boundaries and seen a new way of connecting sellers and buyers.

# ;UIDELINE 2: MONITOR ONLINE
# HANGE INDICATORS . . . . . . . . . . . . . . . . . . . . .

The point is that you have to take a broader view of the markets, processes, and technology, as well as the social and economic landscape. The new online economy has become an equalizer in many ways. Established players are no longer the rulers in the new kingdom; startups can change the rules with the launch of an IPO.

To determine what the new online economy will look like in the next two to three years, several factors have to be explored. The following categories provide a good start for following the rules of the online economy:

- Overall business and commerce landscape
- Change in customer preferences and buying behaviors
- Change in business structure
- Value delivery
- Emerging alliances and interdependencies
- New competition
- Sources of funds
- Advances in technology capability
- Advances in Internet technology
- Advances in IT
- Miscellaneous
- Social/cultural changes
- Regulatory/government

See Table 4.2 for exploring and anticipating online economics.

**Table 4.2**  Template for Exploring and Anticipating Online Economic Changes

| Key Online Economy Indicator | Today's Online Economy | Emerging Online Economy |
| --- | --- | --- |
| I: Overall landscape | Extend business with Internet | Extend Internet into business |
| - Rate of change | - Technology-driven | - Services-driven; e-consumer: |
| - Customers | - Enterprise customers | - Collaborative customers |
| - Focus of sale | - Product-driven | - Services-driven |
| - Pricing | - Fixed | - Fixed + flexible |
| - Demographics | - More male/female/younger | - Equal male/female/all ages |
| - Relationships | - Personalized via contacts | - Online personalized 1:1 |
| - Access | - PC-based | - I-Appliances |
| - Transactions | - EDI, manual | - Online, Internet EDI |
| - Success metrics | - Share of market, short-term sales, repeat sales | - Share of customer, lifetime customer value, repeat site returns |
| II: Customer preferences | - Online purchasing for items with known values, such as PCs. Mostly books and other commodity type items.<br>- Mostly text-based transactions<br>- User interacts with several sites to get total services. | - Expectations approaching "just like walking into a store" experience. Online help expected instantaneously.<br>- Voice-enabled interactive transactions<br>- One click request. Automatic online services collaborate to fill requests. |
| III: Business structures-value delivery | - Based on the core competency/supply chain of an enterprise.<br>- Rigid supply-chain structures optimized by mass production. | - Best of combined core competencies of internal/ - external collaborators<br>- Dynamic value network and intermediaries:<br>- Mass customization-oriented |
| Collaboration | - Along technology or business process lines: IT to IT, banks to banks. | - Cross boundaries: IT, telecom, banks, and intermediaries forming joint capabilities to gain advantage. |

**ble 4.2** (continued)

| ey online economy ndicator | Today's online economy | Emerging online economy |
|---|---|---|
| ompetition | - Traditional products and services-oriented competition.<br>- Competitive basis is individual.<br>- Excellence in technology, services, relationships, operations, innovation-based | - Excellence in online services.<br>- New Internet-driven business models. Competitive basis is collective; service providers, and intermediaries |
| ources of funds ew ventures | - Venture, IT vendors, some Wall Street wealth generated | - Wall Street wealth generated, funding by online economy collaborators such as AT& T and Microsoft |
| V: Use of technology | - Uses Internet for information gathering, buying and selling, building relationships, and connectivity.<br>- Mostly traditional applications accessed with Internet | - Internet is used for acquiring key services, relationships, buying and selling.<br><br>- New unique application sets driven by the Internet.<br>- Application is Internet-based |
| Internet technology frastructure | - Mostly data, graphics, sound, video, html Ipv4 based | - Voice, data, sound, video XML, Enterprise portals Ipv6 |
| Advances in IT solutions | - Three-tier client/server PC access | - N tier Internetworked client/services<br>- Collaboration/brokerage based |
| : Regulatory/government | - Minimal today | - Increasing due to security policies, privacy laws, revenue losses by states and countries. |
| Cultural/social | - National demographics<br>- Within country buying and selling | - Global demographics<br>- Global buying and selling |

The emerging online economy will thrive on the expansion of collaborative cu
tomers rather than just focus on an enterprise's own customers. For exampl
Microsoft's investment in AT&T is partially based on getting a share of the collabor
tive customer's wallet. An enterprise will need to offer more online services that ma
it easier for customers to do business with it, including brokerage/collaborative, ar
self-help. Success metrics will have more to do with customer retention and a great
share of their wallet rather than the number of customers and market share.

Every new wave of technology resets customer expectations. When faxes fir
arrived on the scene, they quickly became the preferred way to transfer informatio
E-mail raised the bar a bit and now it has become the choice for time-sensitive cor
munications. In the emerging online economy, voice, video, and wireless converge
make up the next medium for enhancing customer relationship-building.

Traditional business structures and processes are driven by a mass producti
mentality. This introduces a strict discipline in the supply chain, since the competiti
basis is generally low-cost or operational excellence. The name of the game is
attract as many customers as possible. All major end-to-end processes are part of t
enterprise's internal structure, although the enterprise has to be linked with partn
supplier, and sometimes customer processes.

In the online economy, a Value Network is created, which means we have
accommodate others' processes. Compaq and Dell are two examples of leading ent
prises that share some of their strategies with their suppliers to ensure that they a
fully connected to the manufacturing processes and can guarantee just-in-time deli
ery of OEM parts and equipment.

## Mass Customization

Traditionally, enterprises collaborated with others in similar businesses. IT compani
were partnering with and acquiring IT companies. Their online economy consisted
IT vendors, services, SIs, VARs, resellers, and distributors. Financial companies we
acquiring financial companies. For the most part, companies moved and flourished
their own online economy, much like certain types of sea life flourish in certain d
crete depths of the ocean.

In the developing online economy, you cannot assume that relationships w
technology-only companies will be sufficient for success. Since customer behavior
changing, the new model of alliances is emerging.

A few years ago, it would have been difficult to imagine that Disney, traditic
ally in the entertainment business, would collaborate with the Internet compa
InfoSeek to create a portal, or would work with NBC and Microsoft to cre
MSNBC. But it has.

Compaq's investment in CMGI (an Internet venture firm), Yahoo!'s collaboration with Dell, Microsoft's investments in Comcast, and now AT&T—these are just a few of the unexpected alliances that have evolved out of this new model.

What this means is that you will have to find your own online economy and determine how it will evolve in the future. Depending on your strategy, you may want to be a leader, a player or just be associated with the online economy.

You also have to take a much broader view in singling out your competition. In the past, competition was predictable and easily identified. New competition emerged slowly over a couple of years. It took companies like Digital, Hewlett Packard, Compaq, and others more than a decade to develop any significant competition with IBM.

## Changing Rules of Competition

The rules of competition will be defined by the collective capabilities of the emerging collaborations in the Value Network rather than the capabilities of individual enterprises. Competition will be based more on services than products. For example, recent moves by AT&T and Microsoft point to their collaborative effort to provide cable connections. WebTV solutions and other online information services have been formed by Time Warner, AOL, Worldcom/MCI, and others.

Sometimes competitors become collaborators. LTV Steel, Steel Dynamics, and Weirton—companies that were competitors—have formed MetalExchange.net to effectively sell their products to each other and to customers. Plastics.net is another example of an effective collaboration among former competitors.

The changing rules of business are shaping new models of competition in the online economy.

For example, for years, delivery of services has been based on people's competency, and business models have been developed accordingly. Now the Internet provides a more efficient and effective way to deliver services. It allows faster response to customer needs and faster ramping up of partners' skills.

*Compaq ActiveAnswers*™ rolls up the real-life experiences, shortcuts, and techniques for planning, design, and deployment of key enterprise solutions, such as ERP, and makes them available online to its partners and channels. This program makes answers available whenever they are needed and makes the information much easier and more cost-effective to use. These online services are complemented by using people skills for higher-complexity solutions. This is an example of how innovation in the services business models can be affected by the new online economy.

## IT Advances Fuel Online Economy

As more enterprises recognize the business-creation role of IT, a new online economy will emerge where IT departments are no longer captive within the enterprise but a part of a wider collaborative online economy. It will operate in a way similar today's collaboration of suppliers and partners.

New services will be offered that will make it easier for customers to get the services they want. Infrastructure services will find, access, collaborate with each other and deliver the end results to customers.

What has changed is the IT infrastructure itself. We are already seeing new way to access the Internet beyond the traditional use of PCs. Several new Internet appliances are emerging, including palmtops, WebTV interactive multimedia kiosks, and other specialized devices designed specifically for Internet access. As a result, the consumer will be empowered by technologies that merge the PC, palmtop, wireless and the Internet.

Technologies like the new enterprise portals, application servers, XML, and others may change and play an ever-increasing role in dictating system architectures and in determining the way solutions are delivered to customers. See Figure 4.2 for today and the emerging IT Infrastructure.

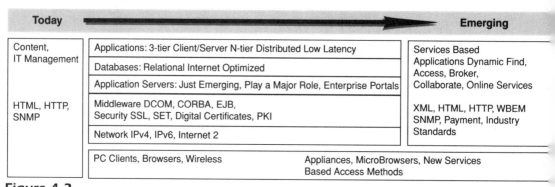

**Figure 4.2**

Today and the Emerging IT Infrastructure

There will be two major types of advances in the emerging Information Technology infrastructure. The first will be based on the integration and extension of the capabilities of traditional types of applications with the power of Internet technology. The Internet-based versions of SAP® R/3® and BaaN's ERP applications and Enterprise portals are examples of advances by extension. The second type of advance will be a new set of online services-based applications that automatically seek, use, and collaborate with other online services to meet the needs of users.

As the online economy emerges, many things will change. The way businesses create advantage with IT, access information and applications, and the services that will be offered over the Internet will look much different than they do today.

The key to success is to anticipate change and respond to it.

# GUIDELINE 3: DEFINE YOUR ROLE AND RELEVANCE IN THE NEW ONLINE ECONOMY . . . . . . . . . . . . . . . . . .

The third guideline—defining your role and relevance—is an important consideration for companies and managers in creating their strategic plan. Consider three probable scenarios:

1. **Your company becomes a leader in the online economy.** For example, Microsoft and Intel have created an online economy where thousands of ISVs, consultants, training, hardware, and services are being developed. In the next few years, AT&T may become another major player in user connectivity with their $100 billion worth of acquisitions. Amazon.com, with its sprawling network of 200,000 associates and new entries into auction, pharmaceuticals, videos, gifts, CDs, and other areas may create another online economy. You want to decide if this is a suitable role for your enterprise.

2. **You become a major participant in a high-growth and profitable online economy driven by others.** In this case, you want to play a major role rather than be the center of the online economy. Dell has benefited from the popularity of Intel and Microsoft. Many infomediaries will play this role.

3. **You become a niche player in the online economy.** In this case, you choose to focus on and excel in your respective area of expertise. Exchange.com, recently purchased by amazon.com for $200+ million, was focused on the rare books niche market. Many infomediaries may assume roles in health care, travel, music, IT or other areas where they can thrive at the depths of online oceans where no large predators exist.

## Lessons to Be Learned:

1. Do not plan only around existing market conditions or follow the lead of others. It may be too late. Anticipate where the ecosystem is going and plan accordingly.

2. The planning cycle has to be much shorter and in lock step with the rate of change.

3. In the new ecosystem, surviving alone will be difficult. Many collaborations and virtual enterprise relationships are being formed to create advantage. Some examples are AT&T and Microsoft's $5 billion investments.

4. Do not look at your immediate and traditional competition. Take a global view of customers and the new market possibilities.

5. You need to define the role you want to play and how you will succeed in the emerging ecosystem as creator, player or niche participant. Be clear about the implications and know your customer base.

## IT Implications:

1. Investigate new IT solutions that have the capability of disrupting the market or changing the preferences of customers.

2. Choose IT suppliers who have an understanding of the global online ecosystem and are investing in Internet-driven, standards-based solutions.

3. Depending on the role you want to play—leader, major player or niche player—your IT strategy has to be defined to accommodate partners and the suppliers.

4. The IT blueprint will have to mirror the requirements for participating collaborators in the online ecosystem. If not, they will seek better terms with your competition.

5. Designing proprietary architectures will make it difficult to become agile and cost-effective in the emerging ecosystem.

6. Scalable, 24/7 solutions will be needed when online markets stay open 365 days a year.

# 5

# he Importance of Customer Management

..........................

*S*ummary: *The customer is always right...at least when it comes to how he or she wants to buy online. While customers are looking for bargains and convenience, airlines and other companies are looking for ways to increase just-in-time sales of commodities that might otherwise go unsold. Enter priceline.com with its recently patented e-commerce system that allows prices for airline tickets, as well as new cars, home mortgages, hotel rooms, rental cars and more, to be set, not by the seller, but by the buyer—in real time. This e-commerce system is transforming a fundamental aspect of economics—supply and demand—into a powerful new business model.*

Let's face it. Customer service and being customer-driven are not new ideas. Taking steps to improve customer satisfaction is not a dramatic new recommendation. The success of every business depends on meeting the needs of customers.

However, being your customer's advocate puts the effort on a different plane. The goal is to think and feel like your customers, to try to develop knowledge of your customer base that can become the basis of a long-term commitment to serving them—and eventually the basis of a relationship—the essence of customer advocacy. It is worth the effort. Customer advocacy builds long-term loyalty among your client base.

In Chapter 4 we introduced the five strategies for gaining instant advantage and discussed the first strategy, "Seize Market Opportunities." In Chapter 5, we explore the second strategy: "Become Your Customer's Advocate."

## TRATEGY #2: BECOME YOUR USTOMER'S ADVOCATE . . . . . . . . . . . . . . . . . . . .

The remarkable power shift in the marketplace—from sellers to buyers—is driving the extraordinary emphasis that online companies are placing on customer loyalty. In the online world, the consumer is king. Customers increasingly make buying decisions

without vendors exercising a formal role. The routine sales process, controlled by t
seller, has no validity in the digital economy. The sales pitch is obsolete. The purpo
of the sales pitch was to convince the customer of the value of a company's produ
or service. That presumed a level of ignorance or naiveté on the part of the prospe
tive customer.

Internet customers have access to sales information without the aid of a sale
person. They tend to know exactly what they want. Being truly empowered, they co
duct their own research and trust their own judgment. This is forcing a changing of t
guard and a shifting of roles in the sales community.

There is growing evidence that customers are going online for complex-soluti
sales. The online purchase offers strong appeal to knowledgeable buyers, even wh
the transaction involves considerable analysis of such factors as risk, services, syste
integration skills, capacity, industry knowledge, and expertise in multiple technolo
disciplines. Based on the spectacular growth of e-commerce just in the last two yea
one thing is clear—customers prefer to shop and buy online.

Customers are looking for easy ways to do business with you. If you can of
an online buying experience that is superior to others, customers will come back
you repeatedly. That's what the new value proposition is.

## A Customer Value Proposition Change

Traditionally, value propositions have evolved from the vendor's point of view. T
old value proposition was based on performance, preferences, price, convenienc
choices, quality, differentiation, and advantage to customers. Delivery was based
the traditional supply chain. This approach is no longer enough...because now t
customer has control.

Power began shifting from the seller to the buyer when supply started to exce
demand, and customers had more choices. Still, in most of those cases there was
opportunity to engage customers in traditional marketing and selling interactions. T
customer did not have the benefit of all the information that can now be gather
online almost instantaneously.

The most dramatic example of shift in customer power is priceline.com. On t
site, the recently patented e-commerce system allows the buyer to set prices for airli
tickets, new cars, home mortgages, hotel rooms, and rental cars—all in real time.

## Customer Demands: Speed and Control

The uniqueness of the digital economy is its ability to provide choice and speed
buyers, with which they can access what they want. They immediately have the inf
mation necessary to make a buying decision.

In this environment, companies don't have a chance to work the conventional sales cycle. It is all over in a matter of minutes, if not seconds, before prospective customers move on to the next better site.

Obviously, sales processes that are complex in nature, such as selling large customized worldwide IT solutions that require services expertise, may not be affected to the same extent as commodity sales.

Even there, changes are taking place. Witness *Compaq ActiveAnwers*™ that provides access to solution knowledge online to reduce the risk and shorten the deployment cycle for leading software solutions like SAP and Lotus.

Customer proposition factors, in the customer buying process, merge with the traditional value proposition. It is a compelling experience at every stage. Information Technology makes the ultimate buying experience a real possibility in this proposition. See Table 5.1.

**ble 5.1**   Traditional Value Proposition and Customer Proposition: A Comparison

| ey Components of a alue Proposition | Traditional Approach | Customer Proposition Approach |
|---|---|---|
| ho is the customer? What e his requirements? | Based on requirements of broad segments. | Individual customers, or as close to that ideal as possible. |
| hat is the unique stomer experience offered? | Usually ignored or not taken seriously as its measurement is difficult. This is because it is the combined result of the engagement of different functional groups. Emphasis is on advantages and benefits. | Very important. Experience starts with log-on to the site. Expectations are driven by what customers would like the experience to be, all the way from first contact to selection and usage to pre and post sales support. In addition, by what is best in class. |
| hat are the price/quality/ rvices/performance-feature nefits? | Driven by vendor assessment of how customers will benefit. Based on a view of how to delight customers. | Value has an additional element of time and impulse buying. Value is often determined by a particular moment's online comparative assessment. |
| ow will value be delivered? | Based on how vendor infrastructure and processes are set up to deliver. | Based on the customer's view of how best to receive value. |

**Table 5.1**    Traditional Value Proposition and Customer Proposition: A Comparison (continued)

| Key Components of a Value Proposition | Traditional Approach | Customer Proposition Approach |
|---|---|---|
| What results are expected? | Based on vendor objectives of what actions they want customers to take next, such as buy more, annuity business, etc. | Based on customers' objective and what actions they want from vendors next, such as ho to get the most ROI from investment. |
| How is this proposition better than the alternatives? | Based on vendor's view of pros and cons and by vendor's competitive analysis. | The superiority of the online experience weighs heavily in the determination of its advantages over the alternative |

The focal point of the New Value Proposition is looking at it from the customer point of view. That is the key to making it easier for him to do business with you.

Ideally, you must think like the customers and see firsthand what your custome experience. It is not enough to do market research to find out their needs. Many tim their experience cannot be interpreted or appreciated until you actually have had t same experience.

The challenge is to merge traditional customer research with information on ho the customer actually clicks through the website. Tools are available from HitList a other vendors to monitor these tasks.

Also, the results of the customer's experience have to be benchmarked with t industry leader. You do not really know how good or bad your experience is until y see what it feels like to experience the best-in-class.

The bottom line of the New Value Proposition is for customers to have a sat fying shopping experience when they are engaged with you.

## Provide Customers with the Ultimate Shopping Experience

If you want customers to keep coming back, some basic things need to be consider You have to make sure that your customer interfaces are flawless. It has to be mu easier for them to do business with you than with your competition. Here are four ru for building strong relationships and brand loyalty:

1.  Excel at each stage of the customer buying cycle. Build relationships.
2.  Match your processes to customers' expectations.
3.  Empower customers to help themselves.
4.  Help them succeed by providing them value-added capability.

# ULE 1. EXCEL AT EACH STAGE OF THE CUSTOMER UYING CYCLE. BUILD RELATIONSHIPS . . . . . . . . . . . .

The whole concept of buying is changing. In the past, vendors targeted customers by using extensive database management tools, data warehouses, data mining, and other marketing techniques. These tools are still important from the vendor's point of view, and we will cover some of these in Chapter 6.

Now, however, customers find vendors by using their own online search methods. This is the reverse of vendor database marketing. It's more like the existing Yellow Pages. The difference is that buyers go to search engines, like AltaVista, and do searches for product categories of their interest. Customers will go to procurement sites like Commerce One and search product categories. They will use intelligent agents from companies like NetBot and Junglee. Junglee was acquired by amazon.com. Other enterprises that provide intelligent agents will be targeted for acquisition by companies like compare.com, buy.com, and bigyellow.com.

## Branding is More Important than Ever

Branding has always been important. Now it is more important than ever, as customers click through the Net, wanting to do business with a known quantity that offers them a sense of trust and a level of comfort.

You need an integrated marketing effort that gives you a presence in key portals and allows you to advertise in the traditional media with online reinforcement. In addition, you need links to key brand name collaborators. More on marketing will be covered in the next section.

Once customers have found you, the next step is to give them a positive experience throughout the buying process. Whenever possible, make the site simple and easy to navigate, make downloads fast, offer the kind of value that keeps customers coming back, and provide powerful searches. Most important of all, establish a relationship, within the boundaries of privacy laws, that allows you to gather information about their preferences. This information will ultimately help you serve them better. These points are covered in Table 5.2.

**Table 5.2** Customer Cycle Buying

| Task | Learn about products | Determine fit with needs | Compare/evaluate | Buy | Repeat buy |
|---|---|---|---|---|---|
| Increase convenience/ easiest to do business with | -Available 24/7 -Up-to-date information -Easy navigation -Downline load -Powerful search -Value Proposition -Comparative info. -Info. from renowned sources | -Create real situation-centric information, rather than vendor oriented info. | -Configure online -Compare online -White papers from experts -Other usage stories | -Simple order process -Acknowledge correct order -Shipment and tracking status -Customer's self tracking at all stages | -One-click orders -Send updates automatically -Send new information as required -Make suggestions based on previous sales |
| Make it fast/ don't keep them waiting | -Fast access times -Real-time info. -Let them know if slow | -Use tools that can help: internal portals, search engines for accelerated information, etc. | -Provide fast responses. If long wait, update on progress -Use powerful configuration tools | -Confirm orders fast –Delivery updates -Configuration short cuts -Software downloads | -Offer free shipping upgrades |
| Provide relevant content | -Create info. on the fly by monitoring clicks. Create scenarios for customers to experience | -Create context -Recommend items that make it better | -Provide visual views of their selections and configurations | -Recommend useful items that complement the sale | -Ask what information would be of interest to them in the future |
| Provide online help | Online option to receive personal help | -Self help -Peer forums -Expert online | -Expert walk-through | -Configuration -Experts | -Interactive training -Experts, |

| Task | Learn about products | Determine fit with needs | Compare/ evaluate | Buy | Repeat buy |
|---|---|---|---|---|---|
| Personalize | -Option to create personalized site -Incentives for info. -Send customized information to suit their learning needs | -Ask them to fill out simple questionnaire and then create suggestions about situations while customer is online exploring | -Offer use of special tools –White papers –Other customized information to help decision-making | -Best way to ship -Lowest cost or fastest delivery options –Options of support | -Build a special welcome page for them to keep track of their buys, project progress, contracts, account status, and other important items in a secure fashion -Real-time appreciation |
| Build trust | -Team up with a known expert of known leaders in the industry | -Offer choice of buying direct, -Auctions -Channels | -Offer access to a wide range of solutions, even competitive | -Acknowledge by e-mail immediately. | -Keep customers informed about latest updates, new solutions, and fixes before they find in press or other sources |
| Cultivate interest | Interactive offer awards | -Interactive | -Chat groups -Auctions | -Awards for discounts | -Offer new services and information. -Request inputs, and reviews |
| Excel at total experience | -Create learning in their own context -Send more info based on request, e-mail answers, voice | -Offer expert, customized help, information packages, catalogs | -Customized choice of solutions and pricing -Tools for decisions | -Ability to track from manufacturing to delivery | -Provide options to keep track of their information or for them to keep their personalized site updated with service information |

# RULE 2. MATCH YOUR PROCESSES
# WITH CUSTOMERS' EXPECTATIONS . . . . . . . . . . . . .

Inconsistencies in processes, communications, and execution are major causes lower operational efficiency, customer dissatisfaction, and the inability to prope understand the needs of the emerging markets. The inconsistencies become magnifi when different groups in the enterprise operate as stovepipe functions.

It is critical that Rule Number Two—Match your Processes with Custome Expectations—be followed, because your competition is working 24 hours a day exploit any weakness your enterprise has. Every good customer experience in the d ital economy should propel your enterprise to provide even better service.

Unforeseen events can create inconsistencies that cause problems with custom satisfaction. Take the simple example of a traveler who has a complete set of tra reservations, including flights, hotels, cars, and events. If he misses the flight, whole itinerary may have to be rearranged. In the traditional environment, this wo take a good deal of effort. In the online world, it might be done with a few clicks.

In the pre-digital world, solutions did not address these issues, due to expense or limitations of the technology. Now, with the real time, interactive power online information technology, many inconsistencies caused by unforeseen events ( be converted to an advantage.

If you can improve your services to help customers minimize discontinuity the buying experience, you will have a significant competitive advantage.

It is relatively easy to achieve consistency when just one company is invol' in the buying and selling process. When you add more players or unusual circu stances, problems can emerge. These problems become even more pronounced wl an increasing number of external parties are involved in the loop.

With the emergence of dynamic Value Networks and the increasing focus enterprises to provide one-stop solutions, the number of different parties involvec a transaction becomes even higher. On one hand, the added power of collabora enterprises enhances the ability to meet customer needs. On the other hand, the cha of inconsistency increases, due to the complexity of the infrastructure.

Looking again at the man with the travel reservations, several enterprises involved, including airlines, car rental companies, hotels, traveler check provid and so on. First, either the customer has to engage with many disparate companies the travel agency may have a unified front, but has to execute many disparate ( cesses. Second, this all works well when the events chain is functioning accordin plan. Nevertheless, when inconsistencies emerge, the recovery processes are always well-defined or effective.

For example, to get an airline passenger on track due to a missed connectio is necessary to have a "manual" intervention. This starts with the passenger callin agent, finding different connections, being rebooked in hotels, transferring luggage, and adjusting fares.

The Internet, with its ubiquitous connectivity and almost real-time response, can turn this discontinuity into continuity almost instantly.

The whole process could be done by dynamically linking the disparate parties and processes without human intervention. All aspects of scheduling, rebooking of hotels, cars, luggage transfers, and financial issues are addressed instantaneously, without inconveniencing the traveler.

In the not too distant future, IT solutions will allow this type of transaction to be routine. Intermediary service providers, specializing in dynamically linking of disparate processes, may also emerge.

Other examples of discontinuities occur in shipping and tracking. For example, when customers' shipments sometimes are changed, invoices and billing information don't track the changes. This causes dissatisfaction and wasted effort. In the online world, one click can ensure that the transaction is handled properly.

In consumer-to-business engagement, matching your processes with those of your customers means that your site, layouts, navigation, billing, shipping, and support must make the consumer feel comfortable.

Other online transactions, such as business-to-business, also need to match as much as possible to the customer's style. Many customers have multiple entry points into the enterprise. They may access a marketing site for products, support sites for services, and another site for billing information. With online providing the customer a complete exposure to your enterprise, it's a win/win for both parties: Customers have a good shopping experience and you get to show them your end-to-end capabilities, and may even be able to sell more products. At Compaq, valuable customers even get access to future product direction, which in most enterprises is highly confidential information.

# ULE 3. EMPOWER CUSTOMERS
# Ɔ HELP THEMSELVES . . . . . . . . . . . . . . . . . .

Most customers like to find out things in their own way and on their own time. It makes them feel that they are in control, rather than being dependent on you. This is another way you can provide the ultimate shopping experience.

Customers can help themselves in identifying sources of information and asking questions. Some questions that customers will ask, and activities from which they can benefit, include:

- Asking "What is the status of my shipment?"
- Asking "Where is my order in the manufacturing cycle?"
- Asking "What is the account status? When are my services contracts expir-ing, how many products do I have on lease, how many licenses do I have and who has them? "
- Chatting with peers to get ideas on how to solve problems
- Updating their own website with relevant information about the above points

These activities not only make customers feel more confident about doing bu ness with you, but they help reduce your operating costs substantially. Cisco has sav more than $500 million over the past few years by providing this kind of self-he capability.

# RULE 4. HELP YOUR CUSTOMERS SUCCEED . . . . . . .

The fourth rule for building strong relationships and brand loyalty is to do everythi possible to make it easier for customers to conduct business online. In so doing, y empower them to be in control of their situation. However, this is only part of the so tion. You also have to help them succeed in their missions. In the past, sales peo would do whatever it took to help their clients succeed. For example, in the world Information Technology, sales people would help customers find the best secur solutions, skilled resources, new ideas, trusted consultants, and contacts with pe who may have similar experiences.

Online solutions can now provide customers with personalized access to t kind of information. Interactive online access also provides you with a means to id tify their needs. You can reach them, learn about their needs online, and get back them promptly with answers. Depending on the needs trends you discover, you create useful sites based on common requirements. For example, you can develop u ful information for purchasing managers, IT managers, finance managers from d based on demographics, interest groups, and so on.

The new enterprise portals, which are now being created, deliver the capabi of the old Enterprise Information Systems (EIS)—but with a different twist. Th new systems are available to customers, so you can gather, sort, and automatically ward information to your clients based on their needs.

# SHIFT IN CUSTOMER POWER . . . . . . . . . . . . . . . . .

## Priceline.com's Pioneering Business Model

Businesses are sparing no effort to leverage the Internet for creating and expanding markets. One example is priceline.com, whose patented e-commerce system is transforming a fundamental aspect of economics—supply and demand—into a powerful new business model.

Until now, purchasing products reflected a centuries-old way of doing business: The seller set the price for the buyer. Priceline.com's e-commerce system turns this paradigm on its ear. The customers are the ones who set the price, and the sellers determine whether to sell at that price.

Priceline.com delivers compelling benefits to buyers and sellers. Buyers can name their own prices for products and guarantee the purchase via credit card. The buyer's "conditional purchase offer" authorizes priceline.com to purchase the product on their behalf—if priceline.com finds a seller willing to meet that price. Sellers can individually and discreetly fill the demand at whatever price point they choose, without publicly announced sales that erode retail fare structures and margins.

Initially, priceline.com focused on two products that share high value and heavy competitive pressures: leisure airline tickets and new cars. By the end of 1999, the company had added name-your-own-price services for home mortgages, hotel rooms, rental cars, groceries, telephone services, and more.

## The Internet Empowers Customers

This concept has struck a chord with buyers and sellers alike, making priceline.com one of the fastest-growing companies and most-recognized names on the Internet.

"The priceline.com e-commerce system is a great mechanism. It simplifies what can be a very complex buying process for consumers," says Ron Rose, priceline.com's CIO. "We provide an outlet for airlines to sell highly perishable inventory to value-minded customers. On U.S. domestic flights, there are up to 500,000 empty seats every day. Each unsold seat means lost revenue."

Priceline.com is also one of most heavily trafficked sites on the Internet. To handle its current volume and anticipated growth, priceline.com architected a system capable of highly personalized customer experiences based, in part, on *Compaq ProLiant* servers, Oracle® databases, and Microsoft® Windows® NT-based Web server tools.

## New Paradigms

Priceline.com evolved from its sister company, Walker Digital. An intellectual p
erties laboratory, Walker Digital developed the concept of buyer-driven e-comme
where priceline.com "harvests" customer demand and presents it to sellers. The c
pany collects customers' offers and payment guarantees—typically, credit card n
bers—and then presents offers to merchants, who make the decision whether to
their products based on the customers' criteria.

For airline tickets, a potential customer goes online, enters the departure p
and destination, days of travel, and a desired purchase price. The customer waives
right to other selection criteria, such as the desired airline, frequent flier miles, or
cific departure/arrival times.

Priceline.com's computer system queries a private, continually changing sec
of the WorldSpan computer reservation system, where 28 major domestic and ir
national airlines have stored seats and fares. If priceline.com can assemble an itine
that meets the buyer's specifications, the ticket is booked immediately. Buyers rec
an answer in one hour.

The priceline.com car buying service, launched in July 1998, works in a sli
ly different manner. Customers select models with preferences, such as colors
options, and the prices they are willing to pay. Priceline.com faxes the request t
factory-authorized dealers in the customer's geographic area. When a dealer acc
the buyer's offer, the paperwork is completed and the deal is closed—without
gling or high-pressure sales tactics. In fact, the only time customers see the auto d
ers is when they pick up their new cars.

"This is an arrangement that benefits both sides," Rose says. "We help
tomers avoid haggling while harvesting demand for dealers and helping them m
expensive inventory off their lots."

## NonStop Service

"There's a lot of money at stake for everyone—the airlines, the customers and p
line.com," says Rose. "Our site is our storefront. The economic impact of down
is both substantial and unacceptable."

Rose identified three critical characteristics for the site's architecture:

1. Availability is crucial to the nature of priceline.com's 24/7 business plan
2. The site needs to support priceline.com's rapid growth, so the architec
   ture's scalability became a decision point.

3. As with any database-driven website, performance is critical as well. With every transaction, priceline.com's systems need to match customer preferences with airline or automobile dealership data in a matter of seconds.

Priceline.com's plans required a flexible architecture that optimized performance in different tasks. Web servers were needed on the front end to perform dedicated tasks, such as creating Web pages on the fly, managing customer service requests and trafficking HTTP requests. "The technology driving priceline.com had to offer high performance for handling significant demand from the outset," concludes Rose. "The architecture had to scale rapidly for future growth."

## Integrating Business and IT Strategies

Priceline.com's plans reflect an IT strategy being adopted by many Internet companies. The architecture is defined by Compaq as the DISA (Distributed Internet Server Array) architecture.

In sites configured with DISA, banks of high-volume application servers are deployed on the front end with availability provided through intelligent server load-balancing technology. Powerful high-end servers and storage arrays drive the mission-critical databases, which are protected with clustered servers.

Previously the domain of expensive proprietary platforms, these sophisticated Internet-based businesses can now use industry-standard building blocks. DISA provides users the ability to affordably and flexibly scale as needed, while delivering performance and reliability for a business environment that never shuts down.

"We decided on a high-volume strategy for our frontline servers," says Rose. "This lets us easily distribute heavy loads and maintain or replace systems without really affecting the performance of the Web site."

As customers access the website, HTTP information flows through a bank of Cisco Local Directors. This Cisco-developed device acts as an intelligent load balancer, distributing traffic across an array of ProLiant servers to optimize performance and availability.

Rose uses the quad-processor Compaq ProLiant 6400 server as the front-end unit. "Compaq rack servers are ideal for our configuration. We can devote a server to one specific task—use it as a Web server, for example, and eliminate worries about conflicts. We can easily bring these servers in and out of commission for maintenance with minimal impact to the site."

Priceline.com has deployed more than 100 *ProLiant* 1850 and 6400 servers. Connectivity is handled through redundant Netelligent 10/100 duplex network interface cards. Priceline.com packs these servers into its New Jersey Exodus data center,

using Compaq racks for space optimization and advanced cable-management featur
necessary when implementing a high-volume server strategy.

## The Internet Equals Mission Critical

As the *ProLiant* servers process customer requests, a custom Java middleware app
cation continuously batches information and sends it to priceline.com's mass
Oracle for Windows NT database. With information on airline schedules and pric
auto dealerships across the country and new car specifications, this database conta
the information priceline.com needs to fulfill customer requests.

The database also processes credit-card transactions and communicates with
central reservation system to retrieve airfare and flight schedule information. "Ora
is a mature, robust database with plenty of development support," says Rose. "We
already started using it for a data warehouse application. With Oracle, we have a cl
upgrade path."

## Seamless Enterprise

Because priceline.com's business model is new, much of the site's engineering ta
place in-house. The specialized programming needed to create priceline.com's uni
customer experience, however, is engineered on easily-managed off-the-shelf ap
cations, such as Microsoft Visual InterDev.

Programmers and site designers use standards-based Compaq Professic
Workstation 5100 systems running Windows NT Workstation. Compaq ProLiant 6
and ProLiant 7000 servers running development and office networking functions s
port the workstations. The enterprise is tied together with support from Com
reseller and field engineering resources.

"We knew that the development platform would be easier to manage if the wc
stations were also Windows NT-based," says Rose. "We develop and stage appl
tions offline, using the security and versioning features of Visual InterDev. When
time to deploy on the main Web site, we just move the application onto the ser
There's none of the porting hassles of using a proprietary workstation. The *Com*
workstations give us great performance and reliability."

## Strategic Thinking

The architecture that priceline.com has deployed is benefiting the company c
strategic level, and in day-to-day operations. "The database information that we g
er from customers during their visits is critical," says Rose. "There is a ton of in

mation at a very granular level about what customers want. This 'demand' information is very valuable beyond the specific transactions. It provides us with an incredibly rich knowledge base that will help us create products and build our business."

"To collect the information we need, we need the utmost in reliability. The Compaq systems deliver," Rose adds. "They give us the redundancy that's required for true 24/7 uptime. The great thing about this configuration is that if one server is brought down for maintenance, we only lose a fraction of our capacity for a short time. If we were using a proprietary architecture, we could lose 50% of our capacity by losing one machine."

# 6

# einvent Your Enterprise

........................

*Summary:* As you continue to evolve your enterprise from a conventional to an Internet-based business, there are several important areas you need to address. In this chapter, we look at a number of ways you can literally reinvent your enterprise. We'll show you why changing your enterprise is only half of the battle—you also need to develop a strong and lasting presence on the Internet. We'll show you how you can build your enterprise's visibility, by taking advantage of the trend toward "intermediation," which means linking customers to the best sources for their information and purchases. And we discuss the importance of unification of products and services, as well as trends in e-marketing, that can engender ongoing customer loyalty. Finally, we talk about e-selling—the techniques that give you a real competitive edge.

## STRATEGY #3: REINVENT YOUR ENTERPRISE . . . . . . . .

Reinventing your enterprise is much more than fine-tuning business models, processes, and methods. When a company commits to reinventing itself, energy is created and released throughout the enterprise. It is a focused, driving energy—the kind of energy that makes change possible.

Many successful online enterprises have been reinvented, evolving from conventional businesses to Internet-based successes. One example is DoveBid, Inc., a 62-year-old auction house based in Foster City, California. DoveBid manages equipment auctions for major corporations—like General Electric—all over the world. Although the family-owned business is profitable (1998 revenues of $15 million on sales of about $100 million), the family became convinced that they would not be able to compete for long with Web-based competitors—unless they went online as well.

And not just go online. They had to reinvent themselves, with a new mission, business plan, financing, and marketing. Their new mission was to become the leading onsite and online business auction company in the industry. In their business plan,

they sought to exploit their superb facilities, their long-term business relationshi
and their 62 years of experience to gain the advantage over the new online comp
tion, which includes iMark.com, TradeOut.com, and AsseTrade.com.

Financing of $12 million was sought and secured from venture capitali
Fremont Ventures and the Mayfield Fund. Financing was essential for implement
their new marketing plan and building their auction site, which was configured w
software from OpenSite Technologies, Inc. Their marketing plan included launch
DoveBid.com in November 1999. This business-to-business auction site offers th
sands of different types of business equipment—from manufacturing to medicine.

DoveBid management is pleased with the results of their efforts. To their way
thinking, they have the best of both worlds: On the Web, they are not hamstrung
the limited amount of products that can be offered to a limited number of buyers
onsite sales. At the same time, they bring a large and loyal customer base from th
onsite business to DoveBid.com—an asset that their new online competitors have
yet been able to match.

When companies entertain the notion of reinventing the enterprise, they typi
ly have business models that fall into one of three categories or situations:

1.  The business model meets current needs but online solutions can make the
    company more efficient.
2.  The business model needs some fine-tuning, with the help of online solu-
    tions.
3.  The business model needs a complete revamping; otherwise, the company
    may not survive in the new economy.

Most decisions will fall in the comfort zone of the first two categories. These
uations are comfort zones because the business model is proven; it works today
requires no major disruption to the existing sales, marketing and other functions.

But the third model is like emergency surgery. Without it, the patient dies.
can revamp your business model by putting a transition plan in place using our "
cute, check, fix and plan" rule. You may also use strategies of complementing y
existing models with online solutions.

## Reinvention in the Digital Economy

In the digital economy, the way things are sold has changed. We have discussed how this is happening with books, cars, PCs, and servers, as well as in such industries as real estate and banking. Virtual banks in the U.S. are now firmly established. Banks in Europe and the Far East are fast approaching the same level of online service.

The Royal Bank of Scotland, one of the UK's largest banks, saw the opportunity. It responded by being the first bank in England to announce an online banking service with 24-hour telephone banking capability.

The bank employs 18,000 people and, in 1996, had assets of more than 61 billion pounds ($98 billion US). The Retail Banking Division of the Royal Bank of Scotland provides financial products and services to more than 3.5 million personal and business customers through 650 branches. The bank has a long history of innovation. It produced Europe's first multicolored banknotes in 1777 to combat fraud and pioneered the double-sided printing of notes in 1826. In recent times, The Royal Bank of Scotland became the first British bank to put its extensive branch network online with a central computer and to put customers' photographs on plastic cards. It continues to innovate with the launching of direct banking by PC.

According to Bill Bougourd, head of electronic communication for the bank's retail banking section, "Currently 11% of UK adults use the Internet, and we believe that over time the Internet will play an increasingly important role in the lives of our customers."

"We chose to implement Internet banking services because it is so widely accessible," said Bougourd.

"Naturally, we were interested in adding online Internet banking to further enhance the range of choice our customers have, but we were also concerned to ensure it was a secure and reliable system."

Direct banking by PC can be accessed through the bank's website at www. rbos.co.uk. Customers can view balances, account details and statements. They can pay bills, transfer money between accounts and order checkbooks.

Looking to the future, The Royal Bank of Scotland plans to refine and expand its online banking service and is re-evaluating its entire sales process. The concept of the virtual branch is at hand.

## Reinvention Begins with the Right Target

In the digital economy, change occurs at breathtaking speed. New types of decisic makers emerge. The decision cycle has collapsed—from months to the mome Today's customers may not turn out to be the best in the long run. For example, i tial Web surfers were technology-oriented, college-educated males, with accessibil to Internet technology. They were intent on discovery rather than purchases. The s ond wave of users was again younger males who grew up playing video games. 1 third wave brought serious consumers who were interested in buying onli Business-to-business commerce came later.

Manufacturing took the early lead in developing business-to-business comme online. According to Frank Gens, Group Vice President of IDC Technology, industr that were slower to capitalize on the Internet, such as health care, financial servi and retail, may outdo the initial inroads made by the manufacturing segment. S Figure 6.1 for the industries the IDC considers to be the best prospects on the Intern

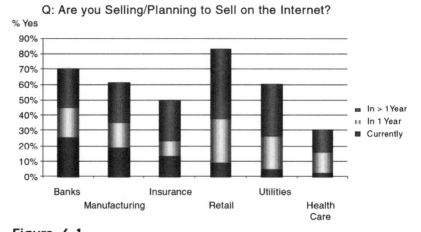

**Figure. 6.1**

**Which industries will be the best prospects?** *Used with the permission of International Data Corporation ©1*

The female audience, which was almost nonexistent in the early days of Internet, is now growing much faster than their male counterparts. Studies show females now are much more likely to buy certain classes of products than males.

According to 1997 *BusinessWeek* and Harris polls, women accounted for 37% Internet users in the US. This number will grow to 46% in 1999. Other surveys e mate that 60% of users in Sweden and 40% in Japan are women. And women demanding a much wider range of services than men.

# EINVENT TO BUILD NEW RELATIONSHIPS . . . . . . . . .

If your strategy is based on low costs, you have to examine the basis for the cost advantages and examine those cost advantages in relation to the impact of the Internet. If your strategy is based on relationships, you have to examine what will change as competition targets one-on-one relationships with your customers.

To reinvent your enterprise, you will have to test all of the business assumptions you have ever made. In the digital economy, the rules have changed. Business assets may become liabilities. ROI may not be relevant. The following short list constitutes the most important rules of the game for reinventing your enterprise:

- Create a Value Network instead of optimizing your supply chain
- Drive e-efficiency and effectiveness
- E-innovate: create new services and products
- Excel in building relationships with e-marketing, e-selling, and e-support

Table 6.1 compares Business Strategy for old model assumptions and online model.

**ble 6.1**    Summary of Business Strategy /Models

| em | Old Model Assumptions | Online Model |
|---|---|---|
| fferentiation factors | Physical operations<br>Own core competency<br>Technology innovation<br>Relationships<br>Geographical coverage<br>Support, services | Online operation, information<br>Collaborative competencies<br>Online services innovations<br>1:1 relationships |
| sets/location | Physical locations critical | Online location critical |
| stribution channels | Must provide solutions, expertise, short delivery time, local support, etc. | Optional in many commodity-type businesses where customers know what they want. New value add needed |
| ermediary | Distribution, retail, wholesale, products, solutions orientation | E-intermediaries, such as<br>-Infomediary<br>-Marketmediaries<br>-Services mediaries |
| rriers to entry | Brand, channels, location, relationships, costs | Brand Name, 1:1 relationships |

**Table 6.1**   Summary of Business Strategy /Models (continued)

| Item | Old Model Assumptions | Online Model |
|---|---|---|
| Switching costs | High: specialized technology, skills | Low: Standardized online technology, skills, short product life cycles |
| Global presence | Difficult to attain | Relatively easy |
| Organization | IT as a function | IT as a strategy |

*Used with the permission of International Data Corp.*

# CREATE A VALUE NETWORK INSTEAD OF OPTIMIZING THE SUPPLY CHAIN . . . . . . . . . . . . . . .

To reinvent your enterprise, you need to create a Value Network, instead of just op mizing the supply chain. In the traditional supply chain, the challenge is to redu inefficiencies, costs, and times between different processes, so that maximum prof can be attained. Activities in the traditional supply chain are generally predictab You can work on optimizing them by re-engineering new processes and deployi new applications, such as ERP.

The traditional supply chain positions the seller in the middle between suppli and customers. Many advances have been made to optimize the chain, by introduci EDI, just-in-time, and electronic connections to suppliers and, in some cases, chann and customers.

This supply chain in the digital economy is being impacted in several ways. I becoming a Dynamic Value Chain, with the buyer in the middle. The supply chair shrinking, with some functions being disintermediated, or e-intermediated, and it new IT components.

Several of these IT components are increasingly grouped under zero-laten strategies, which are aimed at achieving rapid response rates across all enterprise p cesses. In a typical enterprise flow, like manufacturing or distribution, incom orders no longer get routed through a call center. Instead, they are funneled by a we site into an order-entry application, which triggers a build-order or a pick-and-pɛ routine, followed by the appropriate sequence of shipping and distribution activiti

In bypassing the conventional stages of order processing and other subproce es, the overall time-to-customer shipment has been shortened. The time buff between stages in the manufacturing supply chain are eliminated or greatly reduc with proportionate savings in cost and resources. Of course, such a zero-latency st egy is producing benefits in other vertical industries, such as publishing, finance, c

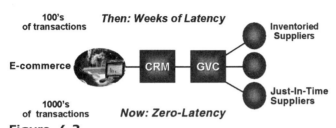

**Unstoppable Enterprise**

**Figure. 6.2**

The Unstoppable Enterprise

tribution, and automotive, aerospace, and consumer goods. Figure 6.2 illustrates the Unstoppable Enterprise.

The foundation of such time-to-solution strategies is an enterprise with an agile and flexible infrastructure that is highly available, scalable, and secure.

The online chain is now controlled by the buyer. Depending upon the situation, the customer approaches different enterprises and they in turn engage the best supplier for the situation. The success of the network is dependent upon the value each step is adding to the customer's buying process. The Value Chain is no longer based simply on reducing friction between steps and adding value to the vendor's processes.

The new economy introduces many different types of discontinuities and degrees of unpredictability into the overall system. It is more of a Value Network than a supply chain. In the new online Value Network, almost everything is online—customers, suppliers, and the manufacturing systems.

The whole nature of transaction is dynamic, in that one transaction may consist of different supply chain participants from the last one. For example, one transaction may have the following participants: the customer, enterprise X, supplier 1, financing institution C. The second transaction with the same customer now may require the same enterprise X to use supplier 2, and financial institution D, to remain competitive and provide personalized service to the customer.

The same customer has a choice to go to Enterprise Y for similar transactions. So the Value Chain has to be optimized around different participants. Transactions are dynamic in nature, requiring the enterprise to build different relationships immediately as required to best satisfy customer needs.

## Delivering Value to Customers

The challenge is to make sure that, while process inefficiencies are being minimize the overall value delivered to customers is being optimized. That will determine t best-in-class service.

Different companies use different strategies today to respond to the need of t Value Network. For example, some institutions are evaluating their supply chain to s if they can re-establish the boundaries of work to provide more value to their cu tomers. Some banks are looking into how much of their clients' work of managi invoices and reconciling payments with purchase orders they can assume to impro personal relationships with their customer base.

The Value Network is also being used to give immediate feedback to supplie and partners on what the most likely usage patterns are, so they can respond to char ing requirements.

*The name of the game in online business is to get to the customers with as f intermediaries as possible.* When the value of the commodity is known, or custome already know what they want to buy, or there are no value added services involve customers will go directly to the vendor, rather than through intermediaries.

## Drive E-Efficiencies and Effectiveness

Another important factor in reinventing your business to win in the digital econo is the use of online capabilities to drive new levels of efficiencies and effectiveness the enterprise.

Here are a few examples of companies achieving different levels of efficienc in the business operation: eBay's and amazon.com's revenues per employee stand $687,000 and $392,000 respectively, according to Morgan Stanley Dean Witter. T transaction costs for retail banking, which now are in the 5-10 cents range, are a fa tor of 10-20% lower than non-electronic transaction costs.

Efficiencies are defined here as a positive impact on costs, productivity, a effectiveness as a measure of the ability to do a better job, or the ability to do thi not possible before.

Here are some of the areas that are being positively impacted by compan using their online capabilities to reduce costs and increase effectiveness:

Efficiency:

- Selling, buying, and other business transaction costs
- Tracking, status checking, configuration, and order entry via self help
- Inventory and delivery costs

- Information access and distributions
- Software fixes, patch distributions
- Support, training costs

Effectiveness:

- Links to suppliers, customers, and partners
- Personalized relationships
- Handling of purchasing and following policies with buy-side solutions
- Demand forecasting, customized to order
- Communications
- Market information gathering, customers, manufacturing
- Others' information search, personalized information, distribution
- One-click services

## E-Innovate: Create New Services and E-Commerce

Reinventing an enterprise means innovation. In the digital economy, e-innovation-driven services create new advantage. This is not to say that focus on products and associated services will not be important. But, as e-commerce, e-business, and e-intermediaries become commonplace, the emphasis will shift to services.

Price comparison services, online expertise in the buying and selling processes, just-in-time inventory assistance and just-in-time sales information are a few of the services that are on the immediate horizon.

Many other innovative services are already appearing: amazon.com recommends books to customers similar to those they order. Garden.com offers an interactive planner to help people plan their gardens. Gap provides "instant styles." Computer Shopper allows users to compare products from multiple vendors.

With the emergence of faster pipes to the consumer's home and business, services possibilities will explode. Today, TV, radio, the Internet, newspapers and magazines usually come from different sources. When the fast pipe delivers all communication with interactivity, it will become the most important information and entertainment center of nearly everyone's household. Training, software distribution, music, and movie distribution services will all change dramatically. Figure 6.3 shows how fast pipe content delivery drives change.

The fastest and highest impact will be on businesses whose content can be digitized easily, as in the entertainment, travel, media, publishing, information, and soft-

**Figure. 6.3**

Fast Pipe Content Delivery Drives Change

ware industries. All industry will be impacted to varying degrees. The services become a major contributor to revenue as well as a differentiator.

## Excel in Building Relationships with E-Marketing, E-Sales, and E-Support

Reinvention of an enterprise for the digital economy requires building new and ferent kinds of relationships with customers. This is necessary because of the ways that business is being conducted in the e-commerce environment.

There are many definitions of electronic commerce. From selling to buying, t include the full range of activities required in the exchange of goods, services information.

The digital economy has a much broader definition of e-commerce.

To establish some meaningful parameters, we have limited the definition o commerce to "a full set of Internet and electronic-based activities required for establishment of relationships and for the exchange of goods, services or informatic

Our definition includes all aspects of marketing, selling and support to gain ly conduct business, share information, and/or collaborate. Many rules of marketi selling and support will change in the digital economy, and will require differ approaches, processes and techniques.

Traditionally, marketing has segmented the market, and then created strateg to win the segments. The 4Ps of marketing—product, place, promotion, and pric have been the guiding principles for effective marketing for years. In the online wo definitions, content, strategies and activities are changing. Sometimes "place" d not have any significance at all.

# HE NEW WORLD OF E-MARKETING . . . . . . . . . . . . .

There are key differences between conventional marketing and what may be called e-marketing.

Traditionally, vendors used different types of segmentation and database marketing techniques to target their customers. In a variation of database marketing, the reverse will happen as well. Customers will find the vendors most suitable for them. Your marketing challenge is to make sure you are on their preferred list. Creating brand identity becomes even more essential when customers begin targeting their choice of vendors. Strong relationships with e-mediaries will also be critical because they may become your direct customers.

The concept of market segmentation becomes dated as new digital capabilities allow for cost-effective micro-segmentation, to the level of individual customers. In the book, *Building 1:1 Relationships*, authors Don Peppers and Martha Rogers argue that even a segment of one is misleading, since the dynamic nature of transactions makes segmentation attributes somewhat less useful.

Yesterday's mass marketing principles become irrelevant when the challenge is how to effectively market to one. Associated phenomena like narrowcasting, as opposed to broadcasting, will begin to establish their importance in delivering targeted messages to a narrow selection of customers.

Mass-marketing efforts were directed at targeting the masses to change perceptions, to bring in the leads, to keep the opportunity pipeline full, and to make the job of sales easier. These marketing models supported the effort of selling a particular product to as many customers as possible.

The task has shifted in the digital economy to effectively market to one, and to try to get the maximum share of wallet. This means selling as many products to one customer as possible, after establishing a 1:1 relationship. In a steady state model, if every marketer is successful in building 1:1 relationships, you have no choice but to get into this mode since, theoretically, everyone keeps their best customers. This is not likely to happen because the behavior of one cannot be predicted and because the customer is in control. Some customers want to deal with more than one supplier as a way to have a built-in contingency plan. Others are moving to standards-based solutions to keep their choices open and to have the option of engaging with a range of suppliers.

Until recently, online marketing to one was inconceivable, because of the prohibitive cost of database marketing. Fortunately, the analogy with Moore's Law is appropriate here. As the cost of the power of computing goes down, so does the cost of data mining targets with an in-depth knowledge of their demographics, psychographics, lifestyles, wants, needs and preferences.

## The Ubiquitous Online Marketplace

"Place" may need to be eliminated from the 4Ps of marketing. In the digital econo
it doesn't have much significance, since customers can reach anywhere at anytir
and you can reach them, wherever they are.

Combined rules of online and traditional "promotion" do apply, however. C
of the fastest growth areas on the Internet is online advertising. Simba and eMarke
have reported that during 1998, $1.5 billion was spent in the US for online adver
ing. Just two years ago, online advertising was at the $40 million level. Simba expe
Web spending to increase to $7.1 billion by the year 2002. Although that is still sm
compared to the $170 billion spent on advertising in the US this year, online adver
ing is growing faster than any medium ever has since the beginning of advertising

"Pricing" is under attack because of the wealth of information available to onl
buyers and the extreme price competitiveness of vendors offering products on
Internet. With more initiatives similar to priceline.com, where the buyer names
price and vendors decide if they want to sell at that price, the whole pricing equat
is being turned upside down.

Marketing is also changing due to the emergence of e-communities that cre
value and thrive in their own ecosystem. For example, e-communities catering
women's issues have begun to emerge. These in turn attract magazines that cate
women and to their travel and banking needs.

Microsoft, for example, has a site called *WomenCentral*. This site will feat
content from another site called women.com, which has major sponsorships fr
enterprises like Unilever, Inc. Women.com formed a joint venture with Hearst N
Media that gives them distribution rights to such magazines as *Redbook*, *G*
*Housekeeping*, and *Cosmopolitan*. Sites like iVillage and many others are targeting
estimated 45-55 million women who are active online.

## E-Marketing and Customer Loyalty

E-marketing will use portals as one of the tools to get to targeted customers. The n
bers continue to change—almost daily—as the popularity of portals grows and con
tition intensifies. In 1998 there were an estimated 35 million registered users
Yahoo!, 28 million on Lycos, 20 million on Excite, and 9 million on Go Network. M
of these sites allow personalization of an individual user's pages like My Yahoo!
are now considering airline-type incentive programs to retain customer loyalty.

Table 6.2 provides a thumbnail sketch and review of the major differer
between traditional marketing and e-marketing.

**able 6.2**   E-Marketing

| Marketing Tasks | Traditional | Global Digital Economy |
| --- | --- | --- |
| General marketing approach | Mass marketing, targeted marketing approaches | Continuum approach: from 1:1 marketing to targeted groups with common needs. Global sensitivities critical. |
| Marketing tactics | Vendor "pull and push" marketing tactics. Pull with advertising and push with sales force. | Blurring division between push and pull. Customer decides. |
| Roles of customer and vendor | Passive marketing. Customers are targets of vendors' activities | Active marketing. Customers are fully engaged via chat groups, moderated forums, etc. |
| Engagement with customers | Mostly one-way marketing from vendor to customer. | Interactive marketing, customers instantly decide what they want. Web pages on the fly, customer opportunity for dialogue. |
| Targeting | You target them: | They target you: |
| | Vendor finds customers by using database marketing. | Customer finds vendors by searching online to learn who meets their needs. |
| | Targeting usually based on existing customers, titles, segments, demographics. | Targeting based on online information. |
| Increasing awareness | Advertising generally. | Mix of online and conventional advertising, links to other sites. |
| Increase interest and knowledge of customers | Direct mail, trade shows, infomercials, general seminars, brand management. | Powerful yet simple websites that can retain customer attention; online targeted mail, online seminars, peer groups, chat forums. |
| Create desire and preference | Powerful demonstrations, testi-monials, focused forums for qualified leads, customer visits. | Online demos, online comparative data, online configurations. |
| Create conviction | Proof of concept, compelling payoff, references. | Online access assisted with support center as customers access you. |
| Favorable action | Request sales person. | Purchase online. |

# E-SELLING . . . . . . . . . . . . . . . . . . . . . . . . . . . . .

E-selling is hot. E-selling is a topic about which everyone seems to have an opini which everyone seems to want to express. Many have proposed that the Internet v disintermediate the sales function. We believe that may happen in some cases, whe the intermediary's value added is minimal—where customers know what they w and can get products just as fast directly from the vendor. In other cases, interme aries will develop new forms of value added.

Ford Motor Company is one of several companies that is moving from strai dealership selling to e-selling. Ford is complementing its dealers' efforts by putting websites that allow individual buyers to choose their new cars online. After collect customer feedback, Ford refers new purchasers to local dealers and sends the colle ed data to their development and marketing organization for improvements.

When an enterprise decides to participate in this emerging business envir ment, it must factor in major changes in three key selling areas:

1. Sales infrastructure
2. Sales process
3. Sales tools

## 1. Sales Infrastructure

Traditional sales infrastructures were organized with sales functions split into dir sales and channels, such as resellers, distributors, VARs, and integrators. Each add its own distinct value, including faster availability, knowledge of solutions, and s vices.

With customers now able to contact manufacturers directly—anytime, a where—the value of some channels has been diminished, or eliminated entirely. I expected that approximately $300 billion worth of sales will be done online in the y 2000. Companies like Dell, Cisco, and Compaq are selling billions of dollars of pr ucts over the Net today. Many others, like amazon.com, ebay.com, barnesai noble.com, and eTrade, have business models that call for 100% of sales online.

To avoid disintermediation, many channel partners are repositioning their va propositions. Major sales channels are focusing on making it easier for their custom to do business with them by providing capabilities that are available directly from v dors and complementing them with services.

New e-mediaries, like Netbuy, have sprung up to address the needs of VARs v feel threatened that retailers will take away their margins. Netbuy acts as an onl super distributor. It has built a system to meet OEM requirements for immediate purchase and delivery to provide rapid order fulfillment.

Depending upon the situation, enterprises engaging in e-commerce have two options: completely revamp their sales strategy or complement existing sales strategy with an online presence—as Ford Motor Company has done—for additional selling effectiveness.

Companies like Compaq Computer Corporation, that have a mix of direct, indirect and online models, have a much more complex task. Compaq has complemented its existing direct and indirect sales channels with online information services through intranets and extranets. The company has also designed specific products exclusively for online selling.

Some vendors, such as egghead.com, have totally revamped their strategy and closed all of their retail stores to go completely online.

## 2. Sales Process

The second sales area to address in an enterprise's transition to e-selling is the sales process itself. New requirements and new rules for new times describes today's e-sales environment. New sales processes are being introduced by marketmediaries such as marketsite.net. Marketsite.net lets companies buy office supplies online from different vendors—Office Depot, Boise Cascade, Graybar and others. This site was developed by and for procurement software vendor Commerce One, Inc. Commerce One created a marketplace by offering products from many vendors, where the customer can compare them, select the products they want, download that information into their systems and route it for approval within their corporation. Once approved, the order is sent to the online intermediary for fulfillment.

In this model, the customer only has to interface with one extranet to compare all the options, instead of logging on and connecting to multiple vendor sites. The intermediaries in this case take a small percentage from the vendors for their service.

The National Transportation Exchange (nte.net) helps shippers find available capacity on trucks and ranks shipment requests in the order of their potential profitability. Intermediaries like Compare.Net provide comparative information on more than 10,000 items, from stereos to common household goods. MetalExchange.net helps steel companies, even competitors, come together to conduct business.

To win decisively, an intermediary must make itself the number-one online source for industry-specific information. MetalSite did that by acquiring online rights to the content of trade publications, including *American Metal Market, Metal Center News* and *New Steel.*

To remain relevant in the face of these new and emerging sales processes, vendors have one of several options:

- Join the intermediaries and offer products through them.
- Create their own marketplace so they can control their own destiny.
- Develop better extranets that offer a compelling value proposition that will keep customers coming back to their site regardless of the marketplace.
- Use a combination of the above options.

E-selling brings a number of changes and requirements to the sales process. T following checklist illustrates these changes, which should be included in the obje tives of every e-sales program:

- Improve view-to-buy ratios.
- Reduce first-time purchaser risk; address security concerns.
- Encourage customer loyalty by offering online incentives.
- Increase repeat buying.
- Place best sellers on home page.
- Use collaborative filtering from firms like Firefly and Net Perceptions.
- Increase trust: use trusted partners for payment and financial transactions.
- Offer discounts to first-time buyers and repeat buyers.
- Reduced-clicks ordering, like amazon.com.
- Provide multiple mechanisms for accepting payment.
- Complement your sales channels with just-in-time and latest information to help close sales.

While many changes have come about because of e-selling, many of the selli fundamentals are still the same. For example:

- Know your customers and their buying decisions; it is essential.
- Target customers with high life-time purchasing value.
- Retain key customers. (It costs four to ten times more to get a new customer than to retain an existing one.)
- Create a mutual learning relationship where sellers and customers learn with, from, and about each other.
- Make sure all your channels have the right information, tools, training, products, and support before you introduce them to customers.

## 3. Sales Tools

Reinventing the enterprise must include the development and refinement of new sales tools. The online world presents new capabilities for increasing sales effectiveness when face-to-face meetings are not possible. Solutions are available today where you can simulate face-to-face sales meetings. For example, you and the customer can look at the same presentation online while talking on the phone, with you in control of flipping the slides. Using today's audio and video streaming technologies, you can also provide remote online demonstrations.

These online capabilities have the additional advantage of keeping the information up to date and conferencing in other key people on the video.

Some companies have deployed extranets to make it easy for their key customers to do business with them and to build better 1:1 relationships. Customers log on with their secure passwords and access their accounts to check the status of orders, shipments, and invoices, or to explore new product directions.

Many leading-edge sites from Compaq and Dell have personalized their extranets and provided their significant customers with access based on the decision-maker's function and the types of content required. For example, sites have been created to meet the needs of purchasing, management, products, information technology, sales and marketing.

Sites for National Semiconductor actually give engineers and designers the capability to track the progress of their projects through the whole development cycle. This service also provides other key information for designing and for project management.

## SUPPORT . . . . . . . . . . . . . . . . . . . . . . . . . . . . . . .

Building 1:1 relationships has been made simpler by the array of opportunities for providing customer support through the Internet. One of the major benefits of e-support is the capability it provides to increase customer satisfaction and loyalty through online support. According to Cisco, their customer satisfaction went up from 3.4 to 4.17, on a scale of 5, after online support was added.

E-support offers companies a key competitive advantage. This online support can take many forms. It can include information gathering and pre-sales support during the buying process or support after the sale has been made. It can be proactive, unsolicited, or in response to a customer's query.

Charles Schwab is a good example of a company that provides proactive support for its customers. Schwab has developed its own software that records changes in customer behavior, based on account activity. The company makes outbound calls to see if customers need advice. They proactively try to save customers money by calli**n** customers who have large concentrations of a particular stock that has significa**n** downward movement.

Clinique, Inc. offers proactive support during the buying process. Its sites su**g** gest that customers fill in a simple questionnaire about themselves and in return, th**e** receive a suggested list of cosmetic products best-suited for their skin type and col**or** ing. Web pages are created on the fly to communicate these suggestions.

A number of advanced capabilities exist for pre-sales support where the cu**s** tomer has questions and with a single click, an operator can be online helping the cu**s** tomer with that question. Many retail companies have online operators ready to ta**ke** calls when customers have questions. The best website approach is to make sure th**at** the Help button is available on all pages.

It is a good idea to have your system's response time checked to see that it **is** functioning properly. Services are available from vendors like Keynote Systems th**at** will monitor your response time and send alerts if performance is degrading.

## Relationship Management Tools

Many of the new Customer Relationship Management (CRM) tools from Siebel a**nd** others have integrated voice and online capabilities where they can simultaneous**ly** answer a customer's questions on the telephone and on the website.

A number of online technologies have emerged to address support needs. The**y** range from interactive online communications to e-mail response systems that aut**o** matically respond to customers' e-mail using artificial intelligence. These tools n**ow** have the sophistication to assess the tone of the letter—whether happy, annoyed **or** mad—and either respond to the letter directly or forward it to the appropriate depa**rt** ment for action. General Interactive, Inc. has sold these kinds of systems to the **U.S.** Senate to help senators reduce the time it takes to respond to their constituents.

NetCall has developed a new kind of support for online companies. When we**b** sites offer a "click here to talk to a representative," the link will automatically sig**nal** NetCall to call the person visiting the website and will also call the support divisi**on** of the company that owns the site. The system sets up a conference-call-like situati**on** to solve the customer's problem.

Post e-sales help also exists for customers who have questions after the sale **has** been made and want information on upgrades or have other post-sale questio**ns.** Compaq is a company that proactively informs its customers of new capabilities rela**ted** to their purchases, and customers can download software with secure access control**s.**

Other companies, including Vantive, Silknet, eCustomers, and BroadVisi**on,** Inc., provide a comprehensive set of online support capabilities for customers.

# UILDING LASTING ONLINE RELATIONSHIPS . . . . . . . .

Building online relationships differs from building conventional business relationships in two ways. First, since the customer is in charge, it is a much more volatile relationship. Second, since everyone has the same objective of keeping their customers, you have to find ways to continue to sell and to get as much of a share of the customer's wallet as possible.

You will need to identify the customers with whom you want to establish relationships. Your choices could be based on the lifetime value of the customers selected, or they could be the customers who are the leaders in their e-community and who work with you closely to provide you with leading-edge ideas. Usually 20% of a company's customers will account for 80% of its sales and most of its profit.

One of the most important actions an enterprise can take in building lasting online relationships is to empower customers to help themselves and to provide them with information that otherwise might be difficult to obtain. Other actions that can have positive effects include providing access to key experts in their fields and providing them with online and offline tools to do their work better and faster. Building trust requires that you give them all the purchasing options, from auctions to intermediaries, and that you provide them with an honest assessment of the comparative advantages of each.

An important factor in retaining long-term relationships is to move the relationships up the chain from a supplier, to partner, to advisor. This approach can be facilitated by building online communities, where customers will return for valuable interaction with their peers. Most major sites allow customers to form community groups that can be open-ended or structured by the enterprise.

Asking people for their opinions is a high compliment that engages customers and moves them up the relationship ladder. Building relationships at multiple levels in the company is also effective. As easy and inexpensive as it is to provide, nothing succeeds in building relationships as much as honest and thoughtful expressions of appreciation. It is important to complement the online efforts with real person contacts. Personal attention in the online world is just as important as it was in the traditional business environment.

Business re-engineering was the mantra of the early 1990s and this evolved into the re-engineering of IT, so that companies can function effectively in the digital economy. One company that has done this extremely well is Best Western. *To stay competitive and gain an instant advantage*, Best Western knew it had to change its infrastructure and make itself futureproof—capable of handling rapid growth and providing fast service to its guests.

## The Reinvention of Best Western
## International to Gain Instant Advantage

Best Western is the world's leading hotel brand, lodging more than 40 million guests
year. It has thrived as a truly international company, but the rise of the Internet pos
some major challenges—namely, being able to offer its services at Internet speeds v
the World Wide Web. Best Western recognized that the 800-calling systems it depen
ed on were still trustworthy, but they were slow and more expensive to maintain th
applications available via the Internet. The company knew it had to upgrade its syster
and maintain a balance between the 800-call system and the newer, faster, and cheap
Web-based systems if it was to stay a world leader in the hotel and travel industry.

Best Western brought in consultants from Compaq to help migrate its reserv
tion system from IBM mainframe technologies to a technologically advanced syste
with ultra-fast response, the highest levels of system availability, and room to gro
Consultants from Compaq Services helped Best Western with overall project ma
agement, systems analysis, and system configuration—all while training the comp
ny's IS staff.

Today, the reservation system runs on a cluster of three Compaq AlphaServ
systems with the Tru64 UNIX operating system, and supports 4,000 of Best Wester
own reservation specialists, as well as 300,000 airline and travel agents, and a fa
growing Internet-based reservation service. The system delivers instant access to roc
availability information—keeping vacancies to an absolute minimum and boosti
room revenue at Best Western properties by an estimated $50 million annually.

"We needed a quick transition from the mainframe environment to the Alp
architecture, and Compaq consultants helped us achieve our goals," says Peter Flac
director of technology at Best Western International. "The new system delivers su
second response to users even during peak periods, and puts vast information resourc
into the hands of reservation specialists, consumers, and our management team."

Best Western uses Compaq Alpha platforms to run the reservation system,
well as critical enterprise applications, including PeopleSoft Financial modul
Internet and intranet solutions, and a corporate e-mail system based on Micros
Exchange Server.

## IT Blueprint for Unlimited Growth

Each Best Western property is individually owned and operated, while the corporati
itself functions as a service organization. Hotel owners join Best Western to gain bra
name recognition, economies in purchasing and, of course, the reservation syste
"When hotels ask about joining Best Western, they want to know how soon their pro
erty can become a part of the reservation system," says Flack. "This alone makes th

visible to hundreds of thousands of agents worldwide—and that translates directly into filled rooms at their properties."

Best Western is growing rapidly, largely due to the popularity of its reservation system. In fact, the company added 360 new member hotels in 1998 alone. It was that level of growth that drove Best Western to move the reservation system off the mainframes to a faster, more scalable computing environment. The company chose to buy, rather than build, its core reservation application and selected software from Executive Technologies, Inc., which uses the Oracle7 database as its underlying data repository. To find the best computing platform for performance, availability, and growth, Best Western sent out an RFP to several major computer suppliers, with instructions that each provide a system to benchmark the Best Western application.

"The Compaq AlphaServer system blew the competition away in both response time and total processing capacity," reports Flack. "We estimate that a single AlphaServer 8400 system could take us beyond the year 2000 without a major hardware upgrade."

## Speedy Response Means Customer Satisfaction, More Bookings

The reservation application—named Lynx after the fast and agile mountain cat—runs on a cluster of three Tru64 UNIX-based AlphaServer 8400 systems, along with other core business applications. The systems are linked with Compaq TruCluster software to ensure continuous computing for critical applications and 99.97% system uptime.

The Lynx system and other business applications depend on rapid access to 3.5TB of data, which resides on the Compaq StorageWorks UltraSCSI disks housed in numerous SW800 RAID systems. The StorageWorks environment provides a flexible, scalable storage environment to meet Best Western's extensive data storage demands. Flack says that in 30 months, he has experienced a failure rate of only 2% on the drives—and no data loss or storage downtime, thanks to the StorageWorks hot-swap capability.

"The reliability of our StorageWorks environment is fabulous," says Flack. "To ensure absolute data integrity on our reservation application, we deploy software mirroring using Logical Storage Manager, so we can mirror data across multiple SCSI buses and have no single point of failure. If we lose a cable, a storage adapter, or a controller, we still have access to the data."

The Lynx system serves Best Western's worldwide reservation centers in Phoenix, Flagstaff, Wichita, Dublin, Sydney, and Milan. All major airline reservation centers have access, as well. "We've spoken with many different airlines, and all are impressed with the Lynx system—in large part because of its speed," said Flack.

For travel agents and airline reservation specialists, fast system response i just a convenience, it's vital. "Agents typically have access to many hotel chains, it's often the agents who decide where to look first for available rooms," says Fla "Once they learn how easy our system is to navigate and how fast it delivei response, they use us over and over again."

Beyond quicker response times, the new system is actually changing the v agents do their jobs. In Best Western's own reservation centers, reservationists, v once depended on printed travel guides and atlases to answer customer questions, r access online information through a Windows-based application. "The system alli our call centers to efficiently handle steady increases in volume, which topped 15 i lion calls in 1998," says Flack.

## Leveraging Web Technology

Two years ago, Best Western extended the reservation system to reach million: users in the consumer market through the World Wide Web. The company's Web in face lets people find the Best Western hotel closest to their travel destination, che room pricing and availability, and make reservations.

For its Web solution, Best Western chose a Windows NT-based Alpha platfc A pair of Alpha workstation-class systems, running AltaVista Firewall software, ke the Web server secure from unauthorized access. The volume of reservations m over the Web grew by 190% in 1998, with some months yielding a 200 to 3C increase in booking volumes.

AltaVista Tunnel software provides secure, encrypted remote access to I Western's network over the Internet. All headquarters support staff now use AltaVista Tunnel for secure remote dial-in, and the company will soon use AltaV Tunnel software and ISP accounts to provide secure network connections to the 1, properties outside the US and Canada. This "extranet" will give Best Western hc access to electronic mail and documents such as policies, procedures, and trair materials. "AltaVista Tunnel software provides a way to streamline communica with our properties and lower our overall cost of operations," says Flack.

## Enterprise-wide Mail and Messaging; Secure Intranet Access

A Windows NT-based Alpha system runs Microsoft Exchange Server software integrated mail and messaging. Nearly 1,000 Best Western employees use Micro Exchange Server software for enterprise-wide communication. Compaq helped I Western with platform configuration while Microsoft assisted with the migration f an Intel-based Microsoft Mail environment to the Microsoft Exchange Server s tion. Simplified management is a major benefit. "Instead of managing 15 post offices on separate servers, Microsoft Exchange Server software provides a centralized mail server on one Alpha system," Flack says.

The platform can easily scale to support planned mail services for property owners and support current Best Western intranet applications as well. The system also supports a Microsoft Internet Information Server (IIS). Microsoft IIS software will provide a powerful platform for new intranet applications, including training solutions for property owners.

To link its 2,300 properties in the US and Canada, Best Western is establishing a network based on very small aperture terminal (VSAT) satellite technology. The IP-based network will support streamlined reservation delivery, messaging and collaboration across the properties and headquarters, and the corporate intranet. AltaVista Firewall technology will allow the properties to access needed services, while protecting core Best Western systems from unauthorized access. Flack estimates that the new community of users will require 4,000 Microsoft Exchange mailboxes initially, and up to 8,000 when fully rolled out.

Flack recalls a few months earlier when Best Western migrated the last of its applications from the IBM mainframe environment to Compaq Alpha systems. The event marked the end of one era and the beginning of the next—and left a vast empty space in the Best Western data center. For Flack, there was a solution that was both practical and symbolic of the new era. "We hired Compaq Services to consult on the design of a smaller data center and to plan the system move," he says. "Compaq engineers then moved our entire server complex into the new data center—with only four hours of downtime."

With all systems running smoothly and new space available to relieve cramped offices, Flack has returned to other projects. The VSAT network and AltaVista Tunnel projects are moving ahead, as is a new Web-based front end for the PeopleSoft supply system, which will allow properties to order supplies online rather than by phone. "We're always looking at ways to provide additional services to the properties," says Flack. "With the platforms we have in place, we can deliver new capabilities with little incremental cost."

## Comprehensive Change Equals Instant Advantage

Once Best Western and other companies make their initial investments to upgrade their Internet-driven infrastructures, they are positioned to grow, to use the latest available Internet applications, and to have unlimited capacity to accomplish these things with "little incremental cost."

Best Western understood that the secret to success in an emerging digital eco omy is making a total commitment to change—to integrating business and IT stra gies. To do it in a piecemeal fashion is to risk failure; to do it in a comprehensive w is to assure success.

# 7

# etting the Stage for Action

..........................

*S*ummary: *Of all the changes you can make to thrive in the digital economy, the most vital is to transform your enterprise into an e-enterprise. In this chapter we'll provide some ideas for merging your core competencies with your e-infrastructure. The entire enterprise has to buy into this new approach...and it starts with top management. We'll show you how CEOs drive successful online transformation. Just as an architect needs a blueprint to properly design a building, you need a blueprint to properly design your online structure. In this chapter, we tell you about the importance of developing an infrastructure blueprint for the global economy. And we'll give you strategies for developing your own e-infrastructure blueprint.*

## RATEGY #4: INTEGRATE BUSINESS ND IT STRATEGIES . . . . . . . . . . . . . . . . . . . . . . . . . . . .

Reinventing an enterprise for the global economy requires genuine integration, which means matching official beliefs and words with actions. If an enterprise made just one change in the new digital economy, the most important would be to transform itself into an e-enterprise. To become an e-enterprise, an organization must change its culture, its metrics and the way it responds to change. It is no longer enough for IT and business strategies to align; they have to merge into one seamless whole. That means working fast, because the pace of change during the Internet years is accelerating. Reinvention involves capturing the combined knowledge of the enterprise and sharing it in a highly efficient way. And perhaps most important to the transformation process, the enterprise's top management has to be involved and committed to drive every aspect of the enterprise into the dynamic world of e-business.

More than ever before, developing a winning strategy in the digital economy means integrating the power of a company's core competencies with its online information technology.

Traditionally, IT has been seen as a strategy for gaining competitive advantag IT strategies reduce costs, improve operations and increase productivity. One of t top CIO challenges is finding effective and efficient ways to integrate IT with the bu ness strategy.

In the digital economy, IT is as likely to create as many new business opportu nities as the conventional business strategies. The primary reason for that is t Internet, which has fundamentally changed the way IT delivers value to the enterpri The Boeing Company is one of the most dramatic cases of online technology creati new opportunities and driving drastic changes in the business model.

Boeing sells more than $1 million worth of spare parts through its B2B e-co merce applications. It is also adding next-generation extranets in support of the co pany's marketing and sales functions, which provide faster and more efficient lir with customers and suppliers. Boeing's hundreds of intranet applications are helpi to knit the company into a truly global enterprise.

Less dramatic, but no less important to the company involved, was the re venting of Square D Co., which was accomplished by totally integrating the comp ny's business and IT strategies. Square D, a manufacturer of industrial electri equipment, has jumped to the front of its old-line industry by implementing a verti Web portal to support its 2,000 independent distributors.

Competition has forced some companies to bring IT managers into the strate planning process. For example, Barnes and Noble was forced to establish an onl presence in response to amazon.com. Dell's online model forced a number of com nies to change their business practices. In 1996, Microsoft made the then-surpris decision to invest in Internet strategies to meet growing competition head-on.

Enterprises can no longer afford to define a business strategy and then con: with IT to see how it will be supported. IT has to be involved from the start; otherw an enterprise risks having an infrastructure that can't support its online direction.

Integrating IT and business strategic planning can reduce planning cycle ti improve the quality of competitive solutions and create best-in-class business cesses. In this case, two heads, or two groups within an organization, are clearly ter than one.

The risk of not working together is that the enterprise will miss the boat on en ing the digital economy and will make investments that don't address all of the iss such as how the customer will interface with the online solution.

Success factors for the digital economy that will help an enterprise benefit f the power of an integrated approach to IT and business strategy include the follow

- Make it easier for customers to do business with you online.
- Create value that puts you on the customer's target list.
- Understand online customer buying behavior.

- Develop business intelligence solutions to target the right customers.
- Develop 1:1 relationships with customers.
- Create the virtual collaborative enterprise.
- Excel in the Value Network.
- Develop new distribution and channel strategies.
- Build real-time learning/sharing enterprise for knowledge management.
- Create advantage with e-marketing, e-sales, and e-support.
- Achieve best-in-class e-commerce.
- Launch new businesses.

## Retain Key Customers/Increase Customer Loyalty

One of the top CIO challenges is finding effective and efficient ways to integrate IT with the business strategy (see Table 7.1).

**le 7.1**   Conventional IT/Business vs. Online E-Business

| y Strategy/Tasks | Conventional Approach | E-Business Approach |
|---|---|---|
| ategy development | IT is aligned with business strategy. | Strategy is a combined output of IT and business capabilities. |
| ʒanization | Several groups, such as the corporate strategy functions, department strategy functions, IT strategy group and disparate Internet activities. | Joint e-enterprise strategy group consisting of business and IT strategy. |
| cesses | Re-engineer business processes, mostly internal end-to-end. IT has a supportive role. Focus on optimizing supply chain. | Redefine total end-to-end process consisting of internal and online partners. Focus on dynamic value chain. |
| hnology | Supports internal needs. The best effort to accommodate partners, suppliers, and customers. IT decisions driven accordingly. | Virtual corporation, which is tightly coupled with economy partners, requires a standards-based IT approach. Otherwise, no agility to respond. |
| ple skills | Mostly back-end technologies, processes. | Knowledge of digital economy solutions. |

**Table 7.1**   Conventional IT/Business vs. Online E-Business (continued)

| Key Strategy/Tasks | Conventional Approach | E-Business Approach |
|---|---|---|
| Key priorities | Driven by internal processes optimization. | Customer facing, 1:1 relationships, integration with legacy. |

## Challenges to Integrating IT and Business Strategies

In the process of integrating IT and business strategies—and the operations associa with each—the ability to excel at information creation is all-important. A newly re vented enterprise must be able to capture, organize, share, and leverage knowledge

When one part of an enterprise does not know what is going on in other depa ments or how their work contributes to the organization, stovepipes and inconsist cies can result.

Several reasons exist for lack of integration in the enterprise. There may be central repositories for information across all functions. There may be no easy way share or easily access information, and no serious effort was made to create relev information that links the experiences. There is some knowledge management w under way, mainly by outside consultants who set up systems for document mana ment, collaborative tools and database information.

The new need for online information technology presents a unique opportu to turn these discontinuities into continuities. But this requires making some chan to the processes, organizations and the culture.

In many enterprises, intranets and extranets have been key to information ation, access and sharing with customers, suppliers and partners. However, th intranets and extranets have been created mostly for corporate communications product, marketing, and selling information. They use more of a bulletin bc approach and are usually disjointed. These were not designed to leverage collec knowledge for competitive advantage.

The processes for capturing and disseminating key information, such as tomer data, sales performance, and support issues, are often in disparate locations, bottled up in as many places are there are departments.

There is no question that fully integrating IT and business strategies is diffi To many companies, that is alien to their corporate culture. Information is treated form of internal currency and a source of power. Business strategy is developed be closed corporate-office doors. IT is a support function, charged with the responsib of providing the tools to carry out business strategies and corporate policy.

Even in the best of circumstances where companies are using their IT resources to reinvent the enterprise and IT managers are full partners in the strategic planning process, integrating business and IT strategies is still a tremendous challenge.

Chevron Corp., the $30 billion petroleum industry giant and one of those "best-of-circumstances" companies, is a case in point. Jeff Moad reported in *PC Week Online* that it took "two years *just getting Chevron into a position to make a credible push into e-business*." The work was accomplished by Dave Clementz, president of Chevron Information Technology, Co., and his 1000+ member IT staff. Clementz will soon be president of a new company, Chevron E-Business Development Co., with responsibility for developing Chevron's IT strategy and for deploying its IT initiatives.

## Design Tools for Enterprise Integration

For most companies, a new approach is needed to remove transactional friction, improve operational efficiencies and integrate the enterprise. Effective tools are thus needed for the integration of content creation, capture, access, sharing and use. To design these tools, it is important to address the following questions:

- What collective information do we need to be effective with customers, suppliers, partners, engineering, selling, marketing, support and manufacturing? What other data—product, financial and legal—are important?
- What key information or processes are inconsistent within the enterprise? Which of those inconsistent processes is making it difficult for us to function as a cohesive, integrated operation?
- What information should be made available so that different functions can be more effective in leveraging partner capabilities?
- Are there communities of people who collectively benefit from certain types of relevant information?
- Should we restructure our information creation, collection, and dissemination based on core processes?
- What would be the payback of creating such an information base?

## Getting Online, On Time

The online world, with its new tools of corporate portals, intranets and extranets, already provides a good starting point for leveraging collective knowledge. This will become increasingly important in the digital economy, especially as the speed of change escalates during the Internet years. Steps you can take to create a seamless strategy for the digital economy include:

*First*: Instead of creating, collecting and disseminating information based on trational functional stovepipes, take a look at all online processes that impact the custom These activities include building 1:1 relationships, selling, marketing and support.

*Second*: Drive for consistency across all functions based on customer-faci needs, rather than the requests for stovepiped information from disparate functions

*Third*: Explore the other key groups that rely on customer and sales inform tion—such as engineering and manufacturing—and create content suitable for co mon information communities. There may be a whole set of information needs fro the supply chain or Value Network perspectives as well.

Information and industry exchanges are now being created to address the sear access and customization of information based on the needs of individuals or u communities. These solutions will capture internal data, as well as data available fre outside portals and news feeds.

Intranets and extranets will be based on enterprise portals and will interoper with other key enterprise technology. These efforts should be integrated with other k enterprise applications, such as ERP and CRM, so that all the information is cons tent. In fact, ERP and CRM vendors are also in the process of designing their own v sions of enterprise portals.

You should always look at the key customer interface and back-end requi ments of systems as you move toward an integrated approach to information captu sharing, and knowledge leveraging to meet customer needs and remain competitiv

# CEOS DRIVE THE TRANSFORMATION . . . . . . . . . . .

It is not enough to have an online function in the enterprise. The whole company, fr the CEO down, has to be actively involved in using the online technology during Internet years. Using the technology is the only way to truly understand its streng weaknesses and possibilities. Unless it is on the CEO's agenda to make sure that company is fully on board, it will be a slow transition—too slow to win in the n phase of the digital economy. If you look at some of the Phase One winners, such Cisco, Dell, Amazon, eBay, Charles Schwab, E* Trade, gardens.com, and Autoby you will see that it was the CEO who was the driver of change.

Many CEOs are understandably reluctant to commit their companies to a per of serious disruptions, unsettling change and major investments in IT infrastruct without a known ROI. They have been through downsizing, outsourcing and re-er neering. Their enthusiasm for innovation has been blunted. As *The Economist* repc they don't know "whether e-business is the most exciting opportunity or the most rifying challenge they have ever faced."

The fact is, they do know. A 1999 Booz-Allen Hamilton survey of 500 large companies showed that "more than 90% of top managers believe the Internet will transform or have a big impact on the global marketplace by 2001." They understand instinctively that, while previous IT investments, particularly ERP, have concentrated on making the company more efficient, the Internet is, according to *The Economist,* "all about communicating, connecting, and transacting with the outside world. The ability to collaborate with others may be just as much of a competitive advantage as the ability to deploy the technology."

CEOs also know that joining the digital economy is as much about survival as it is competitive advantage. Jupiter Communications released a report in October 1999 confirming what many CEOs of traditional companies have feared. Jupiter reported that 94% of online spending represents dollars that previously would have been spent offline. "That's an estimated $11.2 billion that will be taken out of the hands of traditional merchants this year and placed in the hands of their online rivals," says Jupiter's Ken Cassar.

Cassar is less than sanguine about the prospects of companies that continue their business-as-usual course. He says that all successful companies in the future will have strong online operations. "Not having a short-term Internet strategy may not be fatal, but not having a long-term Internet strategy probably will be fatal for many traditional retailers."

To win in the online global economy, you will need an e-enterprise culture, not just some disparate Internet initiatives. To win, you need to create a unified IT and business strategy development culture, and you will need to remove the barriers to information creation, capture, access and sharing.

# TRATEGY #5: CREATE AN E-INFRASTRUCTURE LUEPRINT . . . . . . . . . . . . . . . . . . . . . . . . . . .

The place to begin in transforming your company into an e-enterprise is to develop your own e-infrastructure blueprint. An e-infrastructure is a strategic plan that makes it easy for customers to work with you and accommodates the needs of the digital economy.

Without a powerful infrastructure, all other infrastructure strategies cannot sustain your advantage over the long term. Some suggestions for developing your winning e-infrastructure blueprint follow.

You must be the architect of your own success in developing your e-infrastructure blueprint. An e-infrastructure blueprint should protect your existing investments and add new capabilities to the existing infrastructure, with minimum disruptions to users and customers. Critical to the deployment of any infrastructure solution are services, expertise in best-in-class business processes, and industry knowledge.

Ensure that e-business initiatives—whether for call centers, sales, or procur ment—are aimed at increasing value, while also reducing complexity and overhe costs. This is the litmus test for measuring the business impact of all IT projects. used to be that IT projects were loosely justified under the rubric of innovation a were not subject to rigorous metrics. Today's organizations cannot afford t approach. Your e-infrastructure blueprint must hold up to the same bottom-line scru ny as any other business initiative.

Because technology drives so much of the business in the digital economy, IT by definition part of the business fabric and, therefore, should be focused on the stra gic and tactical goals of the organization.

Commitment and direction must come from the top. Strategy should be tea developed and, once approved, implemented and defended by senior ranks.

**Key Considerations in Developing Your E-Infrastructure Blueprint**
**E-Business**

1.  Align e-business initiatives with strategic priorities (stated goals, user/- market requirements, Year 2000 programs). Assess existing projects, eval- uate competition, analyze market trends, aim for sustained value over the long-term.

2.  Select top three organizations or departments as candidates, based on their potential and vulnerability to competition.
    - Are other companies advancing faster?
    - What are the implied threats to market share, revenue base, and reselle loyalty?

3.  Set achievable goals for e-business
    - Operational (efficiency, lower costs)
    - Financial (revenues, leverage)
    - Business (growth, cost-effective services)
    - Image (progressive, well-managed, technology-savvy, user-friendly)

4.  Develop a framework of working principles built around the Internet and the fast-emerging digital economy. Beware of the traps of conventiona thinking.

5.  Construct a business model for the development and delivery of products and services, online access, electronic payment, and e-records.
    - Balance new investment with proportionate returns
    - E-business must be justified on its own grounds
    - Deliver services on the basis of "cost per use"

6. Plan for new IT infrastructure—costs/resources to design, deploy, and maintain.
   * Servers
   * Storage
   * IP-enabled networks
   * Applications
   * Services

7. Online processes can quickly renovate the "front-end," creating discontinuity with the "back-end" processes. Allow necessary manual processes to coexist with online processes (least amount of breakage).

8. Evaluate the cost of upgrading skills, training people, and changing the culture to ensure smooth transition and success.
   * Leverage existing skills and resources
   * Outsource where feasible

9. Build time scales and metrics for tracking cost-effectiveness of new processes, new investments, and newly trained staff.

10. Partner with established service providers.

There's no reason to wait for the infrastructure to be fully defined before taking advantage of the rapidly changing technologies and business opportunities. Rather, the purpose is to make sure that there is an end goal and a disciplined process in place to reach the end objectives as soon as possible. Table 7.2 summarizes the online attributes and IT requirements for supporting the digital economy.

## Comments on the Chart

From the above chart it is evident that IT needs to be "Internet-agile" to meet the rapid changes of the environment. Standards allow for agility in adding new technologies, new applications and new economy partners. Proprietary infrastructures make it difficult to respond to the changing Value Network needs and global access.

Integrating the front and back-end applications, as well as other internal and Value Network partners' applications, is essential. Systems need to be scalable, manageable, and secure, to meet the performance and affordability needs of the enterprise.

In building your e-infrastructure blueprint first, you give yourself the best opportunity for creating instant advantage in the digital economy.

**Table 7.2**    Requirements for the E-Infrastructure Blueprint for the Global Online Econom

| Digital Economy Attributes | E-Infrastructure Blueprint Requirement |
|---|---|
| Online anywhere, anytime | Support multiple devices, secure 24/7, fast access ADSL, and caching Standards support, security |
| Immediate answers -Interactive Compare/search | Intelligent agents, config. engines Search engines |
| Ultra-rapid change/Internet years Ease-of-doing-business with customer -Support the buying processes -Self-help -Complete view -Make them successful | Standards based, agile infrastructure Customer-centric content 24/7, fast, secure, standards interfaces Online forums, interactive, personal Online/legacy integ., personalized Personalized content, best info. |
| Execute, check, fix, plan | Agility, standards, scalable |
| Value Network | Standards, low-latency, secure Application integration |
| New collaborations | Standards, scalability, 24/7, secure Application integration |
| New online applications | Standards, performance, low latency |
| New competition solutions | Agility to react, better performance |
| Knowledge sharing/management | Enterprise portals, collaboration, New intranet, extranets |
| E-marketing Targeting | Data mining, search engines, Connectivity with infomediaries |
| Create awareness | Online portals |
| -Instant interest | Interactive, Web pages on the fly |
| -Create desire/liking | Personalized, context related |
| -Change preference | Personalization, compare online |
| -Accelerate conviction | Personalization, links to experts |
| -Results measurements | Hit rate/sale conversions |
| E-selling -Processes -Tools | Marketmediaries, interfaces Fast, simple, secure, standards Extranets, intranets, portals, online sales/videos, config. mgmt tools |

ble 7.2 (continued)

| igital Economy Attributes | E-Infrastructure Blueprint Requirement |
|---|---|
| support | Self-support, interactive, voice support, backup person |
| commerce technology | Buy-side, sell-side, EDI |
| eate loyalty | Personalized relationships, 24/7 |
| gh ROI | Fast deployment, low costs |

# HE NET IMPERATIVE · · · · · · · · · · · · · · · · · · · · · ·

Andy Grove, chairman of Intel, says that in five years all companies will be Internet companies, or they won't be companies at all. While it is easy to dismiss such pronouncements from a chip manufacturer as exaggerated hype, it is not so easy to dismiss the growing body of evidence that the Internet has changed business—all business—fundamentally, profoundly and forever.

No company is immune, and nobody can afford to be complacent, regardless of what industry they are in. Successful e-enterprises can emerge overnight, almost full-grown. As *The Economist* observes, "It takes about two years for an innovative start-up to develop its business plan, establish a Web presence, and begin to dominate its chosen marketplace." By then it can be too late for slower-moving traditional businesses to respond.

The risks of betting the company on its ability to compete in the digital economy are real. E-business implementations can be complex and full of hidden costs. There are many obstacles to overcome: steep learning curves, skill gaps, sufficient resources, competitive threats, and the disruption of change.

All of these—and many others—are issues that must be addressed. In the face of these enormous challenges, it is easy to understand why some CEOs have not yet put their ship on that course. They don't want to risk what they have built on something they don't know. As understandable as that is, it is not a tenable position. All the evidence suggests that the greatest risk is to do nothing at all.

Successful online enterprises have recognized and weighed the risks and turned their ship into the storm. They risked their brick-and-mortar businesses, but they knew the risks and the potential rewards. They knew they first needed a plan—a blueprint to balance e-business with traditional business. Charles Schwab's story is one of an enterprise moving boldly and making up for lost time by a risk-taking reinvention of itself.

## Charles Schwab Meets the Online Challenge

Some companies make money by making products. Charles Schwab, America's lar est discount brokerage firm, makes money by making money—for its clients, as w as for itself.

Technology has always been an important part of that formula. How importan Schwab President David Pottruck has gone so far as to say that Schwab is "a techn ogy company in the financial services business," and Schwab backs up that stateme with an aggressive commitment to leading-edge solutions.

Embracing new technology has helped make Schwab the overall market lead in financial services in the United States. Schwab's electronic brokerage busine which has more than one million customers, operates on a scale that befits its positi at the forefront of the financial services industry.

Schwab serves its customers nationwide through more than 260 branch offic that are coordinated through six regional hubs and two central offices in San Francis and Phoenix. Electronic communication connects more than 12,000 Schwab emplc ees and helps disseminate critical information throughout the organization. Managi that communication system presents an ongoing challenge to the small but highly p ficient unit charged with the responsibility for keeping Schwab's e-mail system ru ning smoothly.

## Change: Seeing the Handwriting on the Wall

In 1996, Schwab found itself nearly buried in an increasing volume of electronic ma faxes, and internal and external communication. Its outdated host-based system fre the 1970s was simply not designed for the demands of the information-rich 1990s was time for a change. Senior management committed to replacing the outdated ma frame-based TOSS messaging system and the stopgap SMTP/POP mail service w an integrated solution.

Steve Cropper, managing director of Corporate Messaging at Schwab, says new system is just what they needed. "We wanted to give our users more flexibili the ability to extend the network to customers via the Internet, the ability to comm nicate using rich media and file attachments, and the capacity to increase efficier by enabling functionality on the users' desktops."

## Balancing Risks and Rewards

In financial markets, it is sometimes necessary to take calculated risks to realize spectacular gains. While this philosophy is not as common in the IT field, where reliability is prized above all else, the IT managers at Schwab decided that it was worth investing in a newer product—Microsoft Exchange Server 5.0—because it offered benefits far beyond those of its more established competition.

The risks were mitigated by some comforting factors. Although Microsoft Exchange Server 5.0 was not yet in general release at the time of the decision, Schwab planners and consultants agreed that Microsoft's vision for the product met their need for performance, functionality and ease of use. Furthermore, it promised smooth integration with Schwab's existing Windows NT architecture and would enable Cropper's team to meet an extremely aggressive deployment timetable.

Any good fund manager will tell you that, even in a high-yield portfolio, it is important to balance more aggressive investments with known quantities that have proven their worth over the years. Schwab's IT managers agreed that they would base the new Microsoft Exchange Server on the server platform for Windows NT—Compaq ProLiant servers.

## The Deployment: "Lightning and Thunder"

The pilot program, nicknamed "Lightning," was deployed in December 1996, when approximately 150 users were migrated to the Exchange system. "Thunder," the extended rollout phase, occupied the first quarter of 1997, when users were transferred at the rate of 1,500 to 2,000 *per week*. By the end of April, the extended rollout was basically completed.

Such a massive deployment in such a short period of time required precise logistical planning and extremely dependable equipment. Cropper and his team developed a program for training service center employees to deploy their own equipment, then shipped three servers to each service center office, along with a customized Microsoft Exchange installation CD-ROM.

"We designed, implemented and deployed very rapidly," says David Champine, system architect for Schwab. "Generally, when you move at that pace, you encounter difficulties. Over a four-month period, we put 34 servers into immediate, round-the-clock use, and did not experience a single problem with either the software or the hardware.

"With the Compaq servers, we could put 'em up fast, and once they were up, they stayed up. Needless to say, the savings in terms of time, money, travel and energy were absolutely incredible."

"Communication is absolutely mission-critical for us," says Cropper. "We can effectively serve our customers if we don't have a good flow of information internally

Microsoft Exchange, running on servers, helped Schwab attain its goals improved communication, enhanced productivity and greater efficiency. Unlike th previous text-only system, Exchange allows users to easily attach files; include ho linked URLs in the body of messages; access Exchange functionality from with Microsoft Office applications; and send rich media messages with sound, graphic fonts and colored text. In addition, Schwab's new system is open to send and recei external mail via the Internet, extending the reach of communications beyond th boundaries of the organization directly to the customers.

"The users are overjoyed," says Cropper. "They used the new tools so exte sively in the early deployment that the resources of the mainframe were taxed durir the changeover period." He says a diplomatic set of guidelines and suggestions helpe ease the problem, and now capacity and performance are stabilized at a rate of 6( users per server on the Compaq/Microsoft Exchange Server platform. "The throug put is extraordinary," he says. "Message delivery times are almost instantaneous."

Cropper is most pleased by the way the new solution has empowered users various departments to develop their own applications. A good example, he says, a the employees in the public relations department. They reduced their fax and pho usage and automated repetitive tasks by sending files electronically. This improv their productivity, by allowing them to better manage their time, because they longer need to schedule around constant phone and fax interruptions. All users deve oped calendar and scheduling applications to reserve conference rooms and simpli other administrative chores.

The Charles Schwab story is a behind-the-scenes story of how a compa matched its business and IT strategies to meet the needs of its customers. In the pr cess, it ran the risk of weakening its brick-and-mortar business throughout the cou try. But Schwab took that risk and invested in its IT infrastructure, making sure th the solution it chose—hardware and software customized to meet its needs—wou eventually foster a balanced growth between e-commerce business and its tradition business. It worked. Charles Schwab saw the potential of an Internet-driven econon and is now one of the financial services leaders experiencing an enviable growth revenues and profits.

# Part 3
## Best Practices in the Digital Economy

# 8

# Transition to an E-business

.........................

*Summary: Meeting the heightened expectations of customers in the digital economy requires an enterprise to provide continuous service marked by agility, 24/7 operation, standards, security, scalability, and manageability. These characteristics of a 24/7 business are at the heart of today's successful e-solutions. Enterprises that more rapidly embrace and exploit the Internet and its opportunities will become future market leaders. Critical for success is the ability of corporations to embrace and synthesize this paradigm shift and take advantage of new technologies inspired by adopting the Internet as a new medium for conducting business.*

## E/BUSINESS INTEGRATION: THE NEW BASELINE . . . .

To participate in the digital economy, an enterprise needs to perform at new e-business levels. Its strategies, resources, tactics, plans of action, and its entire staff must work together in sync—and at an intensely quick pace.

E-business began as simple Web presence applications, delivering static content designed to capture the customer's attention. E-business has evolved into storefront applications with basic transaction capability to "take the order." Large enterprises have Internet-enabled their existing applications to better serve their customers, and new Internet businesses have emerged.

What works best in the digital economy is an approach that is governed by the customer engagement or by an analysis of value chain requirements. These should be assigned a higher priority than internally driven initiatives.

Here are the steps that work in planning online business initiatives:

- Define the new customer propositions—existing business and new business strategies/goals that are possible with the emerging online technologies.

These could be increasing share of customer wallet, lowering of costs, deployment of new online "yourbusiness.com" or e-enterprise reinvention initiatives with measurable business objectives.

- Define the Value Network and dependencies that will be necessary for winning collaboratively in the new economy. The new economy will require a collaborative value proposition rather than just your own core-competency-based solutions. Enterprises will have to define the scenarios that a customer will go through in the purchase cycle and determine what else the sale requires.

- Define common requirements, information needs across business units, and necessary strategies. Deploy applications whose results can be measured. Define the infrastructures, architectures, and requirements for information creation, capture, access, and sharing.

- If it is a customer-facing initiative, look at the ease of doing business. Define processes that follow a normal customer interaction scenario. Create end-to-end processes that allow customers to complete transactions seamlessly. Instead of complex flowcharts, ensure alignment of disparate processes.

- Create an e-infrastructure blueprint.

Depending on the objectives and the nature of your business, there may be d ferent strategies for participation in the online world. These may include creating online presence for the following purposes:

- Information dissemination.

- Basic e-commerce sites for doing simple buying/selling.

- E-commerce with sophisticated personalization, interactive services and other capabilities like those of amazon.com, autobytel.com, priceline.com and others.

- E-transformation through new processes like the Value Network, collaboration, sharing of knowledge, and new online services.

The first two activities are quite basic. Today, prepackaged solutions are ava able from IBM, Compaq, and other suppliers. These include prepackaged standar based servers, storage, Internet software, e-commerce software, management so ware, appropriate databases, security, and firewalls. Some companies, like Comp thoroughly test their prepackaged solutions for interoperability, security and for 2 operations. Customers can tailor the solution for their Web hosting, application se er, or e-commerce applications to suit their needs.

To get to the third and fourth stages of e-commerce, you need the above ba components, complemented by higher performance servers, website traffic load lev ing, networks, firewalls and the right level of services skills. Again, many compani like Compaq, IBM, Sun, Systems Integrators and specialized e-commerce VARs p vide the skills for business process, planning, design and deployment, and operations. Skills to integrate with your existing IT systems are vital.

## Resources and Tools

Building an agile infrastructure for the enterprise to meet the needs of 24/7 operations, scalability, performance, security and manageability requires business process, policy, internationalization services and technology expertise. Examine your requirements in terms of the following e-resource categories.

## E-Resource Categories

- Enterprise infrastructure
- Website
- Content management
- Application integration
- Intranets
- Extranets
- E-commerce software
- Enterprise portals
- E-applications

**Enterprise infrastructure**—Figure 8.1, an e-business building block diagram, is useful in the creation of e-solutions. Different types of applications require a different combination of services from these building blocks. For example, e-commerce solutions will use the enterprise infrastructure, commerce services, search engines, intelligent agents, personalization, and e-commerce application software available from Open Markets and Microsoft.

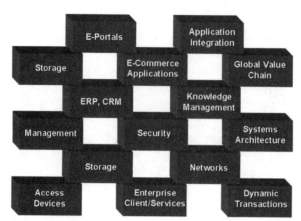

**Figure 8.1**

E-business Building Blocks

As Figure 8.1 suggests, the e-infrastructure blueprint will differ from tradition IT applications in several aspects:

- Access devices will include many kinds of Internet-ready appliances, ranging from PCs to palmtops to wireless appliances.

- Internet-based N-tier client/services computing will emerge, in addition to conventional three-tier client/server computing.

- Instead of pre-defined responses in today's transaction processing, the new transactions will be dynamic in nature. Transactions, with responses created on the fly, will be based on customer requests and customer profiles, click-throughs, the sites they came from, and what was requested on the last visit.

- Online services distributed anywhere in the Internet will find, request, broker and collaborate with other online services to create one-click response to customer requests, which go beyond the capabilities of one enterprise.

- To speed up the response of systems and serving of Web pages, many different caching devices will emerge. Some alternatives already are available from Novell and Inktomi.

- Application servers will be fine-tuned to handle the requirements of dynamic transactions.

- E-portals will emerge as a major component of the e-infrastructure blueprint, and a universal building block for intranets, extranets and knowledge leveraging.

- Zero-latency and application integration services will play a key role in streamlining business processes for shorter time-to-solution in all markets. Many new e-commerce applications will emerge, which are designed specifically for sell side, buy side, or for marketmediaries and infomediaries. New standards for security, like JEPI, digital certificates, OBI, and Internet EDI, will emerge.

- Java and JVM-based solutions, servers, Smart Cards, and applications, with "write once, run anywhere" features, may find a place in the new blueprint.

# TANDARDS-BASED ONLINE INFRASTRUCTURE . . . . . .

Those managing e-enterprises will need to know how to build high-volume, highly integrated, high-availability environments, because these characteristics are the foundation of agile and flexible business systems.

The basic elements of an online infrastructure are the networks, servers, storage, operating platforms, e-business load balancing/optimizers, and middleware (see Figure 8.2). The e-commerce infrastructure components can be added to this infrastructure definition. Such components include security, tracking, measurements, and digital cash payment systems.

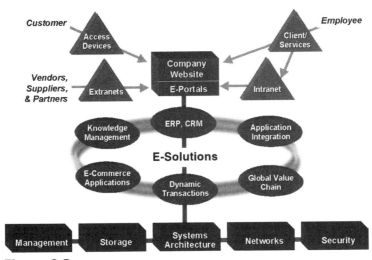

**Figure 8.2**
E-business Framework

# AN EXAMPLE OF AN E-ARCHITECTURE BLUEPRINT  ..

Enterprises need an architecture for building reliable and scalable Internet applicatic
that yield sustained performance. One example is the Compaq Distributed Inter
Server Array (DISA) architecture. Using inexpensive industry-standard servers, DI
can rapidly increase capacity and help an Internet-enabled business cope with s
contingencies as unplanned downtime and sudden peaks in traffic.

# KEY TECHNICAL ATTRIBUTES OF AN ONLINE
# INFRASTRUCTURE ............................

## Connectivity

- Should allow end-to-end flows of data.
- Should distribute online traffic loads to servers that are available. It should
  be standards-based to facilitate links with suppliers', partners', and customers' systems.
- Should feature QoS for meeting service level agreements and COPS-based
  policy management support.

## Interoperability

- Should be able to accommodate next-generation Internet standards.
- Should be able to connect to all types of environments in the Value
  Network.

## Networked Applications Support

- Standards-based Directory Services, LDAP, Active Directories, NDS.
- Web servers, application servers based on standards.
- Networked storage should be available.
- Security services, DCOM, CORBA, EJB support.

## Manageability

- Proactive manageability based on SNMP and WBEM protocols.
- Integrated Directory Services.
- Online backup information with minimum load.

Many leading management solutions vendors have introduced new solutions to maintain availability between Web servers and applications servers that alert administrators to performance issues before an outage occurs. One example is BMC Software's PATROL SafePassage™.

# SCALABILITY . . . . . . . . . . . . . . . . . . . . . . . . . . . . . . .

Scalability is one of the key requirements for the e-infrastructure blueprint. Many e-businesses have found that customer traffic jumps in the online world can grow exponentially and have huge, unpredictable spikes in demand. Scalability to handle additional loads can be achieved in a number of ways:

- Architectural designs where different application servers handle different categories, such as content, transactions, and search. In addition, the data management, business logic and Web interface efforts are segmented.
- Ability to add new servers as demand grows, without having to make changes to other systems' components, such as storage.
- Add load-leveling capabilities in front of the servers so that, as traffic grows, it is distributed equally to maintain the fastest response time. Cisco, HydraWeb, F5 and others supply load-balancing solutions.
- Application servers and software are used to optimize response times, which makes changes based on user trends easy. For development ease, the object should unload the development efforts for security, maintaining session states so they can focus on the business logic efforts.
- The application server software is optimized for working with websites and improving performance. For example, Netdynamics software uses fewer resources and works with Netscape Server at API rather than CGI scripts.

## DESIGNING YOUR WEBSITE . . . . . . . . . . . . . . . .

1. **Purpose**. What is the purpose of your website? Is it simply to provide information or to support a complete line of e-commerce functions (marketing, selling, services, and information) for specific communities? **What exactly will the website provide?** This question raises related issues and considerations. Logistics, shipping, tracking, and integration with legacy data are of great importance. Once online, a website is instantly available for business on a global scale. Issues of pricing and business terms and conditions in various countries must be addressed early in the game.

2. **Different strokes**. Industries, markets, and communities have different needs. Techniques and interface styles that work for one community do not necessarily work for others.

3. **Ease of business.** Give some thought to the ease of doing business. Buy-side criteria needs to be addressed, such as workflow, getting signatures, ease of doing expense reports, and submissions for approvals.

4. **Tracking.** Make provisions for addressing internal considerations and objectives, such as tracking customers' clicks, where they exited the site, what sites they came from, and information gathering on their needs (with proper concerns for privacy issues). The needs of other audiences must be addressed. These include the press, consultants, federal and state government purchasing policies, prospective resellers, and partners.

5. **Visibility**. Ensure that your enterprise focuses its resources on making its site visible on the World Wide Web. Unless end-users visit it, even the best-developed site will not serve any useful purpose. Make use of off-line advertising and free online advertising sites, such as linkages to different portals.

6. **Graphics**. Don't overdesign your site to the point that download speeds are unacceptable. Slow downloads are the number-one reason people give for avoiding a site. Your site should be easy to navigate and require no more than three clicks to access key data, such as the company address, phone number, and support line.

7. **Search functions**. Provide easy search capability for information on your site, based on key words or Boolean queries. The site should allow visitors to move back and forth from the present page to other pages. It should have a site map and easy pull-down menus for people to go directly to the content. It should be easy to link to other related content and partners' sites. Make sure that users have a way to come back to your site so they don't wander off to other locations. A user will generally scan the page for information and will tend to choose options that are visible, without scrolling

down the page. It is a good idea to highlight specific links and draw attention to important areas.

8. **That secure feeling.** Make the buying experience secure for customers. Tell them when they are in secure transactions. Provide all options, from credit cards to online shopping carts. Poor checkout experiences can cause people to abandon shopping in the middle of their purchases. Checkout areas should be clearly marked.

9. **Relevance**. Make your site relevant to user needs. It should be comprehensive and architecturally sound so that new information is easy to add. Provide consistent navigation operations from page to page. Insist on quality content.

10. **Make it fun**. People should have fun on the Internet. Make your site interactive and interesting. You should offer incentives for visitors to come back to the site, such as newsletters, online community forums, games, puzzles, help groups, chat groups, updated material, or other useful information.

Here are some other considerations to keep in mind while developing your website:

- Your Web strategy should be part of the overall business plan.
- Don't simply reproduce your brochures on your website. Use the power of interaction via the online environment. Some of the best examples of effective websites include autobytel.com, priceline.com, ebay.com, and most of the major broadcasting companies—abc.com, cbs.com, nbc.com, and cnn.com.
- Take advantage of the Internet's power to customize pages on the fly while users are browsing your site.
- Keep your site current. Clearly note privacy policies. Some of the leading websites of Internet groups devoted to privacy issues include truste.org, cdt.org, privacy.org, epic.org, eff.org, 2020tech.org, and aclu.
- Many sites provide free analysis and tuning of your site. Consider using some of them to see your site as others see it.

## CONTENT MANAGEMENT  . . . . . . . . . . . . . . . . .

Content creation and management are equally important considerations. Make s that content development, display, and updating processes are uniform and based industry standards.

Content management involves the creation, indexing, storing, access, distri tion and security of information. Today's websites contain an extensive amount of c alogs, personalized information, chat groups, e-mail response, tracking and measu ment information.

Today, content is mostly based on html and other multimedia forms, such audio, video, 3D VRML, MP3 compatible, graphics, animation, Java applets and ot formats. Content has to be downloaded, based on user needs. XML is becoming most important new standard for creating online content.

Content management has to integrate new online-generated information w legacy data. Proper structures have to be put into place to allow for access, integrat and collaboration. Consistent information is a must. For example, a company's pr ing information may be extracted from ERP application databases, product mana ment files, and finance files. The information from these sources must be consiste

Content management also includes managing the advertising and banner disp aspects of content. In those cases, you should ask: Whose ads should be displa based on what kind of user click activity in what sites? How many times should t be displayed and with what links?

Content management requires power databases and management capabilit development environments to create the online information content, collaboration mail, push technologies, search, registration, metering, and tracking capabilities.

## APPLICATION INTEGRATION  . . . . . . . . . . . . . . . . .

Application integration has taken on increased importance in the online environme The need to make it easier for customers to do business with you and have acces critical information about their orders, shipping, order history, and invoices, accure ly and quickly, will require tying together multiple applications across different fu tions in the company. Customers' orders may require many different application: assure delivery, acknowledgement, tracking and ongoing customer support. Al these must be integrated to provide end-to-end customer support.

Internally, e-business extends and leverages the investments made in re-e neered business processes and ERP applications deployed in the last deca Investments in electronic commerce, messaging and collaboration, business inte gence, and industry and enterprise applications must be optimized to achieve busin

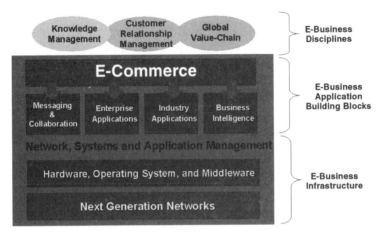

**Figure 8.3**
Compaq's E-business Model

goals. Today's challenge is integrating these applications and creating e-business disciplines focused on Customer Relationship Management (CRM), Knowledge Management (KM), and the Global Value Chain (GVC). These are the building blocks of e-business. Figure 8-3 describes the Compaq NonStop™ e-business model internally, from the perspective of the enterprise.

## In the dynamic value chain, applications need to be integrated across the enterprise

Application integration across the enterprise requires tight integration of multiple-application systems that span organizational and geographic boundaries. These systems must remain agile, flexible and highly scalable. With demanding requirements, the methodology used for application integration becomes a critical choice. Traditional approaches to application integration have the potential impact of slowing down future extension and modification of the integrated system, which is clearly counter-strategic.

Several application integration technologies are currently in use, including:

- Point-to-point integration: Each application is modified to create messages for every other application, which in turn are modified to receive them. Application-to-application communication is often synchronous. Time and resources needed to add the next application grow exponentially with the number of applications integrated. Where large numbers of applications must be integrated, cost can become prohibitive, and the enterprise's ability to react quickly to change can be impaired.

- Master-slave integration: One application (often an Enterprise Requirements Planning application) acts as the master application. Al other applications communicate through the master. This approach greatly simplifies the number of interconnects needed. But it increases message traffic, limits the buyer's portfolio of applications to those that have been certified by the master application vendor, and makes integration of legacy inhouse applications difficult.

- Non-intrusive message bus integration: This approach typically has three components. The first is an asynchronous message-passing facility, which in mature form, provides guaranteed message delivery and high availability. The second is a set of tools for creating object wrappers for existing applications (including newly acquired best-of-breed applications, inhouse developed applications and legacy applications). The third is a logical integration facility that handles data transformation, process transformation and workflow control, external to the applications integrated.

- E-business System Integration will be next. Companies like Matrix One are providing integration frameworks that allow the integration of enterprise applications and services into an end-to-end business system.

Figure 8.4 illustrates the major components in BusinessBus. The Integration Platform is layered on Microsoft Message Queue (MSMQ) on Windows NT and bridge to IBM's MQSeries and BEA's MessageQ for non-Windows NT platforms. *BusinessBus* Integration Manager provides an integrated view of applications vi *BusinessBus* COM interface. The Integration Manager orchestrates the workflow information between any number of applications, using its unique concept of a tra actional business process. Wrappers provide interfaces into the functions of an ap cation, and externalize business events from within applications. Applications that not COM-enabled or cannot be made COM-enabled can still be supported by *BusinessBus* wrapper architecture. *BusinessBus* is suitable, therefore, when addre ing the issues associated with loose integration of computer software systems (par ularly when that integration involves systems in large enterprises that span sev geographies), which involve heterogeneous legacy applications and involve ordered flow of information between otherwise distinct applications.

Application Integration is the current focus of BEA Systems, Inc., with eL which combines their Web and transaction processing middleware with applicat connectors and business processes translators that link the business processes of v ous enterprise applications. IBM has teamed up with Neon, Inc., to tie IBM MQSe and transaction processing middleware to Neon's application integration softw MQSeries broad platform support helps link many applications, regardless of operating environment. Iona Technologies and other vendors also offer applicat integration solutions.

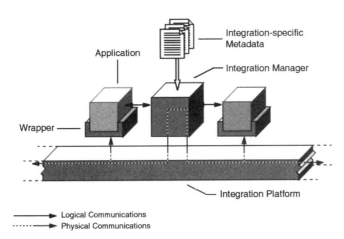

**Figure 8.4**

Major Components In BusinessBus

# TRANET SOLUTIONS . . . . . . . . . . . . . . . . . . . . . . . . . .

Intranets provide access for employees or other people who are authorized to have confidential company information. According to *Information Week* surveys, intranets are being used for many internal activities, including document sharing, training, corporate phone/mail directories, customer information, marketing and sales collateral, and human resource policies and forms.

In many companies, intranets have been added with little corporate supervision. Boeing Co. found that it had in excess of 2300 intranets and websites hosting more than a million pages. While many of these serve useful functions, the drawback may be duplication of resources, unnecessary capital investments and, most important, the issue of exposing information to customers that is obsolete or information that does not conform to the company's policies.

The function of intranets has evolved from providing information to collaborative computing, where information can be shared via e-mail. Collaborative activities for development, marketing or sales can be achieved by using tools like Lotus Notes. Other important functions, like workflow, calendaring, news, and communications, can also by provided by intranets. Intranets will evolve even further, becoming platforms for new decision support and transactional applications.

# MANAGING YOUR INTRANET . . . . . . . . . . . . . . . . . . .

- Define clear goals for the intranet.
- Get organizational buy-in; define support requirements, skills, and bud-getary issues.
- Define user groups, if there is more than one user with proper access authority. Understand their community or individual search and knowledge management requirements.
- Define policies and procedures affecting ownership of the information and sites.
- Define standards for creating, publishing, and managing the content.
- Determine key applications that may be required, such as e-mail, workflow collaboration, DSS, transaction processing, and personalized data/sites.
- Define the architecture as part of the overall e-infrastructure blueprint. In some cases, letting departments create their own solutions makes sense especially when special needs are involved.

# EXTRANETS . . . . . . . . . . . . . . . . . . . . . . . . . . . . .

One of the best ways to build relationships with your customers, suppliers, and p ners is by deploying extranets. These are essentially private networks that use Internet's ubiquitous infrastructure. They are only password-protected.

Personalizing extranets for key customers can put customers in control and build closer relationships with them. Consider providing information that is rele to customers' specific job functions. Offer new ideas or pointers to sources of cri skills. Provide access to the status of their specific orders, history of billing, a spe ic chat group with their peers, and resources for answering critical questions. A v of caution: if direct sales or service representatives are in the loop, keep them up ed in parallel for some of the self-help categories.

Extranets provide connections with suppliers and keep them updated on tomer trends and joint management issues, such as inventory and JIT delive Extranets are also useful for collaborative activities with partners and customers, as joint developments, customized build-to-order initiatives, customer programs, the use of joint selling tools. Buy-side collaborations are also a good idea as lon they are kept within legal boundaries.

A key consideration when deploying extranets is to develop a systematic pla action focused on the business involved, its issues and revenue drivers, its com ment of resources, and its use of technology. As extranets start to build relationships, order entry and inventory management issues may arise concerning the roles of employees. These may include loss of control, ownership of information, lost sales commissions, and finger pointing.

Two extranets, autochain.com and Automotive Network Exchange (anx.com), are used by the automotive industry to make the supply chain more efficient. Their objectives are new ways to improve the supply chain process within their industry and to develop standards for transactions.

# JIDELINES FOR DEVELOPING AN EXTRANET . . . . . .

1. Define extranets for specific capabilities. Avoid having multiple points of entry for customers and partners; these can be confusing and lead to redundancy.
2. Get buy-in from internal functions and partners, suppliers, key customers, and others who will be accessing the site.
3. Make sure the design goals include ways to improve customer satisfaction, relationship, collaboration, and communication, as well as sales, marketing and manufacturing efficiencies.
4. The infrastructure should be 24/7, scalable, secure and based on standards.
5. It should be fast and provide real-time information.
6. Create personalized information, based on individual users and types of functions.
7. Provide content that is relevant and useful.
8. Plan for updates, management changes and improvements.
9. Provide for appropriate applications, search capabilities, security, tracking, and measurements.

# COMMERCE TECHNOLOGIES . . . . . . . . . . . . . . . . . .

When a company broadens its engagement by involving its core business processes in an Internet initiative, it has gone beyond the limits of e-commerce into a new dimension—the e-business dimension. In the first chapter of the Internet, e-commerce was the horizon of most companies seeking to profit from the Internet-driven economy.

With the advent of very powerful technologies, companies were able to integr their back and front office operations and adopt online solutions to bring about c savings and higher service levels. This section is limited to the discussion of busine to-business and business-to-consumer e-commerce.

The precursor of e-commerce was Electronic Data Interchange (EDI), which been around for more than a decade. Many worldwide companies still use EDI will continue to use it for business-to-business transactions. It took more than years for standards to be adopted nationally, and even longer globally. One of biggest hurdles to worldwide acceptance has been the cost involved in implement EDI and the associated value-added networks. Consequently, its implementation been generally limited to large companies and their first-tier partners. There v efforts by some companies to pool their resources and provide EDI capabilities number of smaller companies, especially in the Far East.

Companies will continue to use EDI for forms and data required for legal p poses. However, EDI will increasingly use some of the capabilities of the Inter Internet EDI will use Web-based forms and interfaces instead of computer-to-c puter interfaces. Applications will be integrated with EDI and will use the Web as delivery mechanism. EDI on the Web will support the emerging XML-based con and will become one part of the total end-to-end buying and selling cycles.

Today, e-commerce has three major models: the sell side, which focuses on s ing goods and services to business or consumers; the buy side, to help enterprises cure goods and services efficiently; and the marketmediaries, or marketplaces to b buyers and sellers together.

# E-COMMERCE DEPLOYMENT  . . . . . . . . . . . . . . . . .

Several elements must be considered in an e-commerce implementation. They are of the overall e-infrastructure blueprint diagram. The following are key element the blueprint that relate specifically to the exchange of information, services, bu and selling, and the transfer of money.

These elements include customer services, merchant services, infrastructure, tems services, business logic, payment, administrative, customer support, anal tracking and reporting, links to other intranets, extranets, e-mail, and legacy syst

The customer interface is an essential consideration. For customer satisfac an interface must be easy, engaging, useful, secure, and fast. It should be able to dle different types of transactions based on HTML or XML for browsers.

Interfaces should be intuitive and should be able to support such areas as help, personalization, marketing, customized information, and creating informa suggestions on the fly as customers browse through selections.

- For business-to-business transactions, other standards, such as EDI, EDI on the Internet, Open Buying on Internet (OBI) for purchasing, Open Financial Exchange (OFX) for bill presentment, and Open Trading Protocol (OTP), should be considered.

- Merchant services may include shopping carts, product options, displays, checkout and others. These items are similar to what is available in a physical store.

- Infrastructure/systems services cover all aspects of load balancing, storage, database pooling, servers, networks, and other mechanisms required for 24/7 access.

- Under business logic are the capabilities for inventory management, order-pipeline management, shipment and tracking, and catalog management functions. An important consideration is the proper linkage between the back-end systems and shipping vendors, such as UPS, Federal Express, and USPS.

- Payment systems must accept as many customer options as possible, which include credit cards, debit cards, and checks. Customer data must be secure—from the browser to the authorization processes within banks or other agencies. Payment systems have to support security standards, such as Secured Electronic Transaction (SET), that is being developed by a consortium led by Visa and MasterCard; Joint Electronic Payments Initiative (JEPI), led by the Worldwide Web Consortium, SSL, S-HTTP and others. To protect against merchant fraud, Cybercast and others can help in the credit card or other digital authorization processes. In this instance, the merchant does not see the card but gets authorization to proceed with the transaction, after Cybercast has secured authorization from the credit card source.

- Administration includes such activities as marketing, record keeping, authentication, and maintenance.

Customer support is another essential function of online markets. Customers need confirmations, answers to their questions and easy access to merchants. Some online firms hire tracking services that keep track of the activity, customer behavior, areas where they abandoned their shopping carts, items they were most interested in, and their navigation paths. A number of vendors provide support for the implementation of e-commerce solutions. Some of these vendors include Compaq, IBM, Sun, HP, Microsoft, Netscape, Open Market, Ariba Technologies, Connect, Inc., and Trade'ex Electronic Commerce Systems.

Most Big Five consulting firms offer customers a choice of complete turnkey solutions; or they supply hardware, software, services or specific skills based on user needs.

Most solution providers have a multi-vendor systems integration experience, and can help integrate legacy solutions if desired. Most e-commerce solution providers

have similar relationships or partnerships with software vendors, such as Micros
Oracle, SAP, Siebel, and Lotus. Together, they have pre-tested their e-commerce sc
tions to reduce the risk in deployments.

A vendor's knowledge of vertical industry customers; business process; inter
tional policy; tax laws; legal issues; and planning, design and management service
a serious consideration for companies looking for assistance with their e-comme
solutions. It is also critical that the vendor you select have experience, not only ir
commerce, but also in other areas of the digital economy, such as intranets, extran
e-mail, and integration with legacy systems.

Multi-language support is another important consideration. Companies
excel in partner relationships have partners who can meet the needs of users from
small and medium companies to the largest enterprises.

- Microsoft e-commerce software solutions are designed to provide the bes
  tools available to customers for building their own e-commerce operations
  These solutions offer flexibility for customization, but they require enter
  prises to have knowledge of their own solution needs.

- Other major vendors, such as AOL/Netscape and Open Market, have cho
  sen the strategy of providing pre-packaged and pre-designed modules fo
  the major e-commerce services. This approach makes their deploymen
  easy for enterprises and systems integrators, but it does limit customizatio
  flexibility.

- While most of the financial, inventory updating, and order-pipeline func
  tions have been automated in the new packages, other key aspects of e
  commerce, such as marketing, selling and support, must somehow be inte
  grated into the whole e-commerce value delivery cycle.

- New procurement systems from RightWorks, Ariba, and other vendor
  extend purchasing to company desktops, funnel rogue buyers toward pre
  ferred vendors, and control expenses. Bid systems from Digital Market, Fre
  Markets, and others allow online buyers to obtain lowest prices on RFPs.

In business-to-business e-commerce, companies have found they can save
siderable time and money by decentralizing the purchasing function. Whether
company uses a procurement method or "point" system, or another form of online
chasing, the goal remains the same. Corporations want to empower their employee
make their own decisions. With online purchasing, employees can order the prod
they need online. This process cuts down on the time it takes for divisions with
company to receive needed products. This means faster cycles, improved inven
levels, happier employees, and happier customers.

# NTERPRISE PORTALS . . . . . . . . . . . . . . . . . . . . . .

Enterprise portals should be a strategic component of a company's Internet strategy. In principle, these resemble the Internet portals of pioneers like AltaVista, Yahoo!, Destination, E*Trade, and others. The difference is that Internet portals provide a door to the Internet; enterprise portals provide a window into a company.

Enterprise portals perform such functions as searches, information capture, personalization, and application integration. Users are able to define their personal pages and access relevant information. Portals can capture information from internal, competitive and external sources. They are able to handle structured (database) as well as unstructured data (office documents).

These portals go beyond the sharing of knowledge. They can be used to distribute software or provide updates to existing software. Over the long term, they will play an important role in the dynamic Value Network and may reshape the online architecture of the enterprise.

Plumtree Software has supplied portal solutions to Caterpillar, Inc., and W.W. Grainger. The Plumtree applications use the portal to gather information about specific topics or user community needs and automatically forward it to the appropriate individuals for action. Integrators like AnswerThink are now deploying portal solutions for major corporations.

Traditional ERP vendors have jumped into this market to provide capabilities based on their existing solutions. SAP has solutions that combine data from its R/3 applications with other sources. For example, SAP will allow access to benefits programs, travel reservations and other customized capabilities. It will have extensions to the Internet for business-to-consumer selling and will provide the tools to build storefronts. The business-to-business model will enable the sharing of data with partners and suppliers and the placing of orders in real time.

Many enterprises might be well advised to combine best-of-breed capabilities to create a powerful universal portal, rather than adopt a solution from a single vendor. ERP vendors may have an advantage here, since they have the ability to link frontend, back-end, and manufacturing processes. Business intelligence vendors can provide portals based on their core competencies and integrate ERP data into their solutions. Document management vendors, such as Documentum, Verano, Plumtree Software, and Viador, are working toward similar ends.

# KEY CAPABILITIES OF PORTALS . . . . . . . . . . . . . . . .

- Capture of information, structured and unstructured.
- Cross intranet, Internet, extranets.
- Indexing and storage.
- Aggregation of information from different sources and applications.
- Personalization.
- Single point of access to information; sharing of information.
- Push information.
- Personalized sites. "My Information place".
- Security and management of information.

Ultimately, enterprise portals may serve the purpose of integrating such parate technologies as e-mail, ERP, Knowledge Management, and e-commerce, providing a seamless path for the portal user. Many predict that portals will bec the core technology for building next-generation intranets, extranets, and enterp knowledge systems.

# E-APPLICATIONS . . . . . . . . . . . . . . . . . . . . . . . . .

We see the emergence of three major e-application categories:

1. **Extensions of existing ERP, CRM, e-mail, workflow, collaboratio applications and others with the power of the Internet.** Major playe like Microsoft, SAP, PeopleSoft, Oracle, Baan, and Siebel have alread launched integrated solutions that allow these applications to interopera via the Internet.

2. **Applications that have been created primarily to take advantage online solutions, such as auction sites and multi-vendor malls.** Ma applications will leverage knowledge databases and workflow. Son examples are applications in the areas of personalization, automated e-ma response filtering of information for understanding user preference metering, tracking, and payment systems.

3. **Innovative applications based on brokering and leveraging online se vices.** These will use the Web, rather than traditional operating systems, their platform. The applications are developed to take advantage of W standards, Internet infrastructure, Web content standards, and search too

These applications will drive a new phase of the digital economy where communities collaborate, and users invoke several disparate services to get answers through a process that is transparent to them. These will require enterprises to *think* in terms of user activity application scenarios and to create new applications to meet the needs. These will be popular in the fields of travel, healthcare, entertainment, and other personal services.

# ANAGEMENT AND SECURITY . . . . . . . . . . . . . . . . . .

For e-business, downtime costs customers money, and more importantly, downtime reduces customer satisfaction and increases IT costs. Platform and application management tools address the overall availability, security, and manageability of the infrastructure (hardware, networks, middleware, and applications). These tools help customers maximize system availability and proactively fix problems before they impact system availability and performance.

Companies implementing e-business systems face significant challenges in managing their IT environments. In addition to connecting customers to your company, e-business systems are often interconnected to the business systems of companies' suppliers, which introduces additional issues in managing these environments.

Managing these environments involves managing the availability and performance of business systems, both within the internal IT infrastructure and externally via the Internet. Availability and performance management tools are at the early stages of deployment in the IT infrastructure. Most companies are only now gaining the experience to effectively deploy and utilize these tools, yet they are one of the most important sets of capabilities in implementing a 24/7 business environment.

The internal business infrastructure requires the following set of management capabilities:

- *Platform (servers and desktop) availability tools*, designed to predict and detect hardware failures and to alert system administrators.
- *Application availability and performance management tools*, designed to monitor application, database and O/S availability/performance, and to take proactive recovery actions.
- *Network availability and performance management tools*, designed to monitor and detect network device failure, and designed to monitor and report on the impact of the network on application and network device performance.
- *Service-level administration (SLA) tools*, designed to measure service levels on applications and infrastructure in the business environment.

- *General system management tools*, for job scheduling, backup and recovery, data management, and system administration.
- *Enterprise management frameworks*, for the centralized system and network management of multiple network and PC management.

In addition to these capabilities for the internal infrastructure, the use of Internet requires the following capabilities for Internet-enabled applications:

- *Extranet cross-site availability management tools*, designed to monitor the availability of interconnects between the business applications of trading partners.
- *End-to-end transaction performance monitoring and analysis tools* designed to monitor and measure the transaction performance for the customer of an e-commerce application.
- *Service-level administration (SLA) tools*, designed to monitor and measure service levels of business applications between trading partners and across the extranet.

No single vendor can offer all solutions, so most of them partner with other leading solution suppliers. The key is to check WBEM and SNMP standards complian the degree of joint testing and solution characterization, and the commitment to c tinued enhancements and future solutions.

## SECURITY SOLUTIONS . . . . . . . . . . . . . . . . . . . . . .

Information security makes e-business possible by providing tools to open up in mation to the people who need it, while keeping information assets safe from hack viruses and electronic thieves. Without information security, e-business would b more risks than opportunities; with security solutions, the future of the enterp looks a lot safer.

Typically, the key security objectives are:

- Identification and authentication—Identifying potential computing syste users and authenticating that they are who they say they are.
- Authorization/access control—Once authenticated, specifying wh resources a user can access.
- Privacy—Ensuring that sensitive data is accessible only to authorized partie
- Integrity—Ensuring that information is protected from unauthorize manipulation and alteration.

- Accountability—Providing for accurate, verifiable audit trails of a user's activity on a computing system and protection from repudiation or misrepresentation of actions.

Today, enterprises have a broad range of solution choices to build comprehensive security architecture. Some examples of these solutions are:

- Firewalls
- Virus-filtering
- Intrusion detection
- Virtual Private Networks (VPN)
- Hardware-based encryption acceleration
- Public Key Infrastructure (PKI) / Certificate Authority (CA)
- Vulnerability assessment
- Biometrics (fingerprint) readers
- SmartCards
- Hardware-based security features (CMOS passwords and hard drive passwords)

Security threats can bring e-businesses to a full stop in several different ways: hackers shutting down the firewall through denial-of-service attacks; electronic thieves stealing credit card information; viruses shutting down users, servers, and networks—whether at the enterprise or beyond. Internal users pose the largest security threat of all, through the unauthorized use of information by trusted employees.

Security solutions work to detect, correct and prevent security threats, and thereby provide a safe e-business environment. This means not only stopping hackers from getting into your network, but also catching the ones who do get in. Security also means removing temptation from employees by giving them strong authentication tools, such as SmartCards or fingerprint readers.

Finally, tying all of this together is security management. Most of the large solution providers work with several partners to meet customer security management needs. Compaq, for example, works with AXENT for firewall and VPN; Check Point for firewall and VPN; ISS for intrusion detection and vulnerability assessment; and Trend Micro for centralized, server-based virus filtering. This makes it possible to pull together the best-of-breed security products into a seamless whole, minimizing the gaps available to hackers, while enabling faster, more available, and targeted information to go to the constituencies that need it. In addition, operating system vendors, such as Novell with their Network Directory Services, and Microsoft, with Windows NT, provide additional security services.

While security solutions are essential to availability by preventing security sh
downs, high availability also means preventing single-point-of-failure weakness.
AXENT, through its Microsoft Cluster Server capabilities, and CheckPoint, throu
its partnership with high-availability vendors, such as StoneBeat and RainFini
already provide high-availability solutions for that essential security foundation pie
and Internet gateway, the firewall. In addition, server-based virus solutions from Tre
Micro ensure high availability through layering, which provides virus filtering for
firewall, the application, and the file server through networked computer architectu

For most enterprises, scalability for firewalls is not an issue, since it is not dii
cult to build a firewall that can sustain a throughput far greater than several T-1 or
1 Wide Area Network connections. Compaq testing indicates that firewalls fro
CheckPoint and AXENT are able to maintain greater than 40 megabits per second
throughput, depending on the setup options selected. However, for those enterpri
requiring higher-than-normal traffic, firewalls can be scaled by assigning a separ
firewall to each different type of traffic: HTTP, SMTP, and FTP. In some scenari
load balancing may be feasible.

Scalability has another sense, however, where it applies to human assets:
exponential growth of e-business traffic makes earlier, manual techniques for man
ing security simply unfeasible. Automating tasks—such as the distribution of vi
signatures, monitoring for unauthorized network access, detecting weaknesses in el
tronic security, and updating authorization rights for hundreds or thousands of users
is being accomplished by customers using the tools and vendors mentioned above

# STORAGE ARCHITECTURE . . . . . . . . . . . . . . . . . . . . . . .

Storage architecture enables organizations to combine the benefits of distributed cc
puting in an open, industry-standard environment with the strengths of logically c
tralized data management. At the same time, the storage architecture allows the cc
pany to achieve the highest levels of performance and flexibility at the lowest t
cost of ownership. Compaq, with its Enterprise Network Storage Architec
(ENSA), provides an excellent example of what is happening at the forefron
today's storage technology.

Effective storage architecture begins with a standards-based enterprise archi
ture design. The design goal is to provide unbounded performance and capacity, f
ibility, and simplified management. The standards-based approach will allow org
zations to combine network storage products from multiple vendors to create sha
pools of storage that can be allocated among different applications and needs. The
point of this approach is that these pools can be centrally managed. Not only are t
allocated among applications and needs, they are independent of the computing
tems and those applications.

The architecture will enable companies to adopt the latest in advanced storage technology, such as Open SAN, which is the next development on the horizon in storage architecture. This ensures that organizations can build upon today's investments in storage. It also allows the company to tap a multitude of third-party standards-based products for innovation or cost savings.

Finally, the storage architecture specifies enterprise storage management that enables a small team of administrators to effectively manage a large and rapidly growing pool of storage via the network. Network-based storage management reduces the cost of managing storage because it eliminates the need to duplicate a storage system at multiple sites.

# TORAGE ADVANCES . . . . . . . . . . . . . . . . . . . . . . . . .

Enterprises are benefiting from a host of advances in storage and server technology and strategy, which include:

- Fibre Channel storage interconnect technology.
- Heterogeneous SANs to support multi-vendor server platforms.
- Network attached storage (NAS) for distributed storage.
- Windows NT high-availability clustering.
- High-speed, high-capacity disk drives.
- Fibre channel switches.
- High-speed data replication.
- Fibre channel tape devices.
- Remote vaulting.

Compaq has advanced the concept of storage as a utility—essentially a service on the network, like electricity or water or telephone service.

Someday, when storage becomes a utility, it will simplify the lives of IT professionals and end users. To add storage, just plug it in. Reallocate storage with just a few mouse clicks. Alternatively, define a policy-based scheme and let the storage utility manage itself. High availability, backup, and even disaster recovery all become transparent. Storage administrators define the rules, and the storage utility makes it happen.

## Storage Pooling/Virtualization

Storage pooling/virtualization allows an organization to view its distributed stora
capacity as a single pool of storage. It collects any available storage space in a SA
and then parcels it out to applications as virtual drives. It also provides for the grou
ing of hardware array storage, or physical disks, into a logically linked pool of di
space. Multiple virtual (logical) disks can be created from the pool; they behave a
perform exactly like physical disks. Administrators can allocate and dynamically re
locate this storage capacity as necessary.

Disk virtualization allows system administrators to optimally tailor disk space
the size required by users and their applications. Storage devices can be added to
pool as needed, by increasing the size of the pool. Moreover, storage from multip
hardware array controllers can be bound into a storage pool and a virtual disk can
created that spans them. Up to terabyte-sized individual virtual disks can be create

## The Future Storage System: Open SAN

The Open SAN is the next step in the evolution of storage architecture. Supporti
"many to many" and "any to any" connectivity—application, file system, operating sy
tem, server platform, storage system, tape library, SAN interconnect devices—the op
SAN will use published, open industry standards. But it's not here yet. Today there a
no broad interoperability standards in place, so there is no way to ensure that Fit
Channel storage systems from different vendors can be managed on the same SAN.

Storage systems providers are currently addressing the critical areas of Op
SAN management, Open SAN interoperability, and Open SAN virtualizatic
Compaq was the first to announce new products that can create virtualized Windo
NT storage pools for increased business flexibility, make instant data snapshots
quick recovery leading to higher customer service levels, and replicate data anywhe
in the world over SAN-WAN-SAN connections for reliable business continuance.
rash of similar announcements is anticipated as systems suppliers jockey for positi
in this extraordinarily fast-paced and constantly evolving technology.

The IT market is increasingly focusing on external storage, and today's mar
battleground for storage is software—since storage hardware functionality has esse
tially reached parity for many of the major storage providers. Storage software is a d
ferent story, however, since the advanced functionality required to deliver Open SA
will come from software rather than hardware. Customers are demanding the lat
innovations in the storage-networking arena for improved business velocity. Th
want storage solutions that increase business flexibility, elevate customer service l
els, and streamline operational efficiency. Open SANs hold the promise of deliveri
these strategic results.

The Storage Networking Industry Association (SNIA) has established the Storage Networking Technology Center in Colorado Springs, Colorado. This center will be a state-of-the-art facility for developing and testing open storage networking standards to help expand the use and usefulness of Open SANs. The key to an Open SAN is centralized storage management based on open industry standards. SNIA is working to ensure that this evolving storage technology will be available to meet the market's computing needs during the first decade of 2000.

# STRATEGY FOR THE INTERNET FUTURE . . . . . . . . . .

The challenge of e-business is multifaceted, but the essential principles are the fusion of business and IT planning, the development of a strategic plan, and a phased implementation program that addresses the critical building blocks. The goal is to leverage e-solutions flexibly to make the whole enterprise agile and responsive to changing markets and technologies.

# 9
# Building Your E-Company

.......................

*S*ummary: *Released like a tsunami from out of nowhere, the enormous force of the new digital economy threatens to swamp thousands of established businesses in its wake. However, for those business leaders who saw this new phenomenon as opportunity, it has been an exhilarating—and very profitable—ride. To succeed in this high-stakes environment, with its instant and continuing disruptive change, requires courage. It requires no less than the total transformation of the enterprise. The new incarnation must be a global, agile, e-business, with the ability to act at Internet speed, and whose raison d'être is serving customers' needs.*

## TRANSFORMING THE ENTERPRISE . . . . . . . . . . . . . . .

We have always had choices in business—whether to invest more in marketing or research and development, plant expansion or product enhancements. It was our call. The enterprise flourished and we were rewarded for making the right call most of the time. Perhaps the most difficult concept to grasp about the global online economy is that we are part of it, whether we choose to be or not. It is not our call.

Not only a part of it, we have an urgent mandate to reinvent ourselves—to transform the enterprise into a globally competitive, 24/7, innovative, e-business that embraces change and uses it as a strategic weapon. We cannot choose to pass this one by. We must reinvent the enterprise. We must do it now. It is not a matter of choice. It is a matter of survival.

There are few road maps to follow. The roads are too new. The territory we are entering is unsettled—in constant change and continuous flux, driven by innovation and new collaboration dynamics. What we see in this strange new territory are thousands of other companies, all over the world, feverishly reinventing themselves in a shifting marketplace that is also constantly reinventing itself.

To make a real impact, management must play a leadership role in understan ing, driving, supporting, organizing and preparing for the new global economy. T importance of devising an intelligent strategy with company-wide buy-in cannot overstated. Without a strategic plan, which takes all necessary technology requir ments into account, companies risk losing focus and their ability to compete.

To succeed in the Internet Age, where continuous connections to your cu tomers, partners, suppliers and employees are absolutely essential—and where yo competition is just a click away—you must adapt to:

- The new paradigm of speed and agility.
- Global competition and e-commerce.
- A marketplace that operates 24/7.

## The global economy never stops, and neither can your business

When you think about it, your e-business comes to a stop in the followi instances:

- When a customer logs on to a website and the response time is slow.
- When there is a security breach.
- When you bring a system down to add components.
- When a disaster strikes and the system can't keep going.
- When data is lost or garbled.
- When you can't dynamically recover from a transaction failure.
- When you can't provide quality service.

Multiply all these factors by every supplier and vendor in your extranet sup chain; by all the manufacturing, planning, marketing, sales and customer databas used internally; and by all the networks needed to tie it together, and you quickly s that a fully integrated e-business demands 24/7 e-business solutions.

To compete in the digital economy, your company must be open for business hours a day 7 days a week and be agile, predictable, and secure. Conventional bu nesses handle thousands of orders in a matter of weeks. With today's zero-laten standards, companies must be capable of handling millions of orders in a few secon 24/7, anywhere in the world.

The buffers that exist today will go away. Inventory buffers for work-in-proce channel buffers, and warehouse buffers are changing to just-in-time inventory. C centers will need real-time data to provide service value. All your services and business processes will need to respond to almost real-time triggers.

Companies are learning that there is no room for business disruptions. Their IT environments must perform the following:

- Run without user-visible interruption.
- Change constantly—at Internet speed.
- Scale dynamically and transparently.
- Be easily reconfigured.
- Support secure transactions.

## E-Business Cuts Costs

One saving grace for companies that have committed to transform their traditional businesses to e-businesses is that e-business saves money—lots of it. As businesses restructure themselves to operate online, they are reaping huge cost benefits. Studies show that just-in-time delivery results in lower inventory, with savings of around 20% to 25%. By reducing data entry errors, customer service costs can be reduced up to 50%; and by efficient order processing, time can be shortened by as much as 50% to 96%. E-business lowers transaction costs in every industry.

Examples of lower costs by industry:

- airline ticketing        by a factor of 8
- banking                  by a factor of 8.3
- bill payment             by a factor of 3.5
- life insurance           by a factor of 2
- software                 by a factor of 50
- brokerage                by a factor of 10

## Drivers of the Internet Economy

Business is increasingly driven by the technologies that manage customer information. In the global economy, IT is not just how you operate your business—it is your business.

Companies all over the world are under tremendous pressure to get their own e-businesses up and running because their management and stockholders are confronted by major new challenges in the form of:

- New buyers
- New markets
- Lower cost of sales
- Increased yield per employee
- Shorter time to market
- Reduced cycle time
- Change as a strategic weapon
- More competitive business models

In the digital economy, buyers are going to have a lot of power in defining yo role. You must get into Internet-based sales fast or risk missing the opportunity.

Your portal becomes your Internet brand. Getting people to your site early critical. You must offer product value, service value, and relationship value. Produ value has been the focus in the past. Call centers teach us the value of service. The make sure that Internet buyers can deal with someone who's interested in their situ tion and up-sells where possible. Relationship value is what builds your e-busine through "mass personalization."

The last two holiday shopping seasons unleashed tidal waves of Internet cor merce. Consumer spending on the Internet posted unheard-of dollar amounts and su denly had everyone's attention. While IT managers for these overwhelmed retail sit were scrambling to keep systems running, some companies experienced major glitche

- Customers of some major brokerage firms saw "system temporarily down" on their screens.
- Successful sites took serious hits from multiple outages.
- Companies like amazon.com took business from competitors because other sites couldn't process encrypted transactions fast enough.

In the e-business world, the fast eat the slow, and the small can eat the big. T answer is the same every time: Enterprises of all sizes must innovate or they w evaporate.

## The New Online Model

For many large corporations, the early to mid 1990s saw huge expenditures for Business Process Re-engineering (BPR) initiatives and Enterprise Resource Planning (ERP) software installations targeting the retirement of outdated and costly legacy applications.

Many companies are just now completing their BPR initiatives and major consolidation programs. However, the availability of the Internet and Internet-related technologies during the recent 1990s has had a dramatic impact on the way businesses must view Information Technology and its strategic relationship to business. Corporations must shift from viewing IT as the traditional means for "running the business" to viewing IT as central to the business strategy.

E-business today is a reality, due to the synthesis of IT and business strategy in the context of integrating corporate systems, with the growing global network infrastructure, as represented in Figure 9.1. The International Data Corporation (IDC) defines e-business as "the electronic connection of business operations to customers, suppliers, and partners." Compaq further defines e-business as "the use of the Internet and Internet technologies that enable the transformation of business models to achieve competitive advantage." E-business implies the fully automated, end-to-end integration of the corporation's business systems with partners, suppliers, and service provider business systems.

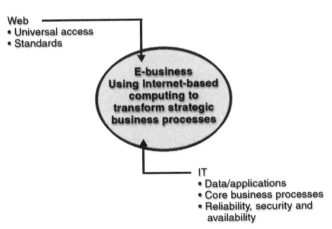

**Figure 9.1**
Merging of Current Business Systems with Internet Technologies

# CHALLENGES OF E-BUSINESS . . . . . . . . . . . . . . . .

Today's dynamic, global marketplace demands instant answers, products, and service Today's educated consumer requires choices, quality, and rapid delivery at competiti prices. The marketplace has changed—it's not shelves loaded with merchandise—i high-tech touchscreens loaded with options 24 hours a day, 365 days a year. Busine hours are now obsolete. What is unfolding before our eyes is a dramatically chang environment, with unprecedented challenges in the marketplace.

**Transition to E-business**—Less than 5% of all companies today understa how to apply e-business and use it as a strategic tool. In fact, 85% of that 5% are ente ing the e-business world by re-facing heritage systems. While they appear to be ahe today, their approach is likely to constrain them and cause them to lose over time. T transformation to an e-business is a process in which the company needs to start sir ple and grow as demand dictates. It is essential that IT systems are architectural designed in a manner that is modular and can support growth and change.

**Rapid new business cycles**—As information technology has become more pe vasive, business cycles and business models have changed significantly. Thirty yea ago the business cycle was 10 to 15 years, and the dominant information technolo was the mainframe computer. In the 1990s, PC usage multiplied and ushered in the e of client/server computing. Business cycles fell to one to three years. Today, we are the edge of perhaps the most significant change of all—change driven by the Intern Business cycles will no longer be measured in years, or even in months. They will measured by the transaction—by the time it takes to deliver a specific product, to me the specific needs of an individual customer—at a specific point in time.

**Unprecedented technology demands**—In this e-business world, businesses w face unprecedented technology demands: high availability, scalability, security, a management. All of these need to be built into the enterprise platforms. They must easy to buy, easy to configure, and ready to plug in and go. Most important, e-busine solutions must be completely predictable in a world where the usage, demand, a stress on e-business solutions will be completely and utterly unpredictable.

E-business is a composite of two sets of infrastructures and systems; those th are internal and those that are external to the enterprise. Businesses implementing business systems should approach e-business from those two perspectives.

# INTERNAL ENTERPRISE PERSPECTIVE . . . . . . . . . . . .

Investments in electronic commerce, messaging, collaboration, business intelligenc and industry and enterprise applications must be optimized to achieve business goa Today's challenge is integrating these applications and creating e-business disciplin focused on Customer Relationship Management (CRM), Knowledge Management (KM), and Global Value Chain (GVC). These are the building blocks of e-business.

**Knowledge Management (KM)**—Simply defined, KM is the ability to leverage the knowledge assets of an extended enterprise, thus enabling management to make the best decisions to maximize competitive advantage (see Figure 9.2).

**Knowledge Management**

**Figure 9.2**

Knowledge Management E-Business Discipline

KM is an emerging business practice that has wide applicability across industries, markets, and professions. It is not a new application or solution domain. KM is an engaging new conceptual model and language for positioning IT and organizational change initiatives. Many companies are feeling increased pressure, during the current shift to a knowledge-based economy, to better manage the following:

- Intangible assets, such as dynamic human expertise.
- Information assets, such as the captured documents, designs, and other physical or electronic fruits of that expertise.
- Corporate strategies that leverage these assets for enhanced profitability.

KM is neither a panacea nor a complete solution to any specific business problem. It can provide perspective and focus for an integrated approach to an identifiable number of specific business needs. Some of the business areas that customers need to see addressed by KM solutions are as follows:

- Innovation and creativity
- Asset protection
- Product development
- Responsiveness

- Knowledge worker productivity
- Organizational learning
- Customer knowledge

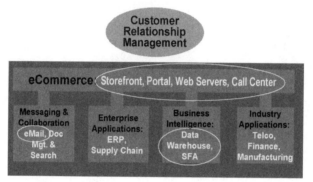

**Figure 9.3**

Customer Relationship E-Business Discipline

**Customer Relationship Management (CRM)**—Figure 9.3 shows how CR builds stronger customer relationships through better understanding of individu needs and preferences and improved customer interactions. This ability includes t following components:

- Maintaining a complete customer view, across all touch points with the organization (paper, Web, call center, and kiosk).
- Developing an integrated view across the organization (departments and databases).
- Deploying customer-focused business processes (help desk, search, targeted information and product offerings).

CRM comprises a set of business processes and enabling systems that suppor business strategy. CRM accomplishes the following:

- Builds and retains long-term, profitable relationships with customers.
- Expands the business to attract new customers.
- Optimizes the share of each customer's business.

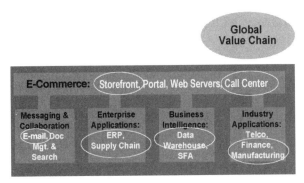

**Figure 9.4**

Global Value Chain E-Business Discipline

**Global Value Chain (GVC)**—GVC is a series of activities that an enterprise pursues, popularly described as a value chain (see Figure 9.4). The value chain is a business model connecting activities that include supply-side relationships, inbound logistics, production processes, and demand-side activities. With the proliferation of Internet technologies and worldwide relationships, enterprises are realizing the importance of managing information. At the same time, they are seeing that the Internet eliminates time and space limitations. Thus, the enterprise global value chain model is one of value-added activity beyond time and space.

GVC enables organizational capability and efficiency through automating business processes and linking suppliers, partners and customers together. As the end-to-end flow of these assets is made more efficient, the cost of inventory management, business process management, time management, and money management is reduced. GVC includes developing efficient supply, transaction, and information chain practices, as well as trading partner enablement.

## External Enterprise Perspective

Externally, e-business is the fully automated, end-to-end integration of the corporation's CRM, KM, and GVC business systems with partners, suppliers, and service provider business systems. E-business is built on the public network infrastructure called the Internet, as well as private networks that have existed for many years. E-business is inclusive of the processes and technologies required for executing secure business transactions between business entities. E-business applications are interdependent and are managed individually by participating business entities which, for IT organizations, introduces a whole new set of concerns centered around availability, scalability, security, and overall manageability.

## Product Engineering and Development

In addition to KM, CRM, and GVC, a fourth operational dimension must be cons‑ ered as one of the four "horizontal applications" that underpin today's e-business. T dimension is Product Engineering and Development (PE&D). PE&D is a prim activity, fundamental to many industries, and it incorporates such subdisciplines design, engineering testing, and manufacturing (or the equivalent series in proc industries such as pharmaceuticals, steel, paper, and consumer goods).

Zero-latency is the operating ideal—the measure of success in the implemen tion of each of the four operational dimensions. Zero-latency is the IT standard t means "operate and execute with the highest speed, with as little delay as possible

In a 24/7 e-business enterprise, reaction to market changes must be fast, syst response time must be fast, changes to applications must be fast, and deployment new applications must be fast.

The Gartner Group observed the growing need for speed and flexibility in seminal series of Research Notes on what it calls the "Zero Latency Enterprise." quote the Gartner Group, "Virtually any activity, from business to war, that combi the work of multiple people in multiple locations can be improved if critical inform tion known by one person can be made available quickly to people or computer s tems operating elsewhere. Virtually all communication advances have improved su latency. However, the idea of using the IS organization to fully enable ZLE is wish thinking until the following conditions can be met:

- Related business activities must be brought online individually before it is practical to tie them together for a ZLE strategy.
- Networks must be fast, inexpensive, reliable and compatible so that differ-ent platforms can exchange files and messages without much customization.
- Application systems must connect easily to the ZLE infrastructure because it is impractical to heavily modify them.
- End users need common mechanisms for interacting with a ZLE infra-structure.
- The hardware must be fast and inexpensive."

A computer system to support the 24/7 e-business enterprise, then, is a glob deployed, tightly integrated, multiple-application system that spans organizational geographic boundaries, *and must still remain agile, flexible, and highly scalable.* W requirements that demanding, the methodology used for application integrat becomes a critical choice.

This is particularly true in the semiconductor industry. A key goal of sup chain integration in the semiconductor industry is the reduction of time-to-market new products. A poor choice of application integration technology will actu increase this critical time. Semiconductor companies must pay close attention, therefore, to the *implementation* speed offered by a technology, and to the impact on total system flexibility of adding another application using that technology.

## IT Values in the 24/7 E-Business Environment

The dynamics of the Internet environment align the enterprise's IT systems directly with the customer. Systems failure in this context is catastrophic. Because of these shifts, business applications will need to run 24/7. Compaq Computer Corporation's definition of NonStop e-business is not just about the availability of the hardware technology that vendors are willing to guarantee. The operation of NonStop e-business systems creates new challenges and opportunities:

- Systems availability depends upon public network availability, partner and service provider availability, and inter-application availability.
- Scalability can become susceptible to last-mile (ISP to customer) and network bottlenecks.
- Application management challenges expand to include cross-partner and application status monitoring and remediation.
- Security architectures must encompass encryption, authentication, and authorization capabilities for system-to-system and internal and partner users.

## Critical Dimensions of E-Business

The new IT environment is all about predictability, and *always* being open for business. The critical dimensions of NonStop e-business are availability, scalability, manageability, and security.

**Availability** for e-businesses is defined as the continuous delivery of accurate business services as measured by the customer of those services (no user-visible failure). Failure of any component, system, application, Internet Service Provider (ISP), Application Service Provider (ASP), or partner/supplier should not cause an outage that prohibits taking and fulfilling a customer's order.

**Scalability** for e-businesses is defined as the ability to meet dynamic capacity requirements without interrupting service operations. The inability to scale server performance resources to meet dynamic Internet user growth, such as has been experienced by some of the major brokerage houses, can cost millions of dollars, in addition to the loss of customers. Selecting the right platform with the scalability headroom to meet these challenges will be key to sustained competitive advantage. In addition, the

inability of your partner or supplier to scale their systems to meet the demand yo
organization generates can result in the reality or the perception that your business
suffering from an outage.

**Security** for e-businesses has even broader consequences. Security for e-bu
ness is defined as the ability to ensure the confidentiality and integrity of a busin
and its customers' assets. Traditional security involves protecting information ins
the enterprise. More difficult is the ability to protect information outside the en
prise. E-business requires sharing information with suppliers, partners, and custome
at any time, from any place. With the increasing need to connect via the Internet
these other entities, security risks increase substantially. These risks run the gam
from receiving destructive viruses or other malicious code, to unauthorized access
your site, to the propagation of corrupt data or financial information. Any one of the
incidents will significantly compromise the availability of your online business.

**Manageability** for e-business is defined as the ability to monitor operational a
application metrics and proactively ensure continuous business operations. The
function is no longer just in the backroom supporting traditional business systems
extends to the front door, the sales floor, and the cash register. IT managers must m
imize the availability of these systems, since small amounts of downtime translate i
lost revenue and lost profits for the company.

# E-COMMERCE IN A GLOBAL VILLAGE . . . . . . . . . . .

The past several years have witnessed the dawn of e-business. Computing a
telecommunications capabilities, enabled by the Internet, arc turning every mar
into an electronic market, where information and commerce are instantaneous, a
transactions are initiated and completed with minimal human intervention. Electro
trade has become an accepted shopping medium, and the rush is on for global c
tomers who want to use the Internet for trading goods and services. One quarter of
stock trades now occur over the Internet, and the leading exchanges are introduc
extended trading hours: global trading, 24 hours a day, 365 days a year.

The communications industry has been growing in both complexity and co
petitiveness as a result of deregulation, aggressive acquisitions, globalization, conv
gence, and more competition. New enabling technologies are also dramatically affe
ing the competitive landscape.

# The New Customer Proposition

E-business is customer-driven. The successful e-company will be as well. Customers are knowledgeable and in control of the electronic transaction. They demand immediate access to your website and instantaneous transactions. To capture your share of customers in this dynamic marketplace, you have to do more than ever before.

Relationship value is the key. It is what keeps them coming back. One example: Compaq has a website called ActiveAnswers. This site allows customers and partners to configure an application server to their specific needs (product value) and have it built and delivered to customer specifications (service value). Additionally, the site contains Application Specific Knowledge-ware that helps customers plan, deploy and operate this system under best-practices methods. This is relationship value.

In building relationships, you need to be creative in gathering customer requirements. Build polls on customer-critical issues and get answers to key customer questions. This is a sensitive area, however, and needs to be kept within reasonable limits, lest it becomes the target of disparate marketing activities and causes customer problems.

Your website is a window into your brand. Many more customers will come to your site for information than actually purchase at your site. Your .com address will be advertised as much as your company's name.

The average conversion of lookers to buyers on e-commerce sites is about 2%. That's rather poor. The most typical reason people leave is that they are having a lousy experience. Pages aren't available, or the site is slow. Although wholesale failures at the biggest sites tend to get the most press coverage, partial outages and "brownouts" that slow down performance are far more common—and, over the long haul, more damaging.

A Zona Research study shows that 30% of a site's visitors "bail out" if downloads go beyond eight seconds. The "eight-second rule" is becoming a guideline for IT managers. Most sites today average nine to 10 seconds. Amazon.com, during the 1998 Christmas season, was able to keep its downloads below eight seconds and stole customers away from the competition.

Preferences vary. Some companies value reliability above all. Some want their site to be available, but are less concerned about performance. Since your site is a reflection of your brand, you want users to have a consistent experience every time. It is all part of building relationship value.

E-business has established the need for business-critical computing at all levels of the enterprise, creating serious challenges for both business and IT executives. Typically, companies find themselves facing one or more of the following challenges:

- Preference for the economic value of industry-standard hardware and software, but continue to require more robust systems.

- Demand for a predictable IT infrastructure, but require the flexibility to allow for dynamic business reconfiguration.

- Easy customer access is mandatory, but tight security and intrusion protection is equally necessary.

- Desire for the systematic installation of one application at a time, but e-business system integrity is essential.

Three critical success factors in building an e-business are:

1. Selecting the right building blocks.
2. Designing an adaptable architecture.
3. Cultivating the necessary professional skills.

## Solution Building Blocks— (Get "Up and Running" Faster)

Servers and storage will continue to be required, but they will be combined into hi er available platforms, such as clustered servers and storage arrays. Examples of are Compaq's recently announced clustered ProLiants and AlphaServers, and 8-v ProLiant and StorageWorks systems. Now, a new class of providers and ready-to-solutions has emerged.

**Service Providers**. These are Internet Service Providers that conform to y architecture, integration, and interoperability requirements. They provide a solution the form of network-delivered processes. Customers will use them in three ways:

- As a global solution (e-mail).
- As a local solution (remote location).
- Buffer service to offset spikes in peak times.

**Application Solutions**. These bundled solutions are pre-tested, factory-integed, fixed-price packages that include hardware, infrastructure software, and appl tion (such as SAP R/3). The bundles, which likely will include a customer-supp database, will be configured with various servers and operating systems and have ferent amounts of memory and storage, depending on the number of users and ant pated application loads.

**Server Appliances**—These are single-function, ready-to-run, highly availa plug-and-play application systems. They are designed for easy deployment and i gration and have the intelligence to be self-discovered and fail-over when do

Compaq has recently announced a caching appliance for HTML pages, which inter-operates with NetWare and Novell's caching software.

## Platform Integrity

When you are a vendor, one way to lower the cost of your platforms is to buy from suppliers with the least expensive components.

When vendors do that, they introduce system level integrity issues. For example, you may be stymied when you need to go from a 40MB disk to an 80MB disk, and you need to swap out the disk controller and the disk drives. While the initial system cost is less, the upgrade and out-of-service adds risk and cost. More importantly, in a world where you must scale fast and maintain availability, this is a huge price to pay and a large risk to take. Quite simply, the cost of downtime with a marginal system easily pays for higher quality designed servers and storage systems.

## Networked System Architecture
## (Design it to Last)

Since many company websites still depend on legacy systems, they continue to face issues of capacity and performance. Some important design issues to consider when you anticipate long-term, constantly changing demands include:

**Design for scalability**. With more than 70 million users currently on the Internet, events that attract even 1% of those people will exceed the capacity of any single e-commerce server. To cope, Web designers must build websites from arrays of standard, high-volume servers—and be prepared to add more for special events.

**Disperse geographically**. Because the Internet has some bottlenecks, creating huge delays even when the servers are up—*"don't put all your eggs in one basket."* Disasters can strike and take down a single system.

**Plan for " flash crowds."** Marketing will cause crowds and spikes. No one can predict when they will occur.

**Contract for additional capacity**. Firms should seek outside resources to meet the unanticipated demand created by flash crowds. Hosting companies, such as Digex and UUNET, have arrays of big pipes and racks of high-performance servers that effectively solve this problem.

**Guarantee service levels**. As more companies become dependent on online business, business managers will demand that CIOs guarantee service levels. Example: "I want three-second, 'anytime, anywhere' delivery of e-mail." This kind of guarantee involves at least two issues: 1) network performance and 2) e-mail application performance. Full-service hosting companies, like US Internetworking, will part-

ner with content distribution firms to distribute network traffic. Alternatively, you ⏺
deploy WBEM (Web-based Enterprise Management) tools to manage your operati⏺
application, and business systems.

## Agile Architecture

**Put intelligence into the architecture**. Internet commerce leaders know that the ra⏺
evolution of technology can make any component obsolete within 12 months. ⏺
cope, e-business leaders start with an architecture that guides them through many g⏺
erations of technological change. Resilient 24/7 architectures include:

**Multiple tiers**. E-business sites split into Web-interface servers, runn⏺
Netscape's Enterprise Server or Microsoft's Site Server; application servers, ▶
Oracle's App Server; and data hosting servers, like Oracle 8. This structure allc⏺
each tier of machines to be scaled independently, with fail-over links allowing op⏺
tions to move to other data centers without affecting users.

**Array of boxes**. Nearly every piece of computer or communications hardw⏺
in the architecture is replicated at least once—and often many times. If user trans⏺
tion requests are distributed among 20 servers, the failure of one system only aff⏺
5% of the users, and new transactions can be handled by the remaining 19 system⏺

**Geographical dispersion**. E-business sites can't know when the next tra⏺
peak will come, nor where congested areas will occur on the Internet. To avoid loc⏺
ized disruptions, leading e-business companies either run geographically disper⏺
data centers or contract with vendors for peak load services.

## Distributed Server Architecture in the E-Business Environment

Many people ask: "I know I can use a mainframe or high-end UNIX system as a hi⏺
availability system, but can I build a 24/7 industry-standards-based site today?" ⏺
answer is yes.

One proven method of adding intelligence to the architecture is to deploy ⏺
Compaq Distributed Internet Server Array (DISA) architecture. Many of the e-cc⏺
merce and e-services companies, including Auto-by-Tel, priceline.com, amazon.cc⏺
Charles Schwab, Netgrocer, Microsoft Network, Lycos, drugstore.com, Excite, ⏺
AltaVista, use this architecture to ensure availability, scalability and service level ⏺
formance.

These companies all have one thing in common—the Internet is the o⏺
entrance to their business. If the door is closed, their business suffers.

# TORAGE ARCHITECTURE FOR
# ODAY'S E-BUSINESS . . . . . . . . . . . . . . . . . . . .

Ensuring your data integrity is an absolute must. Many of today's storage offerings are built around data repository strategies versus virtual information data services. Most systems are built with components from various low-cost suppliers. Each time you want to add capacity, you are required to take down and reconfigure the server. In the absence of system architecture, you risk losing system integrity, interchangeability, and dynamic scalability—a big issue with huge consequences.

**Performance and capacity**—Rapid increases in demand for performance and capacity are accommodated by reallocating resources from the virtual pool. It will be possible to automate this process with policy-based tools.

**Flexibility**—Adding incremental capacity *on the fly* results in more business continuity and lower disaster avoidance. Considered together, this architecture provides the lowest total cost of ownership and the lowest total cost of management.

**Simplified management**—The architecture provides very robust access and control of distributed resources in a centralized manner. Again, many of the standard processes (backup, archive and reallocation) can be automated by policy. Backup windows will become a thing of the past. Data replication occurs instantly—not just for backup and restore—but also for moving data from a transaction server to a data warehouse or for testing.

## Involve Professional Services on Your Team

Some points to keep in mind:

- Companies are placing a high premium on IT professionals.
- IT is now integral to the business, not just supporting the business, and we must reinforce this fact through our decisions.
- We need system experts who know the issues of Internet-based computing and architects who can design unstoppable e-business systems.
- Finally, e-business is NOT a solo performance. You need dependable and qualified partners, especially in the area of 24/7 expertise.

## The Dream Team

In the digital economy, e-business has become a mandate for companies seeking compete successfully. If yours is one of those companies, you must adopt innovat business models that offer product value, service value, and relationship value to c tomers. Or you will lose the race.

And e-business imposes unique requirements on your daily operations. You v need to manage a mixed computer environment to respond to constant changes. ˙ will need to accommodate unplanned growth in demand, while keeping your trans tions secure. Most of all, you will need to set up your e-business environment rapi and build it to last—yet design it to run 24 hours a day, seven days a week.

Unless your company has the in-house expertise to meet those requirements, most important decisions you will make may be the selection of your enterprise sc tions provider and other e-business partners. Your goal, obviously, will be to assen your own dream team of partners, providers, and suppliers that can create a path t business success and competitive advantage that is better, faster and more afford; than any other.

Compaq is one of several leading enterprise solution companies that have capability of providing the experience, expertise, and innovation to get an e-busir up and running fast. An example of this capability is Compaq NonStop e-busin which transcends the transactional nature of e-commerce to involve the core op tions of a company.

# INSUREPOINT: A CASE STUDY  . . . . . . . . . . . . . . . . .

InsurePoint is a prime example of a company that has leveraged Compaq *NonStc* e-business solutions to achieve maximum return on investment. InsurePoint is the full-service Web storefront for commercial insurance. It is revolutionizing a 200-y old industry that is ridden with complex and lengthy paper processes. InsurePoint the Web to cut paperwork, speed coverage and claims handling, and save small c panies time and money.

The process of purchasing commercial insurance has changed little in over years—it remains complicated, paper-intensive and time-consuming. This is espec ly true for small companies that don't have the time or staff to search for the right b ness insurance or to deal with complex claims processes.

InsurePoint brings an innovative approach to the purchasing and claims cessing cycles for its customers—particularly start-up and growing high-tech con nies. As a joint venture between New Jersey-based Atlantic Mutual Insur;

Company and California broker Bolton & Company, InsurePoint provides high-tech companies a fast and easy way to handle their business insurance needs.

While other insurance websites sell personal coverage, commercial insurance involves a far more complex process: one that typically requires alot of human intervention and a trail of exhaustive paperwork. As a result, other commercial insurance companies venture onto the Web in only limited ways. For example, many carriers use the Web to generate online quotes, but require and offline agent contact for all other processes.

With InsurePoint, online features allow customers to apply for coverage, receive quotes, make payments, file claims, renew policies, and tap into loss prevention tips in a secure electronic environment. The only paper-based documents generated are the actual policies. This drastic reduction in paperwork, compared with the time-consuming processes that characterize business insurance, sets InsurePoint apart in the industry.

Before InsurePoint, a company had to fill out stacks of forms to apply for business insurance. This required lengthy meetings with an insurance agent who helped complete the many repetitive forms. Now, these processes are automated and performed in an online environment. Customers apply for coverage through the Web interface, filling in electronic templates. The information feeds into Web and database servers, as well as policy writing and claims systems. An extranet gives 23 independent agencies and 40 underwriters across the country browser-access to the information.

From there, agents and underwriters begin what is otherwise a time-consuming task. Typically, it can take six hours to process a paper application. Using the Web and the extranet, InsurePoint reduces that time to less than an hour. Applicants receive quotes for liability, property, and errors-and-omissions coverage via e-mail within two business days, rather than a month, and instantly receive online binders that verify coverage.

# CROSOFT AND COMPAQ TEAM UP TO PROVIDE VOLUTIONARY TOOLS . . . . . . . . . . . . . . . . . . .

InsurePoint's Web solution is based on *Compaq Proliant* servers and the Microsoft Windows NT Server networking operating system, which keeps InsurePoint's services highly available to its online customers.

Confidentiality is important in the insurance business, and InsurePoint uses the latest security technology to protect customer data. Internet firewalls and passwords restrict access, and secure sockets layer (SSL) encryption and VeriSign digital certificates further safeguard private customer information.

Microsoft Site Server, Commerce Edition, provides customers with sec online transaction processing. This solution integrates with CyberCash software process application fees and policy-renewal fees via credit card.

Industry-standard technology and software, including that offered by Comp Allaire, and Microsoft, enable InsurePoint to manage its online environment wi smaller staff and budget—which contributes to the savings it can pass on to custom

# BENEFITS . . . . . . . . . . . . . . . . . . . . . . . . . . . . . . . . . . . . .

Bolton & Company and Atlantic Mutual Insurance Company joined forces in 199 begin leveraging the Web to drive business. InsurePoint is the "dot com" brainc they came up with. As its target market, InsurePoint founders chose high-technol companies, since they would be far more likely to transact business over the Inter

Both founding companies brought extensive experience and expertise to endeavor—they already provided high-tech businesses with millions of dollar insurance coverage. Combining this experience with the cost-efficiencies of the V InsurePoint further focused its efforts on the small end of the high-tech market—a ment not profitable enough to service with traditional methods. Their strategy paid High-tech companies, which are accustomed to doing business on the Web, re sented a captive audience for the launch of InsurePoint's online business, and rap embraced InsurePoint's revolutionary solution.

As an insurance company, Atlantic Mutual has a high degree of fiduciary res sibility to its customers. Compaq Web and application servers keep information h ly accessible, which helps build customers' trust that InsurePoint will be availab assist customers with information they need on a 24/7 basis. To renew their poli customers no longer have to search through piles of paperwork to find answer wait for an agent to meet with them in person. The answers are readily acces around-the-clock via the Web, which suits the erratic schedules that are com among start-up and emerging companies.

This accelerated process brings real benefits to start-up companies. One be is the opportunity to go after business that might not be available to them unde old insurance procedures. Small and emerging companies don't have a devoted management staff to handle insurance purchasing and claims processes. As a re companies often find themselves in quick need of insurance binders to compet contracts requiring proof of insurance. Not having proof of insurance eliminates from consideration. InsurePoint speeds the application process so their custo have the coverage they need to take on new business.

The Web storefront has been very well received by customers. In its first years of operation, nearly half of InsurePoint's high-tech prospects that were shop for commercial insurance purchased a policy—a figure well beyond the ind norm. The industry buyer-to-shopper ratio varies by company and market segment, but it typically doesn't exceed 20%. Since InsurePoint's launch in 1997, 46% of the company's leads have turned into sales.

And satisfied customers keep coming back: Renewal rates also exceed industry averages. Nearly 90% of InsurePoint's customers renew their policies. This figure compares with the mid-70s percentile for most insurance carriers.

The innovative and effective use of information technology provides a solid benefit to InsurePoint that other industries may find instructive: Without the Internet, InsurePoint could not afford to serve the small-business market, where profit margins are traditionally too low for insurance companies to invest resources to develop. Now, automated and Web-enabled processes lower the cost of servicing this market and make it well worth pursuing.

While Web technology can deliver substantial benefits to the insurance industry, it also defines the industry's newest and biggest challenge. Non-Internet savvy insurance companies will have to come up to speed quickly to stay competitive with Web-based companies. And society as a whole will benefit, as commercial insurance companies change from the paper-driven, procedure-laden enterprises they are today to the leading-edge, Web-wise innovators they can become.

# IO USER-VISIBLE FAILURE—NO BUSINESS SRUPTIONS" . . . . . . . . . . . . . . . . . . . . . . . . . . .

Will we get to the point of 100% system uptime? Maybe not. The systems and procedures are available to prevent users from seeing and experiencing site failures. But it takes people to make these systems and procedures work—trained, dedicated, service professionals.

# Part 4

## Internet Pioneers

# 10

## Online Stories of New and Established Enterprise Players

......................

*Summary: As the Internet continues to radically transform the business landscape, CEOs and their management teams are scrambling to understand and take advantage of new opportunities. While there are many conflicting views of where companies need to move in order to succeed, one thing is certain: there is no turning back. The success of companies ranging from amazon.com to autobytel.com reflects the need for companies to act with a great sense of urgency in developing solid strategies and tactics. In exclusive interviews, four Internet pioneers—the CEOs of Marshall Industries, Lycos, Moai, and SoftBook Press—share their insights into the Internet and the emerging global economy, how their companies seized new opportunities, and how their views have shaped and been shaped by the future of commerce in the digital economy.*

## ROBERT RODIN, CEO AND PRESIDENT, MARSHALL INDUSTRIES . . . . . . . . . . . . . . . . . . . . . . .

Prior to being acquired by Avnet Inc. in 1999, Marshall Industries had become one of the giants in the distribution of industrial electronic components and production supplies. Founded in 1954, this El Monte, California distributor had quietly grown to become a $2 billion company. Robert Rodin was its Chief Executive Officer.

Rodin shifts uncomfortably at the idea of himself as a diviner of the Internet economy. He doesn't mind the discussion, he says. But he's afraid his statements will be fashioned into sound bites, which is anathema to the multi-faceted thinker who attests, "there are no absolutes."

Okay, maybe he harbors a tiny fear that some people might see his ideas as a bit, shall we say, too forward-looking. "When you talk about drawing organizational charts that look like planets," he muses, "people say you're out on one of these planets." Yet, he has reason to believe his convictions. So far, even his most far-out forecasts ha revealed that he can look far over the horizon without taking his feet off the groun

People criticized Rodin when he eliminated Marshall's sales commission co pensation plan in 1992. When he embraced electronic commerce in 1995, long bef the phrase had been coined, people didn't immediately share his vision. Seven ye later, however, those doubters were the ones whose ideas looked alien, while Ro looked like a prophet. He had transformed Marshall Industries from a staid and ti electronics distributor with $500 million in sales into a $2 billion e-commerce pow house by the time it was acquired and integrated into Avnet Global IT.

From the moment Rodin saw Mosaic, he grasped the potential of the Intern And from that moment on, he began moving the company toward what he calls "vi al distribution," which means Marshall not only delivers over 250,000 parts used electrical engineers, but also creates made-to-order products and designs processes solve customers' business problems before they even know they have them. It's a m morphosis he describes in his book, *Free, Perfect, and Now* (Simon & Schuster, 19

When asked about where the world is heading, Rodin forgoes black-and-w predictions. Instead, he asks questions like, "What are the alternatives? What does question mean to the way you run your company? To your life? To the way you c pete? To the way your children will compete? Questions about the future should no designed to elicit 'yes' or 'no' answers," he says. "They are stepping stones to thinki

## Beyond Linear Thinking

Asked about his views on society and industry one to five years out, Rodin redirects question. "We tend to be linear thinkers," he begins, looking out the window of a c ference room in a Milpitas, California, office, an open space with few internal wall dividers. "People tend to make predictions based on today's datapoints," he notes.

Rodin prefers to take a quantum leap out 50 years for a fresh perspective on next few years and ask, "What will be the impact of convergence? Of the blendin 'click and mortar'? The interaction of man and machine?" There will still be pe ("we hope"), he says. Businesses will still have to get their attention and provide s ter, clothing, food, and services. They'll have to manufacture and deliver to tomers' demands and, "unless the physical laws of the world are betrayed," will perform a lot of the same functions they do today.

What will begin to change in the next few years are the companies that h those functions. In the future, we won't find businesses as we know them now, c peting against one another, he predicts. The organization of the future will look r like a "matrix." He's not talking about the virtual-reality, mind-control jail of a K Reeves sci-fi flick, but a constellation of organizational functions dynamically ali to solve a business problem.

## Transformation of the Supply Chain

Rodin offers an example of how this might work at a company. "Marshall is going to be a participant in the supply chain," he explains. At the center of the universe, the "guiding force" in that supply chain may be a company with a concept of some new electronic device they want to bring to market. The people who support that effort, in design, billing and materials management, forecasting, manufacturing, delivery, distribution, marketing, and sales, will be satellites, planets, and moons around this main force. They will take direction based on why that product was invented, what its road map is, what its value proposition is, what its cost imperatives are, all of the design criteria. If everything is aligned with that, he says, "that should be a successful event." At the same time, many of those planets and moons may be connected to other solar systems. "They may be doing multiple functions, so they are going to have to be flexible."

This model, says Rodin, makes more sense than a hierarchy in the "global, mass-customized, built-to-order, 24-hour-a-day, supply chain vs. supply chain world" in which we've come to exist.

He calls this new way of doing business "dynamic alignment." And with a touch of excitement, he warms to his subject, "It's not just about aligning vision, mission, strategy, structure and compensation to result in a single objective. It's about doing it every second of the day. And so, while I'm not entirely sure what the future structure will look like, I'm sure it can't look like something that is a stagnant, staid, bricks-and-mortar, inflexible structure with people making their bosses happy, as opposed to subordinating to what's necessary to service the competitive world market."

## Action Versus Extinction

Asked about which of today's industries face the threat of extinction, Rodin hedges. In an era when the Internet is displacing—or at least redefining the role of—the middleman, Rodin is intimately familiar with the concern. "I would be hesitant to point to any industry," he says. But he concedes that, "the definition of value is constantly changing, and the bar on that is being raised all the time."

What does this mean for today's corporations? That the Internet or other technologies will cannibalize many of the mechanical steps performed by people in today's organizations. "Anybody who is moving something from point A to point B, or asking someone to ask someone to ask someone for a price, [or doing anything that] can be done more efficiently through the network, would be a business or a job function in jeopardy."

The secret to maintaining vitality, he suggests, is to ask the right questions of the right people. Turn to the futurists, he advises. Talk to your receptionist. Grill your accounting clerk. And, perhaps most important, listen to your customers. But don't ask

them leading questions like, "What are you looking for in a distributor?" Instead y
should ask, "What are you worried about?" Their answers, he says, "paint a picture
the future."

When Rodin asks customers that question, rarely do they answer, "price." M
often, they talk about management of resources, capital, talent, and new ideas. Th
are struggling to find engineers and software programmers; they want to know how
beat their competition to market. "Those are the things that are keeping people up
night," he says. And if you dissect any of those issues, he continues, you begin to
that the only way for people to sleep at all is to work together in concert.

As a member of the Board of Directors for Commercenet and Rosettanet, am
other industry associations, Rodin sits at many tables with industry heavyweights, s
as IBM, 3Com, Solectron, Toshiba, American Express and even the US government
doing the work he does, designing standards and efficiency for the years to come,
really becomes clear that the future is not about company-centric solutions," he sa
"It's about your ability to collaborate, to communicate, to pass information and prov
services. I think there is a lot of vision that comes out of this kind of enterprise. A
customers talking about their willingness to do that is very important."

## The Global Online Economy

But what about the rest of the world? As Rodin points out in his book, half the peo
in the world have never made a phone call. "People have been saying that for 10 ye
But I don't think they'll be able to say that 10 years from now," he says.

"Information is moving around the world; people are moving around the wo
40% of the world is under the age of 20, and they are growing up with a differ
knowledge about the world." Rodin points to a country like China, which can skip
copper infrastructure we had to build in the US, and go straight to wireless.

In the future, he adds, the Internet will always be on. "Whatever it's called, w
ever it looks like, it will be something we will always be connected to—your car, y
watch, your credit card, eye glasses, everything can be connected to it." This sens
"always on," he says, "will change the world—with positive and negative results."

Rodin finishes our interview by giving us a small square of paper that says, "
hours/day." "People + technology." "Help @ Once." "Convergence." "Cosmoco
"Interface."

Before the acquisition, Marshall added a new feature to its 24/7 customer ser
site (Help@Once), he explains. The new feature, enabled by video cameras and a p
uct called Cosmocom, lets customers see the service agents who are helping th
Earlier, we had spoken briefly about intelligent agent technology. Rodin emphasized
now, and for the next hundred years, what's critical is not technology per se, but the
riage between people and technology. "Trust is in the interface," he says with a gri

# OB DAVIS, CEO, LYCOS, INC. . . . . . . . . . . . . . . . .

Lycos is currently one of the most visited hubs on the Internet, reaching one out of every two Internet users. Its network of sites includes lycos.com, HotBot, Tripod, Angelfire, Quote.com, WhoWhere, MailCity, Wired News, and Gamesville, among others. The Lycos network provides leading Web search and navigation, communications and personalization tools, homepage building and Web community services, and a cutting-edge shopping center.

Robert J. Davis, President and Chief Executive Officer of Lycos, Inc., was the company's first employee, in June 1995. Davis has helped Lycos evolve from an Internet search engine to one of the most powerful Internet hubs and Web media companies worldwide. In just four years, Davis has led Lycos from a small start-up company to a multi-billion dollar business.

It takes an athlete's stamina and vision to build the New Economy. Davis, a former freestyle swimmer for Northeastern University, is both fatigued and invigorated by the Internet's potential to change the way people communicate and the way companies do business. Davis is weary. He has just returned from Asia where he launched Lycos Korea and Lycos Japan, and he recently ended negotiations to merge with Barry Diller's USA Networks and TicketMaster Online-CitySearch, a deal that collapsed in a high-profile disappointment. Yet for the pioneering Internet CEO, this is a temporary setback. He sees an exhilarating future, in which geographic boundaries disappear, local cultures thrive, and "speed is life."

Over the past four years, Davis has transformed Lycos from a search engine into what has become an online network used by 30 million people a month, a number he is not too modest to mention at any given opportunity. Almost from the start, he plunged headfirst into uncharted waters, only to watch competitors dive in behind him. Instead of buying audience, he bolted on "eyeballs" by assembling a network of disaggregated websites, while retaining each of their brands and identities.

In trying to merge Lycos with USA Networks, Davis provided a glaring example of just how difficult it can be to marry Web and non-Web assets. In the process, he also showed the world just how fragile strategic planning has become.

With that deal in his wake, and hundreds of others in his path, what does Davis see when he looks at tomorrow? In a word, diversity. He's optimistic, he says, that the Internet will not encourage a vanilla world in which everyone speaks English, wears Nikes, and eats Kentucky Fried Chicken. Unlike television and film, he says, the Internet brings people together from different countries and cultures, allowing them to exchange stories, traditions and experiences.

Not exactly a radical idea. But Davis is no blue-sky visionary. The 43-year-old first-time CEO is laying the groundwork for the colorful future he describes. As he expands the Lycos network into far-flung territories, he's doing it with local partners. He explains that it would be "totally arrogant of us to think we can jump over to any

country and understand local products, services, and interactions." And while la
guage translation software is "fine for selling components," Lycos is providing ne
and information for a cross-section of society. And that, he maintains, requires inp
from the same cross-section.

Having said that, Davis admits that he was surprised recently by a student
EWAH University in Korea. During a Q&A session, the student stood up and asked ho
Lycos could help Koreans better understand English, "the language of the Internet."

"I thought it was telling," Davis reflects. "When he started asking the questic
I thought it was going in the other direction—that the student would be resentful of
the English on the Net." Still, the incident did not dissuade Davis that the Internet v
more likely enable local culture than erase it.

But while cultures flourish, some jobs will be displaced, he suggests. "We ha
all these new-world jobs being created, and traditional brick-and-mortar jobs that w
go away by the millions and millions. How we as a country fare depends on how w
we adapt and bring the workforce along in these changing lifestyles and business p
cesses." And he's spent a lot of time on Capitol Hill, advocating education and tra
ing to help America deal with the displacement of these jobs. Traditional retail jo
customer service people, and inbound telemarketers will feel the effects of more c
tomers buying goods and services over the Internet, he predicts. Meanwhile, sales jo
will go from order processing to customer relationship management.

Combine this view with the mushrooming global economy, and the ramifi
tions are daunting. Already, says Lester Thurow, MIT professor of economics a
author of *Building Wealth*, wages are beginning to even out globally. "If you look
America in the 90s," says Thurow, "those in the top 20% in terms of skills made
like bandits, but for the bottom 60%, wages have gone down. That is likely to cont
ue for as long as people don't have skills."

## Disruptions and Opportunities

Davis believes the Internet is a "new medium in the making." In his eyes, portals
"hubs" of activity) will become the mega-media companies of the future. But unl
television or the traditional news media, these content aggregators will rely not just
audience but on commerce. "I fully believe the 21st century's media companie
whoever they may be—are being established today," he says. "Think about
world's largest entertainment venue, the world's largest library, and a party [pho
line of all the people in the world. A portal can bring some order to what would c
erwise be chaos. We become the librarian; we become the operator; we become
community organizer."

But will they also become the mall? Some people are skeptical. So far, the
little evidence that portals can make it in e-commerce space. They aren't seen a
shopping destination. And, unlike vertical business-to-business marketplaces, t

aren't integrating inventories. If a company already takes credit cards, why does it need Lycos to process the transaction? Even heavyweights like IBM have tried and failed to provide a truly useful storefront-creation service.

What makes Lycos any different?

Davis replies that skeptics are looking backward, not forward. It won't take a magician to transform the millions of people who use Lycos' services each month into purchasers, he says emphatically. "To think that the millions of people coming through our front door right now don't want to shop is not a realistic perspective. Taking consumers and turning them into buyers doesn't require changing our patterns, it becomes an extension of what we are."

Of course, he's talking about doing more than building an electronic mall where retailers can build their own online stores. He's talking about providing a transaction-processing engine so that the stores can take credit cards, hire back-end reporting, and accept a universal e-wallet. That way, customers can buy goods from one store and have "one-click buying" at any other store in the market. And he's just launched LYCOShop.com, which is a comprehensive online shopping destination, and a Lycos MasterCard with Fleet Bank, as well as a shoppers' rewards program. "A mall by itself is a piece of what Lycos is offering. Unlike a traditional retail mall, I'm the real estate developer and the infrastructure partner that helps you do business on a day-to-day basis."

However, capturing people's time, attention, and dollars is no easy task, especially with all the choices that confront them. As Davis concedes, people can opt to read a book, flip through a magazine, listen to the radio, watch TV, do nothing...or log on to one of the 400 million websites that are now available. The mission of Lycos—and most Internet companies—is to meet this challenge by offering a "compelling user experience," says Davis.

How does one create such an experience? There's no magic bullet, he cautions. At Lycos, the answer is to continually innovate, bringing new products and services to market. In the short term, that means putting effort into navigation, so that customers can find whatever they're looking for, in whatever form. For example, if they search for "Red Sox," says the Boston-area native, they might want the baseball team's homepage, but they might also be looking for scores of the last game or the team roster or directions to Fenway Park. "To have all of that as a logically integrated experience is what navigation is all about."

Community and personalization are also a vital part of the plan, he adds. Whether that means allowing consumers to build their own versions of "MyLycos," with customized news feeds, weather feeds, and stock portfolios, or letting them use the Lycos service to connect with other people, these are the activities that will turn today's portals into tomorrow's hubs.

While the traditional media undergo a transformation, Davis strongly believes that other facets of business don't change simply because you add the Web. He sub-

scribes to the theory of the power of multiple brands—exemplified by things li
Time-Warner's Time, CNN and Warner Brothers, or Honda's Acura division. "Mul
branding," he says, "will be as feasible in the Internet world as in the world of ca
and sport utility vehicles."

## Speed is of the Essence

So many of today's Internet companies are grappling with the unprecedented pace
change. Lycos is no exception. The company is growing at well over 100% a year, a
has offices around the world and data centers in Germany, Tokyo, Seoul, S
Francisco, Boston, and Pittsburgh. "The downside," says Davis, "is that virtua
everything we establish breaks after a reasonably short period of time."

It isn't products that malfunction; it's processes. At Lycos, for example, t
accounting system was designed for 100 employees, not the 900 that the compa
employs today. Meanwhile, developers can no longer work individually, and t
human resources system needs an overhaul. It requires new measurements of opp
tunities, a new compensation plan, and a new benefits package.

Davis, like most CEOs today, has no time to rest or become complacent. "T
'speed of life' concept has to be so much of a driver that we're constantly looking
everything and saying, 'does it still work?' and we're constantly challenging ourselves
certain service standards." To facilitate this process, Davis has just hired Lycos' first Ch

The 'speed of life' concept extends beyond systems and processes, though. T
days of leisurely planning and unhurried decision-making are over. There's not ti
to order a variety of alternative business scenarios. Business models and plans t
can't be hatched and revised in 30 minutes may be useless in today's supercharg
environment. "There's not a day that goes by when we're not presented with oppor
nities to align, to partner, to work with a host of different companies," says Dav
breathlessly. "Literally, a day doesn't go by when someone isn't calling, all across
company, saying, 'Take our content and put it on your service,' 'Let's take our tra
tional media company and align it with yours,' and 'Let's create a new product and
it on the Web.'"

"But all that opportunity comes with a threat," says Davis. Even for this de
maker, legendary for his ability to keep multiple balls aloft, the reality is "that we ca
do all of those things." And picking the winners is "a never-ending task." For ev
success in a partnership that fits, there's the opportunity cost of the one he didn't pi
And it's a cost that's hard to measure. "Speed is life" has become his mantra. An
succinctly explains the difference between an Internet business and an old-world co
pany. Winning demands understanding that, in this new world, "Traditional proces
don't apply. Things happen, and they have to happen very fast."

And Davis is swimming toward the finish line, reacting to every opportu
with steady, lightning-fast strokes. He embraces the fast-paced Internet lifestyle

"more of an opportunity than a threat." Suddenly pensive, he looks out the window at the Cambridge Reservoir below and says matter-of-factly, "The Internet changes everything; the way we buy, sell, and capture information—more so than anything we've ever seen."

# ɪNNE PERLMAN, PRESIDENT AND CEO, MOAI  . . . . . .

Founded in 1994, Moai designs and delivers powerful, scalable, and highly configurable software and services for implementing a variety of dynamic electronic commerce applications. Moai's flagship product, LiveExchange, allows corporations to host their own private Web-based auctions with key customers, as well as enabling organizations to conduct open public auctions directly with consumers. Moai President and CEO Anne Perlman brought 21 years of experience in Silicon Valley to her role at Moai's helm. Just prior to joining Moai, Anne had been a strategic management consultant, assisting Internet start-ups and other high-tech companies. Before that, she was employed at Tandem Computers as VP and General Manager of Multimedia, VP of Marketing, and President of Tandem Source Company. She joined Computer Curriculum Corporation immediately after graduate school and was Director of Marketing, among other roles.

With a sly smile, Anne Perlman owns up to having "almost missed the Internet." Seven years ago, she confesses, she would have put her money on interactive television. The Internet, she assumed, was a passing fad.

It's an oversight she never forgets as she steers her upstart electronic auction software company through turbulent seas. "We may not be right about everything today," she concedes, "but what's more important is to miss as little as possible." When you're living in Internet time, missing The Big One is a far more dangerous threat than not "approaching every opportunity specifically, precisely, correctly."

Those who survive must be able to head into the wind, and alter their course at a moment's notice. Perlman understands that intimately. In less than two years with Moai, she's already had to shift her concept of Moai's primary customer base at least once. Instead of Fortune 500-type companies, those most interested in Moai's LiveExchange business-to-business and business-to-consumer software have turned out to be "micromarkets," or companies that aggregate buyers and sellers online around a vertical industry or product. And, she reports, she's learned to think in three-month increments, "because the way the market uses technology changes the requirements."

Unlike many CEOs of Internet startups, Perlman is a grounded captain. She's "able to keep from being too starry-eyed," says Vernon Keenan, Internet analyst and founder of the Keenan Vision research firm. "She has been able to translate her experience in big business into marketing a completely new kind of technology. And she's able to match the technology with the marketplace very well."

Moai's LiveExchange software connects to a corporation's legacy databases, a dot.com's databases, pulling information such as inventory, or goods that are to auctioned, as well as customer information, or data about the people for whom y want to hold an auction. LiveExchange might send an e-mail to all the customers the database, or a segment of those customers that meet certain criteria, informi them that an auction is going to take place and providing them with information abc how to log in.

When the auction for each item closes, the order is sent to the company's ord processing system and is processed, in whatever way the company normally do business. Does the company accept credit cards, or should they check with the co pany's credit system to find out whether this customer is credit-worthy? "There ar number of ways that this can work," says Perlman, which is why native database co nectivity, open application programming interfaces, and the fact that this is written an open language like Java are important. "It's unpredictable what the customer w want to do because the market is evolving."

## E-Auctions and New Paradigms

Electronic auctions may serve a variety of purposes. In their first iteration, they w used to sell surplus goods, says Perlman, who is seated in Moai's airy brick he quarters in a former meat packing plant, just down the street from the new ballpark SoMa, San Francisco's new media district. "Then companies realized they could u auctions to sell aging goods." Eventually the dynamic pricing model turned out to a good way to price goods, by determining what the market will pay. In addition, co panies have begun using auctions more recently to establish the price of products t are scarce. That, she says, "is a brilliant way of using auctions." Because it's not t different from what companies have done in the past when they put their best c tomers on allocation. The latest use of the solution is for procuring goods in reve auctions.

Perlman believes a real-time trading environment is just around the corner almost every industry. Leading the way are high-tech companies, as well as distri tors and other intermediaries. One customer, ShoeNet, has aggregated manufactur and retailers of shoes. It's a traditional industry with close-knit relationships, and "even that industry can benefit from dynamic pricing, or from just having a mark place where they come together to buy from electronic catalogs or hold auctions real-time," says Perlman.

Without too much of a stretch, one can apply the concept to any firm that sta between buyers and sellers: real estate agents, financial brokers, even companies t find jobs for day laborers. Today, in most cities, contractors meet at a designated lo tion to find out who needs how many people for what jobs. "If you think about w the barriers are to those people using [technology to manage this process] today," s

Perlman, "you come up with cost and availability." And, she adds, those obstacles are only a year from being cleared. "In fact, our newest customers are offering services, not just goods, using dynamic commerce," she says.

Dynamic pricing won't work for every industry and product, she acknowledges. Buying or selling low-cost goods by auction may not be worth the time involved in setting one up.

## Reassessing Total Economic Value

According to Forrester Research, e-auctions have gone from a gimmick to a given. Today they are considered part of a good e-commerce site, a far cry from the position the market took just six months ago.

Over the next six months, Perlman says, electronic auctions will likely be used to conduct full exchanges, in which price and quantity are not the only variables. "You may even have a series of auctions for an item, leading up to one buyer being awarded the item, or one vendor being selected in a procurement situation," she says.

ShoeNet, for example, may find that some shoe manufacturers will hold an auction to sell scarce goods, or those in demand. Or retailers could hold a reverse auction to procure them. Say patent leather pumps are the latest craze. Retailers might face a shortage in Mary Janes. In that situation, a retailer might say, "We're looking for shoes that are of the following description…" Any manufacturer with excess capacity could bid on the request. The retailer might then choose ten of its favorite suppliers and hold a second auction to discuss the timing of shipments and payment terms.

Perlman calls that a "tiered auction." And it's doable today. But if you take it to its next level, you could apply it to, say, bandwidth, where someone puts out a request with the amount and the time frame, and a supplier could use that as a starting point for negotiations. The seller might reply, "I'm willing to provide what you want at $.015 a minute, but if you will agree to take some data circuits and expand the number of minutes you want, I'll supply it to you for $.0125." And they might also offer to provide it in a shortened time frame. This, says Perlman, is where auctions are going. "From simple auctions to a true exchange, where there are multiple variables and multiple steps before a decision is reached."

## New Tools for the Digital Economy

When asked about agent technology, or "bots," Perlman comes to life. Bots are bits of code that roam the Web, doing what they're asked to do. Perlman is fascinated with bots. She confesses to having been enamored with the concept of robots as a child. At that point, she says, she dreamed about them as, "something that would do exactly what I wanted."

While physical robots may not have taken root—at least, not in the consum
world—electronic bots have come along to take their place in the virtual world. The
tiny, yet sophisticated software applications, "will go out and find exactly what I"
looking for with the parameters that are important to me," Perlman predicts. In o
case it might be a particular type of goods, for example, a 12-foot conference tab
with a laminate finish. In other cases, it might find the best price for name-brand goo
with a particular model number. But that's just the beginning.

There will also be bots that go out and complete the transaction for their "ma
ter." It might contain information about the person, even his or her preferences. T
most intelligent bots, however, will go out and act as proxy for a person, filling c
paperwork or bidding on a product, while the person does whatever else he or s
needs to do.

But this view of bot usage raises a host of issues, one of which is privacy. T
most powerful bots will not only search for information for us, but will carry inf
mation about us as well. Perlman doesn't see this as a showstopper. In the future, s
says, people are likely to value efficiency over privacy.

## The Internet Creates Level Playing Fields

Some people are concerned that the Internet is exacerbating inequalities—amo
countries, among people. Left unassisted, Perlman agrees that this trend could conti
ue. However, she sees a number of what she calls "hopeful signs." First are the effor
at least in the US, to make sure that all schools are wired. "If all schools are wired,
children, regardless of economics or geographic circumstances, will know somethi
about technology and know about the Internet, and they are very likely to grow up
especially with price points falling the way they are—with the Internet affordable
them," she says.

Second, in some countries the Internet is becoming more affordable. In the U
for example, Internet access is now free, and the price of local calls has come do
substantially. Combined with $500 computers, the Internet is much more afforda
than even a year ago.

The third development is alternative computing devices, combined voice and
mail, and voice-driven interfaces. She continues, her words spilling out in unabash
enthusiasm: "That opens it up much more to the masses. Because, whether you
using a cell phone because your country has skipped a generation or you only hav
telephone, you obviously have access to technology."

She also points to the work being done to make sure that all libraries have
access, as well as the venture capital community's funding of startups in Easte
Europe. The whole world, she says, needs to be able to share, not only in the use
technology, but in its development.

How does Perlman cope with the pace of change? "First, we hire the most talented people we can find," she says. "Then we talk to customers, prospects, partners, experts in the industry, industry analysts. We read as much as we can, and we try to make the best decisions anticipating what we can anticipate." All the while, she admits, knowing that they will look back on some decisions and laugh. But, "hopefully, at least 50% of the time or more we'll have made the right decision, and thought correctly about the future."

At the same time, she says, "I have dropped the words 'mature' and 'maturing' from my vocabulary. I now use the word 'evolving.' Maturing implies that there's an end. And I don't see that at all."

# M SACHS, CHAIRMAN AND CEO,
# OFTBOOK PRESS . . . . . . . . . . . . . . . . . . . . . . . .

Founded in 1996, SoftBook® Press, Inc., has emerged as a front-runner in the race to win a dominant share of the potentially huge electronic book market. The company's SoftBook Reader, a lightweight portable reading device, along with the SoftBook Network™, an Internet-based content delivery service, functions as a complete paperless reading system. James Sachs has 20 years of design and management experience in computer-based industrial and consumer products and has developed more than 100 high-volume electronic products. He is co-designer and patent holder of the Macintosh mouse. Prior to founding SoftBook Press, Sachs was Vice President and General Manager of the Hasbro, Inc., technology group, where he created the company's pre-school multimedia software business and developed several popular software titles.

Sachs envisions a rosy future in which our dollars go further, inefficient businesses disappear, and junk e-mail gets under control. He believes that, within the next five years, information will be exchanged globally—among businesses and among children—and that people will use the Internet without even knowing it. The Internet, he predicts, will improve education—worldwide.

His optimism doesn't stop there. He believes that good technologies will surface sooner, while inferior technologies—even with brand names like Microsoft—will face stiffer competition. And he imagines a leveling effect. Within three years, he says, a best-selling book will be published on the Internet; the Internet will have launched a number-one rock band; and an award will go to a company that was birthed on the Internet.

With the same boyish spirit of adventure, Sachs co-founded a company he hopes will be in the vanguard of this brave, new wired world. Starting SoftBook, he says, was the biggest risk he's ever taken. This young CEO with a laser-sharp mind left a safe and rewarding job to create what he hopes will become the next evolution in reading and distributing written documents.

But, while it may be his biggest gamble to date, it's hardly his first. Sachs w
also a co-founder of Elfin Technologies, a failed robot company that, in Sachs' wor(
"was 20 years ahead of its time." As a former executive at Worlds of Wonder, In
where he directed the development of more than 60 consumer electronic products a
toys, Sachs first hit the big time with his best-selling Teddy Ruxpin doll, a talki
teddy bear. He was later a founding principal of IDEO, the nation's leading prod(
development company.

## 'Be' Your Customer

The idea for the SoftBook Reader, he says, sprang from a personal need. He had be
doing research on and about the Internet for months and had accumulated an en(
mous stack of information. He downloaded and printed it, but it sat unread next to
desk. When he'd tell people about his stack of research, he recalls, most would n
knowingly and hold their hands out at least a foot apart, emphasizing that their o
paper stacks were even bigger than his.

The seminal moment came on August 6, 1995, says Sachs. He was flying
Hong Kong for a consulting project. "I finished all my reading materials with 12 ho
left," he says, his expressive face breaking into a slow smile, "and I thought about t
stack." He searched Hong Kong for a reading gadget for the flight home and fou
nothing. At that moment, he says, "I realized there's a need and there's no solution a
I know I can make the solution." Almost the moment he got home, he went to
garage and built a model—of what is now called a SoftBook Reader—out of sprink
tubing and plastic. The rest, as they say, is history (or, as Sachs hopes, the future).

The SoftBook Reader looks like a sideways notebook computer, and sport:
640x480 Passive Matrix LCD screen and a protective leather cover, giving it the lo
and feel of a hefty hardcover book. It provides a bookish experience by displayin;
full-page in portrait with fully formatted text and graphics. Like a computer, it l
users search, annotate, click on hyperlinks, and connect to the SoftBook Network
modem, or Ethernet directly without a modem, but instead of page scrolling, it allo
for page "turning," which gives it the "feel" of reading a book.

It's a sexy little device that received a gold medal in *Business Week*'s ann
design awards. But it's really just an icon, says Sachs. He likens it to a cell pho
where the real value (and expense) isn't in the phone, but in the service. "For 5
years since Gutenburg created movable type, there's been a maturation of the proc(
of authoring works, of printing and distributing them, and people consuming then
he says, sounding professorial. "And yet, with everything that's going on with
Internet and computers, there's never been a parallel path having to do with electr(
ic distribution." That parallel path is what SoftBook's business is all about.

The real power of SoftBook Press resides in the content and distribution syste
which comprises three "layers." The content layer consists of relationships with p

lishers and tools for taking a book, or other reading material, and transferring it into an electronic format that can be sent securely over the Internet—the distribution layer—and consumed on the SoftBook Reader (the consumption layer).

Content partners include the New York Times, the Wall Street Journal, McGraw Hill, and Simon & Schuster. SoftBook, Microsoft, and another e-book company, NuvoMedia, have created the Open eBook Publication Structure, a specifications standard for electronic publishing that hundreds of companies have agreed to use.

## In the Footsteps of Fred Smith: Looking Beyond the Surface

In explaining the concept behind the SoftBook Press electronic publishing system, Sachs conjures the image of a pioneer with whom he identifies, Fred Smith, founder of Federal Express. The analogy carries a certain logic. Smith, he explains, saw that buried within the new world of air transportation lay the future of delivering packages. Similarly, says Sachs, SoftBook Press views the Internet, not only as something with websites and browsers, but as an infrastructure for sending and receiving documents securely.

Corporate uses range from educational training materials that are customized, searchable, and readily updated, to information stored in databases and to legal briefs and other confidential documents that would otherwise need to be shredded. One early customer, a newspaper delivery company called Central News, gives SoftBook Readers to its carriers and alerts them every morning of any changes on their routes.

Why not simply use a PC? According to Sachs, "that's the old way." In the future, he believes, computers will carry less weight, figuratively as well as literally. (Note: Recent statistics seem to support this. Although computer purchases are up, computer use is down.) Instead of a PC in every home, people will have a microprocessor in every device, much the way the fractional horsepower motor took off a century ago, he believes.

The SoftBook Reader, Sachs explains, is an example of what fractional computing can look like. "It makes people stop and think about what a computer is." Sometime in the future, Sachs predicts, electronic books will come in different shapes and sizes. There will be executive ones, yellow waterproof ones, little paperbacks—and that's just in electronic books. There will be other kinds of devices with other uses as well.

## A Global Online World

It's hard not to be swept up in Sachs' enthusiasm. Especially when his boyish face lights up, and he says something like, "I honestly believe it's a wonderful time to be alive right now!" He explains: "There was the Stone Age, there was the Bronze Age, man learned to walk, man had fire, harnessed the horse, transportation, communica-

tion, the Gutenburg press, television, telephone…The Internet is absolutely as fund
mental as all of those, because now you have global transfer of information whi
wasn't available until the last few years." He's still amazed that someone in Russia c
read about his son "who promotes on his own website a good summer drink made w
Coke®, milk and orange juice!"

Perhaps this helps explain Sachs' conviction that the Internet will improve ec
cation by the mere fact that it gives children access to more information and me
resources for pursuing their own dreams.

He doesn't confine his glowing predictions to kids. Within two years, he sa
with confidence, we'll start to see global distribution of products and services via
Internet. People in the US might buy a French wine from France because "some co
pany will emerge that will be able to provide that service. In five years, someone
going to say the world is starting to look like one [world]. The distances have be
eliminated. It is just as easy to get something—information, products, services—fro
around the globe as around the corner."

Of course, this isn't good news for everyone. Some industries and businesses,
says, will be "toast." Here's what, in Sachs' mind, is about to get crispy: any mar
that doesn't take advantage of Internet communication or distribution, publishi
companies that don't innovate, overpriced retailers who don't add value, and retail
that charge more because of geographic proximity.

"Retailers will have to make money in other ways than simply making produ
available," he predicts. "We might see some strange new services. For instance, y
might be willing to pay money to test drive a car, because who knows where you
going to buy it." Financial services will become commodities. "Oh, and high pric
text books, too, are toast in the long term, because they're so expensive, so stude
buy fewer of them, so publishers print fewer, and they go up in price."

Today's pace of change will continue, he concludes. But the opportunities
limitless. "Anybody who says that all of the Web technologies and the cool webs
concepts already have been thought of, they're dead wrong. For those who are thi
ing it's too late to get into the Internet, Ha!" He whoops with wicked glee. "
haven't even started!"

# 11

# New Players Lead the Online Revolution

..........................

*S*ummary: *The Internet has started to open the doors to paradigm-shifting business models. In the world of Internet commerce, companies live or die on the strength of their customer service. Market leaders in every industry depend on their information systems to streamline business processes, open new markets, and create agile, demand-driven organizations that can adapt quickly to customer requirements. In this chapter, we hear from some of the e-commerce pioneers who are delivering products and services the way their customers want to buy. Dot.com companies such as amazon.com, priceline.com, autobytel.com, drugstore.com, Motley Fool, and Net Grocer are capturing market share and customer loyalty through innovative online marketing—at the expense of established companies that have been slow to recognize the opportunities spawned by Internet technologies and applications.*

## AMAZON.COM REVOLUTIONIZES CUSTOMER SERVICE ........................

As we learned in Chapters 3 and 4, amazon.com is one of the most successful online retailers in the Internet's short history. Amazon.com plunged into the digital economy with a new concept and a bold new marketing plan that included an online book megastore featuring a virtual catalogue of practically every title in print. The key was the development of software capable of finding, capturing, and indexing the enormous volume of available information about published books.

The primary thrust of the development process involved integrating AltaVista search technology with amazon.com's own information repositories. Amazon.com captures data from a variety of places, such as book distributors, book publishers, and content reviewers. That data is then reconciled and coalesced into a form that is indexed

by the AltaVista software. The system uses a combination of full-text retrieval a
fielded-text retrieval, creating a set of indexes tuned for the current content on the si

"We have large data sources," explains Dwayne Bowman, Director of Enginee
ing at amazon.com. "For example, on the book side of our business, we mainta
information on 4.5 million titles, including title, author, subject, table of conten
reviews, and excerpts. For the music side of the business, we offer about 250,0
titles, indexed by artist, title, label, and list of tracks."

## Mass Customization

As a result of Internet technologies and associated applications, the expectations
customers have been raised significantly. Empowered customers are demanding mo
and more as enterprises offer them new, better, faster, and more efficient products, se
vices, and solutions.

Mass customization has arrived and is here to stay. By using the AltaVista sear
and retrieval software, amazon.com has been able to customize the online shoppi
experience for each user. For example, a user might only be interested in hardcov
books. Before amazon.com had AltaVista software, it didn't have an easy way
accommodate this type of search. Extra indexes and extra development work we
required to satisfy these types of requests. With the AltaVista solution, users can qu
the data in different ways from a single index. A user can query just the hardcover p
tion of the book catalogue, for example, and have the results sorted by publicati
date, author, or title.

"Today, we can offer more options to users for how they search and how th
would like to view results," says Bowman. "We have created a reliable and high
flexible system that gives customers a better search experience."

Behind the scenes, the software governs where a product is coming from, a
thus how long it will take to reach a user. Depending on the shopper's requirements,
AltaVista solution can push the distribution method that makes the most sense at a
given time. Similarly, it can be used to promote specific offers, or to recommend tit
related to the ones that users request. Another useful feature is the support for displ
ing the results of customer searches. "This is especially useful with classical mus
where you might want to search by orchestra or performer, rather than just artist
title," says Bowman. "We now have a better way to support these unique rankings."

## Enhanced International Language Capabilities

Recently, when amazon.com brought up satellite websites in Germany and the UK, AltaVista software enabled the retailer to extend its existing catalogues without getting bogged down in linguistic issues. For example, German users can include unique diacritic characters, yet these words and characters will be properly identified by AltaVista software. "The AltaVista solution helped us get our products out to these international markets more quickly," says Bowman. "It understands how to correctly index and retrieve foreign words, which significantly reduced our development work."

Amazon.com is particularly concerned with how well its technology assets perform in a heavy production setting. Thus, when evaluating AltaVista software, the company was encouraged by the software's proven ability to work well under extremely high user loads. Another reference came from a large government agency, which used the AltaVista software to dramatically improve search and retrieval performance for an Oracle database that contains over 250 million records.

"We knew we were purchasing mature technology with proven ability to handle a heavy load," says Bowman. "Reliability and availability are strict requirements for us. All of our hardware and software must perform well, 24 hours a day, 365 days a year."

The AltaVista solution proved amazon.com's capabilities during the busy 1998 holiday shopping season, when more than a million customers shopped at amazon.com for the first time. In a six-week period, the company shipped more than 7.5 million items, as customers searched for and purchased enough videos, DVDs, CDs, and books to fill a shelf 101 miles long.

He pauses, reflecting on the recent flurry of activity. "Finding and discovering great things is one of the core attractions of our store," concludes Bowman. "It is what defines amazon.com and makes its services useful to customers. It's hard to put a value on such a critical piece of our infrastructure. Thanks to the AltaVista software, we've improved the customer experience and raised the bar for our competitors."

# RICELINE.COM'S PIONEERING BUSINESS MODEL . . . .

E-business pioneers are leveraging the Internet to create and expand markets. One of the best examples—introduced in Chapter 5—is priceline.com. Priceline.com turned e-commerce upside down when the company introduced its "name your own price" Internet business model in 1998. Buyers have responded by the millions, leaving priceline.com executives scrambling to keep up with the frenetic pace.

If priceline.com's CIO Ron Rose could name his own price for a little peace and quiet, no telling how high he would bid. But there's no chance of that happening any-

time soon with the soaring demand for his company's Internet pricing service
aggressive expansion into new lines of business, and Rose's determination to kee
priceline.com's information platform one step ahead of rising demand. While there
little peace in the world of a 24/7 e-business like priceline.com, more than a hundr
Compaq ProLiant servers supporting the company's front-end Web interface and cr
ical middleware functions offer, at a minimum, a little peace-of-mind.

Priceline.com calls its patented business process a "demand collection system
It has certainly been collecting demand. "We've experienced staggeringly go
growth," says Rose. Priceline.com today brokers the sale of about 2% of all leisure a
line tickets sold in the US (up to 10,000 tickets a day), 16,000 hotel rooms a night, $
million a month in home finance loans and a growing number of automobile purcha
es. Priceline.com's site is one of the Internet's most heavily trafficked websites, w
more than 1.5 million hits a week. And the numbers keep growing, with sales routine
jumping 50% per month.

What's drawing millions to priceline.com's services is its unorthodox approa
to e-commerce, in which buyers—not sellers—set the prices. Priceline.com serves
a kind of online super-agent, allowing consumers to name their own prices for goo
and services like airline tickets and automobiles. Priceline.com collects these cc
sumer offers and electronically presents them to sellers, who either accept or reject t
offers. Potential buyers are notified electronically whether their offers have be
accepted, usually within hours rather than days. By serving as the ultimate Intern
middleman, explains Rose, priceline.com benefits both sides in a transaction. "V
help buyers save money and allow sellers to get rid of inventory without upsetti
their traditional distribution channels."

Priceline.com currently brings buyers and sellers together in three main lines
business: travel services, which includes airline tickets and hotel rooms; hor
finance, which allows shoppers to name their preferred interest rates and terms
mortgages and other personal loans; and automotive services, which extends t
name-your-own-price model to new-car shopping. The business model is even fle
ble enough to add a variety of other markets, like grocery shopping—a business tl
priceline.com has recently entered.

## Keeping the Doors Open

To support an environment where millions of consumers bid for items as diverse
cans of tuna and $40,000 automobiles, priceline.com's information platform had to
designed from the ground up, to bend and stretch, but never break. That means h
service availability, even as traffic surges and new product lines are added. "This
our storefront," explains Rose. "If we don't stay up and running, it's like closing
doors and turning away sales."

For priceline.com, keeping its store open for business also means continually knocking down walls, literally, and expanding the size of its virtual facility. "System scalability is extremely important. We have to be able to reconfigure object servers, add processors, bring in new servers—all without bringing the system down to do it," says Rose.

The twin goals of availability and scalability led priceline.com to adopt Compaq's DISA front-end system architecture. DISA helps ensure availability by balancing traffic loads across multiple application servers, rather than relying on a single server with lots of memory and processors. "The horizontal redundancy provided by DISA is the key to system uptime—and it offers a plug-and-play architecture that we can use to reconfigure our servers on the fly," says Rose.

## Compaq Out Front

An architecture is only as good as its component parts, however, so priceline.com decided to anchor its front-end Windows NT and middleware platforms with what Rose calls "premier Wintel servers." Explains Rose, "Compaq ProLiant servers are well-designed and well-built. Their reliability is superb, and they'll run Microsoft applications as well as they can be run."

The current mix of Compaq ProLiant 1850Rs and 6400s running the Microsoft Internet Information Server (IIS) handle the all-important interfaces with priceline.com customers, including Web page creation, trafficking of HTTP requests, and processing customer-service requests. Purchase offers initiated by buyers on the website are distributed across the array of ProLiant servers via a bank of Cisco Local Directors, which provide intelligent load balancing functionality.

## More Bang for the Buck

The addition of ProLiant servers on the front end highlights priceline.com's determination to accommodate surging traffic without breaking the bank. "It's easy enough to throw servers at every problem, but that can get expensive, especially when you have to double the IT staff needed to manage the servers. It's hard to keep a thousand of anything going. As we continue to add product lines and experience staggering traffic growth, we're looking for more processing power from fewer servers. So we're moving in the direction of multiple-processor servers, like the ProLiant 6400."

If four processors are better than two, then eight processors are four times better, especially when that means enhanced processing power, fewer servers to manage, and a rack-mountable, compact form factor. "We're also investigating the benefits of integrating ProLiant servers equipped with 8-way processing," says Rose. "Our ulti-

mate objective is to increase performance, decrease the cost of maintenance, and ke
our site up and running."

Forget the peace and quiet. Ron Rose doesn't even look for it anytime soon. He a
the rest of priceline.com would prefer the steady hum of a thriving business.

# DRUGSTORE.COM, INC. . . . . . . . . . . . . . . . . . . . .

Drugstore.com, Inc. (www.drugstore.com) was introduced in Chapter 3 as a leadi
online source for health, beauty and wellness products. The company's prescripti
for healthy business is quality products and excellent service—fronted by the best po
sible customer Web experience. Drugstore.com's Chief Information Officer I
Raman says that a high-performance, highly available Internet infrastructure is cr
cal to the success of the business. "High availability is as important to e-commerce
breathing is to humans," says Raman. "Our servers stay highly available to custome
giving us an advantage for e-commerce."

That high-availability advantage pays off. Media Metrix, Inc., the leader
Internet and digital media measurement services, rates drugstore.com among the t
50 e-commerce sites. *PC Magazine* also named drugstore.com as one of the top 1
e-commerce sites.

## IT Integration for Uninterrupted Performance

Today, drugstore.com offers consumers thousands of personal healthcare products
wealth of decision-making resources, personal services and a licensed pharmacy.
NonStop e-business environment of multi-tiered Compaq servers provides the perf
mance, availability and scalability.

At the front-end, intelligent load balancers distribute requests to a redund.
array of high-volume Web and database servers—keeping response high as custom
browse, place orders, or consult with beauty experts and pharmacists via e-mail. Ev
during peak traffic loads, the solution transitions requests smoothly and reliably to
available server for continuous customer interaction. A firewall at each tier, coup
with message encryption, protects personal information, like prescription data.

Compaq StorageWorks systems keeps this private information protected,
readily accessible when needed. Microsoft solutions provide advanced e-comme
capabilities for online transactions with secure order capture, management, and ro
ing, as well as integration with core business processes. Fully integrated operatic
make business flow quickly and smoothly—from online ordering to fulfillment.

The scalable-server architecture allows the company to add additional systems flexibly and affordably as workloads increase. "We've already added at least 50% more servers since the time we launched the store," says Raman.

## Creating an E-Infrastructure Enterprise Blueprint

Compaq consultants and engineers helped drugstore.com Web-enable its business from top to bottom—all within a week. Consultants helped plan the architecture, determine server capacity for the best performance, and install and configure the Windows NT environment.

Drugstore.com has its finger on the pulse of the wellness and beauty market and a healthy outlook for the future. "Our mission is to empower our customers, and to fulfill their health and beauty needs online," Raman says.

# UTOBYTEL.COM REVOLUTIONIZES SELLING ND BUYING AUTOMOBILES . . . . . . . . . . . . . . . . .

The Internet-driven economy that is emerging before our eyes touches every area of commerce ranging from trucking companies, as we noted earlier, to financial services organizations. One critical area is the automobile industry, one of the top 10 industries in the US. Using Internet technologies and newly developed applications, one new dot.com company is revolutionizing the purchase and sale of automobiles.

For most people, buying a car ranks up there with going to the dentist or filling out tax returns. It's no fun spending a Saturday afternoon traipsing through car lots and haggling with salespeople.

Pete Ellis, a former car dealer, knew the problem firsthand. In February 1995, he set out to reinvent the way people buy and sell cars. His idea? Take information from potential car buyers, then go out and find the best deal for them. Launched just a few years ago, this service, which became Autobytel.com, has revolutionized the $1 trillion-a-year automotive industry.

Ellis started Autobytel.com with advertisements in the newspaper and on CompuServe. A month later, impressed with the online response, he decided that cyberspace was the place to be. Prodigy wanted to increase its automotive content and offered his company a free slot online. Ellis thought he'd get 500 requests a week but ended up with more than 1,300 a day.

Before long, Ellis had launched the Autobytel.com website on the Internet and business grew exponentially. Autobytel.com has over 3,000 dealers in its North

American network and is more than three times the size of its next biggest Internet co:
petitor—with sales representing 45% percent of the Internet new car-buying market.

Along the way, Autobytel.com has increased its offerings to include the ent
life cycle of car ownership, including: leasing, insurance, financing, warranties, aft
market products, service and maintenance, and vehicle resale. "We offer our c
tomers a complete automotive solution," says Marc Benjamin, Autobytel.com's Ch
Marketing Officer. The company is also blazing trails globally, with websites in
UK, Japan and Sweden. Autobytel.com has upcoming launches in Finland, Norw
and Denmark, and plans are under way for Australia, Holland and other countries
Europe.

Autobytel.com charges dealers sign-up and monthly fees ranging from $500
$7,500. In 1999, for the second year in a row, dealers ranked Autobytel.com tops
terms of satisfaction among Internet auto-buying services, according to a report p
lished by JD Power & Associates.

## Expanding Customer Horizons

Why is Autobytel rated so high? The company's site lets customers research th
dream vehicles—including pricing, dealer comparisons and even digital photos
before filling out a purchase request. Not only can shoppers browse without comn
ment, but a more knowledgeable consumer leads to better-qualified customers
dealers.

Autobytel.com's innovations have radically altered the economics of the au
buying business. For one, it has sliced dealers' marketing costs tremendously. T
average cost of selling 100 cars through its system can be as little as $18,500 ver:
$101,500 through the traditional system.

For another, buying through Autobytel.com can result in major discounts
consumers. Since dealers aren't spending lots of cash on advertising and commissio
they can pass the savings along to consumers. As a result, the Autobytel.com car b
ers often pay 1 or 2% above the invoice price that the dealer paid for the car, ver:
7-14% when buying through normal dealer channels.

## 4 Million-Plus Customers

The company sells, on average, 50,000 cars a month, generating $1.6 million an h
in car sales through its network of dealers—which represented and is on track to g
erate nearly $14.5 billion in car sales in for 1999. Autobytel.com has processed o
4 million purchase requests since inception and receives, on average, over a mil
new, unique visitors a month.

With that kind of traffic pouring in from the Internet every day, the company needed reliable equipment to power the site. Autobytel.com uses four Compaq ProLiant servers for its database and over thirty other ProLiant systems to handle Web traffic, according to Ann Delligatta, Autobytel.com's COO. With Compaq, the company has found that it can scale up by adding more database and Web servers as the business grows.

Autobytel.com chose Compaq for one simple reason—reliability. "As the most recognized, and most successful, automotive e-commerce provider, it is crucial that our website is up and running 24 hours a day. Our brand represents the highest standard of service to consumers," she says. "Compaq provides us with stable systems that allow us to grow incrementally."

Will consumers ever be able to actually buy a car over the Internet from start to finish? Delligatta says it's headed in that direction. "We already deliver cars to our customers' doorsteps, and we will continue to innovate to offer customers a seamless, pleasant car-buying experience. Whether through an Internet specialist in a dealership, 'direct' online sales, or auction, we will provide consumers with the automotive sales experience they demand," she says.

Like the automotive industry, the dynamics of auctions and flea markets changed forever with the introduction of the Internet. If you were considering going into the auction business today, you would look at it a lot differently than you would have three years ago.

# ONEERS CREATE A MOTLEY FOOL . . . . . . . . . . . . . . .

David and Tom Gardner are unlikely Internet innovators. Six years ago, the two English majors started a monthly newsletter called *Motley Fool* in a shack behind David's house in Alexandria, Virginia. Its purpose? To dispense financial information and advice to individual investors like themselves.

After six months, with 40 subscribers and sales of only $20,000, they were struggling to make ends meet. Fate intervened in April 1994, when a *Motley Fool* prank caught the attention of *The Wall Street Journal*. The brothers posted a phony stock tip on Prodigy about a fictional company called Zeigletics selling portable toilets to Eastern Africa—an event that sent gullible readers scrambling for more details.

Executives at America Online liked the joke, apparently, and offered to include the newsletter as part of its service. Non-fools that they are, the Gardner brothers launched their online version a few months later, hauling in 20% of the $3-per-hour tariff America Online charged readers at their site.

By January 1996, with a solid audience behind them, the Gardner brothers opened shop on the Web in time to coincide with the release of their first book, *The*

*Motley Fool Investment Guide.* The new site marketed their book and grew to of
features like Fool Mart, which sells everything from books and computer software
*Motley Fool* baseball caps and boxer shorts. About 30% of the company's rever
comes from e-commerce on Fool Mart and transactional agreements with other co
panies, such as online bookseller amazon.com. Advertising generates the rest.

The Gardner brothers have changed the stock advice game by making the s
ject more interesting, interactive, and fun. And they find that the Web is changing th
mission. "There's a real place for financial reporting going forward," Tom says. "I
right now, it's not done by talking to the experts. It's really done by being a mode
tor for conversations online and doing research for people." Along those lines,
newsletter recently added sections on home, insurance, and car buying.

*Motley Fool* currently receives 16 million page views a month between its sites
the Web and America Online. That translates into roughly one million readers a mor
or 12 million a year. To handle the volume and provide faster response times for th
burgeoning audience, they have now opened a mirrored website on the West Coast.

Since its debut on the Web three years ago, *Motley Fool* has been fueled
Compaq equipment, with eleven ProLiant 6000 and ProLiant 6500 servers currer
online. The company's technology needs are growing at the rate of 20% per mor
and Compaq servers provide the scalability to meet the extra demand. The comp;
will soon add several ProLiant 3000R systems to expand Fool Mart and its rece;
launched British version of the stock newsletter. "The Compaq boxes rock," s
Dwight Gibbs, whose title at *Motley Fool* is Chief Techie Geek. "They're really r
solid. We could have easily found less expensive equipment; that's a no-brainer. Co
we have found better equipment? I don't think so."

## NETGROCER.COM'S ONLINE SHOPPING CART
## REVOLUTIONIZES FOOD INDUSTRY . . . . . . . . . . . . .

Another dot.com company to lead an industry—in this case, the food industry-
NetGrocer. Its founders saw the changing environment and instinctively underst
the potential of new Internet technologies. They developed and ran with a concept
is changing the way established companies are doing business.

Nearly everyone has been in this situation: standing in a long checkout line
supermarket, shelling out more than $100 for a week's worth of groceries, and
lugging the bags home. The people at NetGrocer know that today's shoppers are s
on time, money, and patience. So they came up with an alternative: online gro
shopping. In fact, it's the first nationwide supermarket on the Internet.

Unlike regional Internet supermarkets such as Peapod—which takes gro
orders online, does the shopping for you at your favorite grocery store, and delive

your door—NetGrocer buys its products directly from the manufacturer and ships directly to the consumer. Right now, it only offers dry groceries, not perishables such as meat, milk or produce.

Here's how it works: You go to the company's website, select from the 2,000 items in stock, then type in your credit card number. The items are shipped to your door the next day via Federal Express. The charge? A mere $2.99 for orders less than $50, or $4.99 for larger orders. The delivery fee more than pays for itself, once you start comparing prices.

By buying directly from manufacturers, NetGrocer saves its customers up to 20% off typical supermarket prices. In New York City, where the company is based, NetGrocer undercuts grocery store prices by 42% for an average basket of goods.

NetGrocer was founded in the fall of 1995 by two men who know a lot about both computers and consumer products. Fred Adler is a venture capitalist and one of the first investors in the computer giant, Data General. His partner, Uri Evan, started USA Detergents, which marketed the value-brand Extra to supermarkets. They recruited Daniel Nissan, formerly with VocalTec, to be President and CEO.

The two entrepreneurs figured they could save shoppers money by replacing the lengthy chain of wholesalers, distributors, and supermarkets with the Internet. "Why should a product change hands 13 times between the manufacturer and the consumer?" asks Jeffrey Steinberg, NetGrocer's Vice President of Marketing. "Using the Internet, the product changes hands only two or three times, and you deal directly with consumers."

NetGrocer helps manufacturers as much as it helps consumers: a central distribution facility in New Jersey helps reduce inventory throughout the supply chain.

## Groceries on the Net: Instant Advantage

More important, NetGrocer helps manufacturers test new products online, with advertising directly targeted to its select group of consumers. "Instead of putting a coupon in every Sunday paper and expecting 1% of the people to redeem it, they can target those people who have purchased their product or a competitor's product," Steinberg says. "So there's lots of savings from the manufacturers' end. Best of all, marketing over the Internet is immediately measurable."

As a result, NetGrocer has vastly shortened the time it takes to roll out a new product and have it sampled by a nationwide audience, allowing regional players to become national distributors instantly. "It's been difficult for a small company to get a product into the pipeline, because you have to pay slotting fees to supermarkets to get your product on the shelf," Steinberg says. "With NetGrocer, you're instantly nationwide."

Are supermarkets and manufacturers thinking about adopting the NetGro
concept themselves? Not right away, Steinberg says. "They don't think in those terr
They think in terms of real estate and store space; they don't think of Internet spac
he says. "We hope they don't change their opinions, because we're currently pre
small compared with them." But NetGrocer has changed the way the industry thin
about the whole shopping experience. "We've altered our industry's cost and mark
ing structure," Steinberg says. "For certain commodity items, there's just no need
go to a store."

This is the kind of savvy thinking that pays off. After spending eighteen mon
in the development stage, NetGrocer launched its service in July 1997. Since then, sa
have doubled every month. So far, approximately 5,000 customers have purchased g
ceries using the NetGrocer service, which receives about 45,000 online visits a day

The key to NetGrocer's success is the integration of its business and IT strateg
and having an e-infrastructure enterprise blueprint. "If our systems go down, we
closed for business," says Steinberg. But the IT infrastructure now in place enab
NetGrocer to serve its customers non-stop. Our systems "warn you of potential pr
lems even before they become problems," adds Steinberg. NetGrocer doesn't want
shoppers to have to wait in line—even in cyberspace—to buy their week's worth
groceries.

# E-COMMERCE PIONEERS AROUND THE WORLD . . . .

The Internet explosion is truly global, and e-commerce pioneers around the world
moving at breathtaking speed to bring their own countries into the digital econo
This rapid deployment of Internet technology around the world is being made po
ble by the partnering of these international entrepreneurs with the leading soluti
providers, including Compaq, Microsoft, Nortel, Cisco, Lucent and others. Se
examples of how such partnerships are taking the Internet to the world follow.

**Malaysia**—Maxis Communications formed a strategic partnership with a c
sortium led by Compaq Computer Corporation Malaysia Sdn. Bhd., as Maxis gea
become a major provider of Internet services in Malaysia.

For this project, Compaq Malaysia will build, operate, and transfer the ISP inf
tructure to Maxis. Compaq's Professional Services will plan, construct, and deploy
infrastructure, comprising 50 units of Compaq Proliant fault-tolerant servers.

Compaq is also involved in building the ISP billing system and working o
call center solutions. Compaq will place its employees on-site to operate the envi
ment and ensure uptime of its systems, help desk, and call center.

"We have chosen to work with Compaq-based on their strong track recor
systems integration and outsourcing in general, and Internet services in particu

said Maxis' CEO En. Jamaludin Ibrahim. "Compaq's worldwide expertise includes providing Internet solutions for 1,000 enterprise customers, managing ISP sites for 2.5 million subscribers, and completing 20,000 enterprise network projects. We believe that Compaq will be able to create and deliver the products, solutions, and services to support Maxis' ISP infrastructure effectively."

He added, "We also chose Compaq because of the other partners that they brought together with their expertise and solutions. These partners include Microsoft, Nortel, Cisco, Lucent and Kenan." Microsoft will be the main software vendor and provider of the operating system, while Northern Telecom, Cisco Systems, Lucent Technology and Kenan Systems will provide the network equipment.

Maxis also commissioned Compaq for the operation and management of its call center for the Maxis Internet services. Located in Sungai Besi, the call center will have state-of-the-art equipment to provide the highest level of service to Maxis customers. Maxis has already completed the construction of the data center there.

"We are setting up all the necessary infrastructure and support services to provide Internet services to our customers," said Jamaludin. Maxis plans to provide a high-quality service capable of supporting 200,000 to 300,000 customers within the next two years.

Maxis currently offers a full suite of data and voice services, which ranges from basic telephony services to more advanced services, such as frame relay, international private-leased lines, domestic-leased circuit, trunk services, toll-free services, VSAT services, and Smart Access.

**China**—The Guangdong Post and Telecom Administration (GPTA), the largest telecommunications company in China, is relying on Compaq services and systems to develop and deploy a secure e-commerce infrastructure to serve the 90 million citizens of the Guangdong province.

Through its e-commerce service company, GPTA will deliver Internet EDI for the trading companies of the province and provide secure electronic-funds transfer. Compaq has contracted to complete a major e-commerce pilot implementation, providing a secure transaction infrastructure among 10 banking institutions, 10 governmental entities, and 200,000 customers with electronic wallets.

The Guangdong Province Postal Savings and Remittance Bank is currently one of China's largest users of Compaq NonStop Integrity platforms, which support retail banking and a province-wide ATM and point-of-sale network. This financial network infrastructure, in concert with the Guangdong Gold Card Switch Center, will ease deployment of the Internet payment systems.

Compaq is also partnering with GPTA in a recently established e-commerce technology center. Through the center, Compaq and GPTA will work together to accelerate the growth of e-commerce in China.

**Spain**—Servicio Andaluz de la Salud (SAS) is the public healthcare organization of southern Spain. With Compaq Services in the lead, SAS is creating one of the largest intranet-linked extranets in Europe. By 2001, the SAS "superNet" will li▪ 30,000 medical and administrative personnel at 88 facilities across the Andalus province and provide Web-based information services, such as scheduling of appoi▪ ments, to the province's 8 million residents.

IS Manager Luis Gallego describes the process for choosing a service and tec▪ nology partner: "We gave several corporations a set of complex tasks to be acco▪ plished in a short time, and also at a difficult time of year in Spain—vacation tin▪ Compaq accomplished these tasks splendidly, with far more expertise and creativi▪ than the other corporations. Compaq clearly demonstrated that it is a reliable partne▪

Compaq Services is designing and implementing a high-performance, bro▪ band extranet with security, search, and workflow capabilities based on AltaVi▪ products, Microsoft Exchange, and Compaq Work Expeditor. Platforms include fc▪ Compaq AlphaServer systems, 90 Proliant servers, and 2,100 Compaq DeskPro P(▪ Compaq is also creating a public website and is developing an interactive site ▪ young patients at SAS hospitals.

The superNet roll-out continues, and SAS management is pleased with ▪ results Compaq has delivered so far. "Compaq has the knowledge, the attitude, and ▪ professional skills and experience to ensure our success," says José Antonio Cobe▪ SAS, CIO and COO. "For big projects, big companies are required. Compaq is a▪ to meet all of the SAS requirements."

**Europe and North America**—TelePost is a young company with high am▪ tions and a clear vision. Today, thanks to system infrastructure and consulting exp▪ tise from Compaq, TelePost is moving swiftly ahead with its worldwide deploym▪ of "Web-centric" messaging, collaboration, and computer telephony services.

TelePost and Compaq have already rolled out the services in select US ▪ European markets. The TelePost Office 2000 services use the Internet to manage ▪ control the public switched telephone network (PSTN). Mobile professionals, sn▪ and medium businesses, and corporate collaborators are key targets for TelePost ▪ vices. The services TelePost offers include audio conferencing; hosting Web-ba▪ PowerPoint presentations; a unified message center for integrated voice, fax, anc▪ mail; and e-mail or Web-initiated toll-free callback capability via interactive busir▪ cards or a website.

The uniqueness and strengths of the services led the *Financial Times* to no▪ nate TelePost Office 2000 as the 1998 Internet Telephony Product of the Year.

TelePost first engaged Compaq Services in 1997 to implement several pil▪ TelePost then enlisted Compaq Services to assist with the specification, certificat▪ and rapid implementation of major network infrastructure components. In 1▪ Compaq and TelePost deployed six TelePost network nodes built on Micro▪ Windows NT-based ProLiant servers with Dialogic voice processing, Excel switcl▪ platforms, and distributed Oracle8 databases. Today, these nodes serve m▪

European markets and are being expanded to cover 22 major metropolitan areas in North America.

The smoothness and speed of these deployments led TelePost to further expand its agreement with Compaq. Early in 1999, TelePost inked a multi-year contract that calls for Compaq Services to assist TelePost with the logistical coordination of the next wave of node deployments, and to assume complete responsibility to build, integrate, deploy, and manage the TelePost worldwide network.

"We've essentially outsourced the management and day-to-day operation of our network to Compaq," says Bruce Runyan, TelePost President and COO. "Compaq will provide 24/7 monitoring from its network operations centers, along with hands-on support in over 20 countries. With this service infrastructure in place, TelePost can focus on rapid deployment of its services."

In March of 1999, Compaq and TelePost entered into a worldwide distribution agreement to deploy TelePost services through Compaq.com in the US, UK, France, and Germany. Runyan says that TelePost has plans to roll out at least 65 network nodes worldwide and will also deploy database farms in the US, UK, and Japan.

# 12

# stablished Players Concede Nothing
# Dot.com Companies

.........................

*Summary: Business managers know the importance of responding quickly to changing markets and seizing new opportunities. The introduction of Internet technologies and their myriad applications have forced companies to change strategies and tactics ten, twenty, and thirty times faster than they are accustomed to. They have had no choice, as new dot.com companies have rapidly gained marketshare at the expense of established titans. But the better run, more established companies have been playing catch-up; some have seen the Internet's big picture, recognized opportunities, and have become Internet leaders on their own terms. According to one study sponsored by the Boston Consulting Group and Shop.org, a trade association of Internet retailers, consumers will spend $36 billion with retail websites in 1999, more than double the $14.9 billion they spent in 1998. Most of the spending will be with retailers who already have a brand presence through their brick-and-mortar stores—and now on the Web.*

*In this chapter, we share some of the stories of companies that listened to their customers, read the key signs and indicators of the emerging global economy correctly, and are taking advantage of new opportunities to grow their businesses and maintain their leadership status in a wide variety of industries.*

## S EVERYONE'S INTERNET:
## TRUCKING COMPANY EXCELS ................

If you think that the Internet is only for retailers, entertainment entities, and high-tech enterprises, think again. Consider the story of Schneider National.

You're cruising down the interstate at 70 miles an hour, minding your own business, bopping along to your favorite CD. "Born to be wild," you think to yourself, "king of the road." But suddenly, as if from nowhere, a massive 18-wheeler is flashing its lights in your rear-view mirror—not menacingly, but with enough photonic force to say "Excuse me," and then some. Graciously, you slide over to the right, ting the big rig get on down the highway.

Most likely, and probably without knowing it, you've just had a close encou with one of the most technologically savvy organizations in the world—Schnei National, the leading trucking company in America, and the most aggressive, by in aligning information technologies with high-level business strategies. Schnei National is so far ahead of the pack, in fact, that many technology firms would b in a head-to-head comparison. From microprocessors measuring the wear-and-tea every axle and camshaft of its trucks, to a football field-sized, NASA-like miss control center in Green Bay, Wisconsin, to satellites communicating from abov geosynchronous orbit, Schneider is a seriously wired company.

## "Technology is the Future of our Company"

It couldn't be any other way, according to Chris Lofgren, CIO of the Green Bay fre company. "Technology is the future of our company," says Lofgren. "It is critical to positioning. Just look at the portion of our SG&A costs that are taken up by techn gy. We make a significantly larger investment [in IT] than any of our competitors.'

As a family-owned business, Schneider doesn't release detailed financial st ments. But even without such data, it's easy to see that this is an organization that l and breathes computing and communications—because it has to. Only with the si silicon machines can it wring the most profit and customer satisfaction possible f the diesel-driven, rolling steel machines that actually generate the revenue.

"Technology gives us the opportunity to do things for customers that can' done any other way," says Steve Matheys, Vice President of Applica Development. Schneider currently employs more than 350 people in its IT dep ment, half of whom are focused on developing a steady stream of new applicat and information systems. So far, they've written more than 200 proprietary syste composed of some 17 million lines of code—right up there with the major playe banking, insurance, and other information-based industries.

Another 450 people spend their workdays in front of PCs, using all those ho brewed applications, and others purchased from software companies, to mo Schneider's fleet of 15,000 tractors and 43,000 trailers and to get customers the ir mation they need about everything from truck availability to expected time of deli

Rating is a core business process for all shipping companies, whether they m loads by air, sea, or land. The objective is simple: Prepare the most-competitive p quote possible and still make a profit. The process of calculating a rate, thoug enormously complex, for it must take into account dozens of factors, including type of goods the customer wants shipped, how much the shipment weighs, whe must be delivered and by when, and what size truck is required.

Add the fact that Schneider works closely with some 3,000 other freight carriers, and the amount of data—to organize, maintain, and search—quickly escalates. Without a superior rating system, Schneider would find itself increasingly vulnerable to competition. Customers would take their business elsewhere—to Federal Express and UPS, for instance, which are part of the new breed of technology-driven shippers.

## Competitive Advantage

"We're always looking for ways of using technology to gain a sustainable competitive advantage," says Matheys. So, having determined in 1997 that the various off-the-shelf rating systems were not what was needed, Schneider built its own—a project that top company officials believe has pushed Schneider well ahead of its rivals.

The problem with the packaged rating systems was their lack of detail. The rates they calculated were based on estimated transit times and distances, and carrying capacities. Worse, these canned programs were inefficient in the way they sifted through mountains of fuzzy data, taking several minutes to generate a single rate. That was unacceptable, since Schneider's technicians were already handling scores of concurrent phone calls at any given time.

The rating system Schneider built for itself is a winner. Using a database structure optimized just for its purposes, the software runs about 2,000 times faster than the packaged code—in fractions of a second instead of minutes. It doesn't deal in estimated data; it deals in live, constantly refreshed information that describes some 2 million different rates. Total development cost: $300,000. Initial payback period: a little more than three months.

The success of this new rating system points to the future of Schneider. Instead of actually owning, maintaining, and operating large fleets of trucks, Schneider's business is gradually shifting more to managing information about trucks and the shipments they carry.

Today's customer thinks in terms of just-in-time deliveries, vendor-managed inventories, and other forms of the digitally enhanced Value Chain. He wants to know exactly where his freight is and exactly when it will get to its intended destination. To supply that information, and to squeeze the maximum ROI from its assets, a trucking company needs to know where its trucks are, at any given moment, and what state they are in—fully loaded with the meter ticking or empty while waiting for the next assignment.

For shipping companies, logistics is the science of managing transportation assets within the constraints of schedules, budgets, and the availability of people and equipment. Logistics is where Schneider sees most of its future growth. The company already organizes the movement of more than $1 billion in freight each year.

For a customer like General Motors, Schneider is under contract to manage movement of service parts at every step of the way, from the factory to every a mechanic in the country. CIO Lofgren also carries the title of Chief Logistics Offi a further clue as to how interrelated IT and business strategy have become Schneider National.

A growing portion of the company's revenue comes from helping arrange movement of freight—whether full truckloads or small packages—via other carri Schneider is positioning itself as the industry's master scheduler, a vital hub of in pensable information about virtually everything to do with shipping.

## A Visit with 21st Century Truckers

Schneider, and the thousands of big rigs it operates, would probably dispel any gering romantic notions you might have about truckers. Sure, just like Humph Bogart in that great old John Huston movie, they still ride through the night, and ing the daytime, too. They still live a somewhat lonesome, solitary life out there the highways and byways of America. They may even be the last of the cowboys some songwriters and poets suggest.

However, for all practical purposes, today's truckers are as digitally tethered— empowered—as your typical 9-to-5 office worker. In 1999, Schneider began outfit its vast fleet of trailers with on-board computer communications systems that autom cally report back to Green Bay on virtually everything that goes on in and around th Open the trailer's door and a proximity switch takes note. Hook or unhook the tra from its tractor, or place it on a railcar, and more data are beamed back to central. trailer's temperature can be monitored from Greenbay, along with its precise loca (via a miniature GPS device) and its consumption of electrical power.

Like an earthbound spacecraft, the typical Schneider trailer will soon repor amazing detail, its every move and change of state. What makes all this possible i fact, a spacecraft—a fleet of them—moving silently overhead in very low and, th fore, maximally visible orbits.

Working with Orbcomm, a company that specializes in exploiting such l earth-orbit (LEO) satellites, Schneider has once again leaped ahead of its competi With this trailer tracking system, the company can manage these extremely valu but widely dispersed assets almost as if they were all locked up and sitting on the c pany's airport-sized parking lot in Green Bay.

"It's all a matter of asset visibility," says Paul Mueller, the trucking firm's President of Communications Technology Services. "If a shipper doesn't notify us a the status of our asset (a particular trailer) we have no way of understanding how to cute our next move." Sometimes, it's simply a matter of making sure a driver can a ally find the trailer he has been assigned. Many drivers work essentially freelance, on a mileage-per-load basis and, if they're forced to waste time scouring a lot looking for a lost trailer, they may think twice the next time about driving for Schneider.

## Digital Satellite Communications

Trailer tracking follows a long history of using in-cab communications systems. Schneider cabs are equipped with digital, satellite communications systems that allow drivers to receive and respond to detailed dispatch messages. The technology proved to be popular with drivers, because they no longer had to spend hours waiting in line to use a phone at a truck stop. Soon, this system was monitoring the tractor's engine performance, including RPM and idling speed. The system also constantly measured the rig's braking capacity. The system's advantages: improved safety, optimized maintenance schedules, and happier drivers.

Schneider's main logistics-related challenge now is to better integrate its systems with those of its customers. The goal, as always, is to further streamline operations on both sides of the fence—to put in sync all their interdependent activities, such as deliveries of raw materials and consumer demand. With better visibility into Schneider's freight management systems, customers can better manage their overall supply chains.

There is already a good amount of EDI traffic flowing between Schneider and its customers, but the Internet holds the promise of even tighter integration and an even clearer, more high-fidelity window in both directions. "We're always trying to be proactive, not reactive," says Mueller.

## Integration of Business and IT Strategies

If anyone embodies the culture of technology that pervades Schneider National, it is CIO Lofgren. Like many such executives these days, Lofgren reports directly to the company's CEO, Don Schneider. And just as important, the IT steering committee, which Lofgren heads, meets every two weeks to decide the next point at which IT can best be applied to achieve strategic objectives.

Don Schneider and his management team recognized early on the importance of technology and saw the advantages they would have by embracing new, emerging Internet capabilities and applications. They also stayed focused on their customers and the need to adapt constantly to meet customer needs. In reinventing their enterprise, they integrated their business and IT strategies and aligned their resources accordingly. The results are straightforward: Schneider has maintained its leadership position in the Internet-driven economy and is prepared to change gears at the drop of a hat in response to continuously changing market conditions. That's why they are in the enviable position they are in today.

# BARNES AND NOBLE STAYS ON TOP WITH BARNESANDNOBLE.COM . . . . . . . . . . . . . . . .

We have seen that Barnes and Noble is an established book publisher/booksell whose name is known and respected around the world. Like many established con panies, it was suffering from the adroit use of the Internet by its competitors and w faced with how to stay competitive and reassert its leadership—and how to do that Internet speeds. Every day that Barnes and Noble delayed entry into the e-commerc marketplace was a day it was losing ground.

The 1998 holiday season was anything but a season of peace for the country electronic-commerce marketers. Some $5 billion in US goods and services were so over the Internet during the holiday period in an online frenzy that surpassed even t most optimistic predictions and strained the physical and virtual infrastructures many e-commerce vendors.

At barnesandnoble.com, the division that the company established to participa in the online economy, executives were holding their collective breath. While sor online businesses were facing IT capacity bottlenecks and unfilled orders, Barnes a Noble's two-month-old, technologically advanced back-office e-commerce platfo was facing its most critical test.

Whether the new platform—powered by Microsoft Windows NT Server 4.0 a Microsoft SQL Server 7.0 running on Compaq ProLiant 7000 clusters—could survi the strain would also test the nerves of the teams of technicians from Barnes a Noble, Compaq, and Microsoft. They had designed and implemented the entire dist bution and fulfillment infrastructure in a matter of months. E-commerce had fina hit the big time. The question was, would barnesandnoble.com be ready?

## 24/7 E-Business

However the holiday crunch turned out, the company had, in fact, already come a lc way in a short time. Just 18 months earlier, Barnes and Noble took its first tentati steps into the e-commerce arena. The barnesandnoble.com website, launched in m 1997, was part of the strategy to expand the reach of the world's largest booksell "The site got its start when Barnes and Noble realized that e-commerce was the w of the future, and that we needed to take our brand to the Web. We needed to build our heritage of delivering books and content to a growing number of consumer explains Ben Boyd, Vice President of Communications.

As a subsidiary of a company with 505 retail bookstores in 49 states, barnesar noble.com had the brand recognition. It just needed the back-office IT infrastruct that could support such make-or-break functions as order fulfillment, customer-s vice and accounting.

By early 1998, more than 300,000 customers were already testing the limits of the original back-office platform. With the 1998 holiday season looming, barnesand-noble.com executives knew they had about six months to design and deploy a new platform, and they had one chance to get it right. That meant setting clear goals. "Reliability, scalability and usability are the key characteristics we were after," says Gary King, Chief Information Officer at barnesandnoble.com.

"We wanted a platform that could handle the peaks in terms of volume loading. We wanted a platform that allowed us to bring in new technologies and do mainte-nance while continuing to operate 24 hours a day, seven days a week. When we talk about Internet time, we really mean it. There is no allowance for down time with the kinds of changes that happen in the retail world," King said.

King says the customer experience was also key. "With the incredible increases in traffic, we were getting a lot of new users. So there's a constant need to focus on the site's usability and ease-of-access for customers, as well as the prompt tracking and filling of customer orders."

"The back-office platform needs to support several key functions—functions that customers don't notice unless something goes wrong," adds Alan Bourassa, Director of Distribution and Fulfillment Systems. "The fulfillment process—what we call picking, packing and shipping—involves taking customers' orders and figuring out the fastest and most cost-effective ways of getting books from warehouses to our distribution centers to customers' doorsteps. The accounting function makes sure we keep track of costs and handle credit card transactions correctly. And our back-office platform needs to support customer service reps at our three call centers, by giving them instant information on customer orders."

## The 24/7 IT Team

With these priorities set, the barnesandnoble.com IT staff next looked to the team that could help them pull off the complicated platform design and tight implementation schedule. That meant turning to software and hardware systems-providers who had already proven their ability to work with Barnes and Noble—and with each other.

"We had made a choice early on to go the Microsoft route in terms of tools and software," says King. "It's a choice that has worked well for us for the type of site we run, for the high number of pages we need to publish on a daily basis, and for the high volume of customer transactions we have to deal with."

With Microsoft on the software side, Compaq was the natural hardware choice, explains King. "One of the key benefits to us is the alignment of the two organizations from a development standpoint, how they leverage the capability of the hardware and match it nicely to the software. The high degree of collaboration between Compaq and Microsoft made us confident to partner with the two companies for critical compo-nents of our business activity."

Compaq and Microsoft contributed much more than hardware and softwa Engineers and technical consultants from the two companies worked with barnesan noble.com's IT staff to design, implement, and troubleshoot the new back-office pl form that became known as PRISM. Consultants from Compaq Services helped dra up design and implementation plans, while technicians from Compaq Netwc Integration Services designed and installed the physical infrastructure, including t wiring of hubs and routers that connect the platform's wide-area network.

The distribution and fulfillment solution would certainly have to span a "wi area." Electronic links were needed to connect the company's primary data center New Jersey to other segments of the company's supply chain. These segments inclu third-party warehouses, where books are stored; the company's new Dayton, Ne Jersey, distribution center, where Compaq servers would control the packing and sh ping of orders, and even the movement of conveyor belts; shipping companies, whc tracking and delivery systems would ensure that orders get to customers; and to t company's customer-service call centers around the country.

## 24/7 Availability and Growth

In early October, the implementation partners unveiled the fruits of their intensi team effort as the platform went online. The new platform employs an unusual thre tiered architecture, with Microsoft Internet Information Server 4.0 linking to the fro end client, Microsoft Transaction Server 2.0 providing business functionality, a Microsoft SQL Server 7.0 serving as the database engine, all running on Windows N Server 4.0. "The three tiers offer maximum scalability and fault tolerance," explai Bourassa. "And SQL Server 7.0 in particular helps meet our needs for highly scalab high-volume database transactions. SQL's new row-level locking feature helps update the database without causing data concurrency problems."

The platform's Compaq hardware foundation also employs some forward-thir ing technology solutions designed to address the project's goals of reliability, sca bility, and usability. "We selected Compaq ProLiant 7000 servers with four-way In Pentium Xeon™ processors and Fibre Channel storage arrays, clustered together allow us the redundancy that we need," says Bourassa.

Clustering involves interconnecting two or more servers in a way that enables the to share processing tasks, but still present a single interface to network clients. Fil Channel storage is a Compaq technology that replaces traditional copper SCSI cab with higher speed fiber-optic connections between servers and external storage device

"When you operate a website, having the site unavailable, even temporarily, c permanently cost you customers. Your top priority is system reliability and availab ity," continues Bourassa. "We selected Compaq because the hardware is extreme reliable. If a server ever fails, though, this configuration offers us three lines defense. First, Compaq Insight Manager gives us pre-failure warnings for our CPl power supplies, or disk drives. Second, the cluster services offer failover protection, and features in the ProLiant servers allow for hardware to be swapped in and out without bringing down the entire infrastructure. As an added safeguard, we've got Compaq Fibre Channel storage for faster backup and recovery of data."

Bourassa adds, "The Xeon processors have actually given us a lot of headroom to grow, and we still have a lot of capacity on our Compaq ProLiant servers. We have many folks who come in and look at PRISM, and they just say, 'Yes, this is highly scalable. It's not a throwaway.' And it's a platform that's probably going to be used for the next five to seven years."

Further ensuring the growth potential of the platform, he says, will be the incorporation of a new eight-way processing technology, which barnesandnoble.com is currently testing. Says Bourassa, "With eight-way, you get a bigger bang for the buck. You need fewer boxes taking up less real estate, but you gain greater processing power and simplified management."

The new platform is designed to enhance the customer experience, too. "We want to be able to have a seamless shipment for our customers from beginning to end," emphasizes Bourassa. "In fact, we want to get the notifications back to them with their tracking number, the carrier we're using, and the date the products will arrive at their homes. This platform not only allows us to send e-mail notifications the same day the customer places an order, it also provides more real-time information to customer-service reps and helps reduce our time to ship."

## The Big Test

How did the barnesandnoble.com IT infrastructure stand up in the real world, under the pressure of the biggest online Christmas shopping rush in the short history of Internet commerce?

"Beautifully," says Bourassa. At the same time that volume overwhelmed many competitors' systems, barnesandnoble.com managed to fill orders without a major hitch. "We've had no outages or downtime since we deployed the new systems last October," he says. "And with a 380% annual user-growth curve, that's a major accomplishment."

# ANK OF AMERICA OFFERS
# RETAILING BUNDLE . . . . . . . . . . . . . . . . . . . .

Banks and other financial service companies were among the first to recognize and exploit the power of the Internet to help them grow their businesses. Bank of America was one of the first in the industry to take that trend a step further—by focusing on e-

business solutions for new online retailers. Bank of America recently took the wra
off its Internet Order Center, an e-commerce solution for small to midsize compani
it says will increase customer loyalty and trust on the Internet.

The Internet Order Center consists of a bundle of products aimed at providi
online merchants with an end-to-end e-business solution, from initial Web connecti
to the creation of an online store. Users have the option of building an e-store frc
scratch or connecting an existing online store with a checkout process that incluc
shopping cart, billing, and payment-entry options. Users are also provided with toc
that monitor sales activity, inventory, and shipping information.

Bank of America executives say that online merchants will no longer have
worry about processing credit card transactions. Once customers decide to make a p
chase, they enter a Bank of America branded area of the merchant's site, and the ba
processes all financial transactions.

"The co-brand is certainly a unique aspect of the product offering in that it cc
veys a sense of trust to customers, because of the integrity of the Bank of Amer
name," says Andrew Efstathiou, Senior Analyst with the Yankee Group.

EMS, an application service provider in Burbank, California, developed ▪
Internet Order Center service. Pricing ranges from $100 to $250 per month, depen
ing on the package selected.

# OLD LINE ASIA PACIFIC COMPANIES JOIN
# THE DIGITAL ECONOMY  ....................

## South China Morning Post

*South China Morning Post*, Hong Kong's largest and most prestigious newspaper, ▪
the hot breath of Internet-empowered competitors building a niche as instant inf
mation providers. Not to be left behind, *SCMP* mounted a strategic offensive to rec
ture long-term customers who had been wooed away by the up-to-the-minute ne
availability provided by *SCMP*'s upstart rivals.

In planning its own Internet-driven news service, *SCMP* needed a platform t
could cost-effectively scale up as its online business developed. *SCMP's* investm
in a robust, scalable Internet architecture, based on Compaq NonStop™ solutions z
a Microsoft solution, not only yields benefits of performance and reliability, but pa
the way for the newspaper to meet many of its longer-term strategic objectives.

"The dissemination of news in Hong Kong is very, very important," says Ov
Jonathan, CEO of *SCMP*. "There is heightened interest in Hong Kong in the Engli

speaking world since the handover, and the Internet allows us to reach a much wider audience. There's also keen interest in Hong Kong as a gateway to China and the Chinese market." Moreover, the Web business provides *SCMP* with new sources of revenue in a competitive and uncertain market.

"One component of our strategy is aggregating content into our Internet umbrella to generate more interest to readers," says Jonathan. "We are looking at providing Chinese language content through our Internet site, and we are experimenting with a number of niche products to provide advertisers with a specific portal for e-commerce activities and other opportunities." And the opportunities are paying off. According to Jonathan, "People are approaching us saying, 'You've got the traffic, you've got the demographics, we have products that would be interesting to your readers. Can you sell them for us?' And we say 'sure'—because, thanks to Compaq and Microsoft, we've got the systems in place so we can actually do this."

While *SCMP* is experimenting with B2B portals, they are also looking at Compaq's new B2E, or business-to-employee, megaportal concept. As the latest example of what Compaq is doing to leverage the Internet, the company now offers— as of January 2000—a website that will allow individuals to customize a portal site that is organized around their job function (marketing, engineering, manufacturing, HR, and IT). The customized portal will improve employees' access to job-related content and will provide a conduit for technical support, while enhancing an employee's ability to conduct work from home and take care of personal responsibilities from the office. The concept is a natural evolution in the trend toward the increasing integration of work and personal lives.

## The Hong Kong and China Gas Company, Ltd. (or Towngas)

There are few markets that are more competitive, more dynamic and more uncertain than those in Hong Kong. The Hong Kong and China Gas Company, Ltd. (or Towngas) is the city's largest and oldest gas utility company, serving Hong Kong's energy needs since 1862. Rarely in its long history has Towngas faced a more daunting challenge than the current combination of increased competition, a shrinking economic base, rising consumer expectations, and a workforce uncertain about the future.

Towngas is mastering these challenges because of an aggressive strategic plan built largely on enhancing customer value and increasing the productivity of its operations. Central to this plan is its choice of IT partners: SAP R/3 management systems running on Microsoft Windows NT and anchored on a stable hardware platform of high-performance, high-availability servers from Compaq.

# ALLTEL USES THE INTERNET AS LEVERAGE TO
# MAINTAIN MARKET LEADERSHIP  . . . . . . . . . . . . . . .

Consumers are getting faster and better service in all areas, but especially in financ
services. Without a responsive infrastructure that supports the right applicatio
financial institutions could not keep up with consumer demand.

ALLTEL Residential Lending Solutions is the largest mortgage loan serv
bureau in the United States, and more than half of all the mortgage loans outstandi
in the United States are on file in ALLTEL's software and systems. ALLTEL works
keep ahead of the competition, which is no easy task in an environment where co
panies can rise up almost overnight and offer pioneering applications, taking aw
business from market leaders.

To stay out front as a leader in its field and continue to meet growing custor
demand for Internet-based applications, ALLTEL contracted with Compaq to repo
tion its current infrastructure, maximize its existing capital investments, and prep
for the e-commerce wave.

Mortgage credit processing involves reliable, around-the-clock communicat
between customers seeking loans and mortgage bankers, credit agencies, appraisers, t
companies, and other organizations involved in the complicated, time-sensitive proce

As the only value-added network specializing in the mortgage industry, Al
TEL InterChange enables companies that support the mortgage industry to excha
business transactions via electronic data interchange (EDI) to get their jobs done m
accurately and efficiently than a paper-based system allows.

"The ALLTEL InterChange network is a very vital part of the organization, a
our customers view it as mission-critical. It's one of the primary services that
deliver," says Rob Lee, Executive Vice President with ALLTEL Information Servic
"The infrastructure that we've built gives us an essential building block for taking r
services out to our customers via the Internet."

## Scalability for Internet Growth

ALLTEL entered the Mortgage EDI transaction business in 1993 with a Com
NonStop Himalaya K1000 two-processor system and the MPACT MessageWay s
ware. Customers quickly grasped the value of instant electronic mortgage credit p
cessing through EDI, and by 1995 the growing transaction volume justified
upgrade to a four-processor system.

This upgrade allowed ALLTEL to expand its client base from 300 mortgage t
kers to approximately 3,500 throughout the US. The message count jumped fr
about 1,100 messages per week to between 42,000 and 48,000 by the end of 1°

With this volume increase, ALLTEL began realizing substantial revenue growth from the four-processor system at the core of the ALLTEL InterChange network.

"Through the years, we didn't always have a good idea of what our growth would be. We've literally seen traffic increase 30 to 40% in a day," says Lee. "Compaq has always been able to help us increase our capacity 'on the fly,' so we could grow our business significantly. We've been able to pick up the phone and have Compaq respond very quickly to bring incremental hardware and people on-site to help us manage that growth."

Lee adds that without Compaq's quick response and ability to scale, "our customers wouldn't have come to rely on our service. If they had felt that we couldn't handle their growth or get their transactions through, we'd be out of business."

## Availability 24/7

Craig Foote, Vice President and Product Manager for ALLTEL's InterChange network, explains that the Compaq NonStop Himalaya server was originally chosen as the core of the ALLTEL InterChange system because of the server's continuous availability.

"We needed the reliability to keep our network up and running 24 hours a day, seven days a week, because the transactions are critical to our users who are trying to write new mortgage loans or perform important servicing transactions," says Foote. "Today, we have thousands of users connected around the country in different time zones. "Not only do we move trillions of bytes of data each year, but every byte needs to be in the right place or it doesn't work at the other end," he adds.

In addition to the scalability and reliability that's built into the Compaq platform at the core of ALLTEL InterChange, Lee says the ability to leverage that platform to capture new Internet opportunities is a huge benefit for ALLTEL.

Jay Archibald, System Manager for ALLTEL, agrees. "The Internet is the future for us. We have to be there for our clients. When it comes down to Web-enablement, we have to understand the functionality of the system and what it's going to take to satisfy our clients."

## Clients Aren't What They Used to Be

Compaq and ALLTEL have co-designed another architecture to meet the ATM outsourcing needs of some of ALLTEL's banking clientele. This solution uses the recently purchased Compaq NonStop Himalaya S-series server. Rather than supporting remote systems and support personnel, this server will enable ALLTEL to bring an ATM application inside its Jacksonville Technology Center and manage ATM devices anywhere in the world.

Although the EDI application running on the Compaq NonStop system is pro
itable, the complicated transaction flow and networking environment present limit
tions. The cost of maintaining the environment, for example, is very high. Th
Compaq Services group reviewed ALLTEL's business plan and the existing fram
relay infrastructure. They recommended the Compaq NonStop Himalaya S7000 ser
er as a Web-serving front-end to provide secure terminal access to the EDI applicatic
via standard Web browser technologies.

ALLTEL formed a collaborative strategic agreement with Compaq to help wi
redeployment of its client/server loan-processing system in a remote Web-based pr
cessing environment. The goal is to simplify and streamline the current process, whic
entails bringing all the Microsoft SQL server applications and equipment, located
the lender's offices, inside ALLTEL's computer room, where the process can be sta
dardized on Compaq ProLiant and Compaq Alpha-based servers. The change w
facilitate quick and cost-effective maintenance. Customers will be able to connect
ALLTEL's InterChange application across a Wide Area Network, as though th
servers were still local to the lender's facility.

"As our business continues to grow, Compaq is helping us extend our existi
platform to address the Internet," emphasizes Lee. "As Internet opportunities cor
up, we don't have to go out and build a new platform to address the Internet. We'
leveraging the investment that we began making in 1993, without a fundamental rei
vestment. Our new Internet focus is just taking our existing business and using the ne
work to fundamentally change the way we deliver that business.

# LEXIS-NEXIS—INFORMATION AT THE
# WORLD'S FINGERTIPS . . . . . . . . . . . . . . . . . . . . .

One of the biggest challenges for any company, new or established, is the storage
information, and having an infrastructure that makes that information instantly acce
sible. Since the Internet, by its nature, gives new meaning to the word "expansive
companies in the information business need undreamed of storage and retrieval capa
ity if they are going to operate successfully in an Internet environment.

But where does a company go for an Internet state-of-the-art infrastructure to me
its clients needs? And even if a company finds a partner to help, can that partner wc
quickly enough to give the company instant advantage? The question is a critical one
an e-commerce environment, where speed is the lifeblood of the digital economy.

The Lexis-Nexis story is a story of an established company that is no slou
when it comes to the use of technology—but a company that knew it had to rea
beyond its organizational structure to keep ahead of some of its upstart competitor

It's hard to walk into the Lexis-Nexis 65,000-square-foot data center near Dayton, Ohio, and not speak in superlatives. Lexis-Nexis' online data repository is big. Really big.

"We offer six times the content of the Internet online at any given time," contends Jeff Biggs, Senior Director of Commercial Internet Services at Lexis-Nexis. In fact, inside the information company's data center are nearly two billion documents, spread across 8,600 databases.

The vast data repository grows at the rate of about four-and-a-half million documents a week, providing one-million-and-a-half professionals—attorneys, journalists, accountants, law enforcement officials, and academicians—with the specialized research data they need to do their jobs.

## Creating an Internet Niche

Despite its scale, the company—which for 25 years has been charging subscribers for access to all this information—is feeling the impact of the Internet. "We've been at the top of the information pyramid for a long time. But we saw our business dramatically change with the rise of the Internet," says Biggs. "With the Web, almost anybody with a computer, a modem, and a database can become an information publisher and provider."

Not only does the Internet enable smaller competitors to dream of nibbling away at segments of Lexis-Nexis' customer base, the availability of free information on the Web prompted Lexis-Nexis to find new ways to add value to its subscription service.

Lexis-Nexis responded to the Internet challenge by capitalizing on its open technology. In mid-1997, the company rolled out a new Web-based interface—powered by Compaq ProLiant servers and Microsoft Windows NT 4.0 applications—that transformed the way subscribers retrieved information. "Our customers are willing to pay for premium content, but the navigational experience is of prime importance to them," says Eugene Pierce, Chief Technology Officer for Lexis-Nexis.

For years, explains Biggs, subscribers used proprietary software that allowed them to dial-up and use a search engine to get information processed through the company's powerful MVS mainframe system. "Although the basic customer-interface software served our customers well over the years, we wanted to present our customers with a more friendly navigation experience—similar to what they were used to on the Web," says Biggs.

Another key requirement of the new front-end system was its ability to bridge the heterogeneous Lexis-Nexis IT architecture. "On the back-end, we have a mainframe environment, which has our search engine. In the middle, we have what we call a transaction administration environment that houses our UNIX® systems and processes queries. The front-end houses our Web servers. There needs to be interoperability among all three systems," Biggs explains.

Finding the right fit meant choosing between two distinctly different Web ser
er platforms: Netscape®, running on UNIX servers, and a Windows NT-based syste
running on Compaq ProLiant servers. "We did extensive testing and analysis, a
when we considered things like price-performance, cost-to-support, and the ramific
tions of a long-term partnership, we determined that Compaq and Microsoft provid
the best possible advantages in leveraging the Internet market," remembers Biggs.

"Microsoft was an easy choice: You only have to tour the MSN (Microsc
Network) or IT Group data centers to see that Microsoft understands how a very lar
corporate infrastructure can deliver a product to the Web. And we already had mad
corporate-wide strategic decision to use Microsoft SQL for database applications,
we were able to leverage our investment in Microsoft SQL with the new Microsoft a
Compaq platform."

## A Clear Compaq and Microsoft Message

"We didn't have any previous experience with Compaq, but when we toured the MS
and ITG data centers, we saw nothing but racks and racks of Compaq servers—mc
than a thousand of them. It certainly sent a clear message that Compaq and Micros
are closely aligned, and that they leverage and exploit each other's technology," sa
Biggs. The Lexis-Nexis front-end platform—which was launched in mid-1997 a
fully deployed by late 1998—integrates several Microsoft applications, includi
Internet Information Server 4.0, Site Server 3.0, Transaction Server 4.0 and Syste
Management Server 1.2.

The applications run on approximately 200 Compaq ProLiant servers. Repo
Biggs, "In our production environment associated with the Web front-end, we
ProLiant 1600 servers to host the Web environment. The back-end servers—where
have Microsoft SQL applications and membership, and things like that—are hosted
ProLiant 6500 servers. They provide us both the capacity within the server and
scale across many servers to meet our needs."

## Solutions at Internet Speeds

"The deployment went smoothly, " Biggs adds. "The systems are almost turnkey, and the support from both Microsoft and Compaq was superb. We were able to leverage Microsoft's Premier support infrastructure so that we had one-to-one relationships between our Microsoft SQL database analysts and their Microsoft SQL experts, between our IIS experts here and their IIS experts. The Compaq engineers, too, were extremely fluent in technocrat problems."

Kurt Walk, manager of Windows NT Systems at Lexis-Nexis, and the person responsible for managing the company's websites, agrees that support from the two partners was instrumental. "There's definitely an advantage with the Compaq and Microsoft relationship and that's most noticeable when we get a server in, get the basic operating system loaded on it, get other applications loaded on top of that, and basically get our products as fast as possible to market."

Perhaps most importantly, subscribers seem to embrace the more friendly Web interface. "We're seeing more and more users go to the Web," says Biggs. "Our subscribers are professionals like lawyers and journalists who don't hesitate to give us feedback, and we're getting good reactions from them."

## Internet-driven Opportunities

"This is a good time to be in the IT business," says Biggs, "because the technology advances we're seeing today seem to be outpacing the problems we're encountering. We're getting new hardware and new technology delivered by Compaq and Microsoft that help us push the performance envelope so that we can, in turn, deliver more product in a shorter period of time."

Pierce believes that the Internet will be the venue for building on the momentum Biggs describes. "The IT business in the future is going to be one of leveraging architecture to provide the best total cost of ownership," predicts Pierce. "I see thin clients and big, fat servers providing high-end value, but total low cost of ownership. And over time, almost every function within a business will become, effectively, an electronic commerce function. "If you're not doing business using Web-based technology," Pierce states emphatically, "you're probably not going to be doing business at all."

# Epilogue

The Internet has leveled the playing field for start-ups and has opened up new markets for established companies. While the former implement new business models, the latter need to destroy current business models in favor of new ones that demonstrate a totally new economic value. That new value consists of the combined economic resources of an enterprise, its impact on a virtual network of collaborators—such as suppliers and distributors—and its ability to serve customers, attract new partners and win in the digital economy. The old brick-and-mortar measurements—percentage of gross margins and tangible assets—are no longer sufficient to establish value.

As we enter the second phase, or early maturation stage, of the Internet, winners of the first phase are scrambling to protect their new positions. Others, who have been eliminated or "disintermediated" from traditional supply chains, are struggling to play catch-up.

## INCREASED PROFITABILITY A REALISTIC EXPECTATION?

That's the question on the minds of business executives who have just come out from under the Y2K crunch and must now rationalize their competitive strategies for e-business. These executives are being bounced between a state of anxiety on the one hand and skepticism on the other. The urgency of being on the Web keeps them awake at night, but their doubts about hard payback sharpen the dilemma. What should they do?

In the first place, they should remember that e-business implementations can be complex and full of hidden costs and risks. Companies must ensure high-level executive commitment and direction before heading down the path to a full-blown strategy. We have suggested a number of issues that must be addressed as part of formulating a business/IT plan. Some of these involve the threat of competition, the scope of resources and expertise required for success, and the specific needs that an e-business plan must fulfill.

Experts also point to issues that arise out of the need to bridge from existing processes and models to new ones demanded by the e-business paradigm. Will the organization be able to accommodate changes without falling prey to concealed weaknesses in the business structure, steep learning curves, skill gaps, IT compatibility issues, and the competitive threats of the new economy?

Lastly, as the Gartner Group points out, the overwhelming question always is this: Can the Internet create sustainable shareholder value by increasing profits, accelerating growth, reducing time-to-market for products and services, improving customer service, or improving the public perception of our company? (*Executive Edge* July/Sept. 1999, p.10).

# WINNERS AND LOSERS

The winners in the new economy will be constantly planning, sizing up the environment, and quickly making changes to stay ahead of the competition. There is no turning back, and there are no guarantees of success.

As you and the enterprises you are part of move forward in this new century, there are several thoughts we would like to re-emphasize in closing:

**Competition will intensify**, no matter what industry you are in. It will escalate with each new technological advance, spawning new and bolder competitors. The companies now dominating e-business, for example, have a take-no-prisoners mentality and are driving down prices dramatically at every stage of the supplier and distribution chain. They are gaining at the considerable expense of laggards.

**Businesses can grow at dizzying speeds because of outsourcing**. Those succeeding in the digital economy are able to outsource everything that does not represent a core competency. Their operating costs are lowered by an estimated 10 to 30%, helping them to stay focused on their primary mission. What's more, these enterprises are positioned to access newly emerging technologies, applications, and services. At Compaq, this is called FutureSourcing—an expanded relationship with customers that helps them meet their present and future needs.

**Customers are rulers, not subjects**. Because of the new online marketplace, the balance of power has shifted from manufacturers and retailers to customers

Customers have more choices than ever, have raised expectations with each new Internet-related technology application, and are demanding that more businesses custom-tailor products and services to meet their individual needs—mass customization.

**Leading with actions, not words, CEOs must integrate IT with business processes**. In a recent poll by Booz-Allen & Hamilton, nine out of 10 CEOs surveyed agreed that the Internet is re-shaping the global marketplace. But only four out of 10 had already implemented an e-business plan. Success in the digital economy calls for IT operations to be fully integrated with business processes. If IT is not integrated, an enterprise will not have the infrastructure to support the company's online direction. Integrating IT and business strategic planning will reduce planning cycle time, improve the quality of competitive solutions, and create best-in-class business processes. In addition, the whole company—from the CEO down—has to be actively involved in leading the company forward, using Internet technology consistently. This is the only way to understand the Internet's strengths, weaknesses and possibilities. If you look at some of the early successes—Cisco, Dell, Amazon, eBay, Charles Schwab, E*Trade, Gardens.com, Autobytel and others—you will see that the CEOs were the drivers of change.

**Branding and connecting are keys to Internet success**. Trust is still the determining factor in a customer doing business with any enterprise. A recognized name and outstanding service are basic requirements for customer retention and loyalty. However, more is needed in online transactions—namely, connecting. For that, an enterprise needs a website that is easy to use and delivers information, services, and access to relevant links. One measure of the site's effectiveness is how often, and for how long, users visit the site. According to a recent survey by Media Metrix, for example, eBay ranked first, with its average user spending more than two hours a month visiting its site. E*Trade was second, with users averaging a little over an hour per month.

# XECUTE, CHECK, FIX AND PLAN

The velocity of change in the digital economy is lightning fast. We've not seen anything like this at any other time in history. To succeed, an enterprise must move quickly—and must be prepared to make changes as conditions in the market change. After listening to presentations by Michael Dell and John Chambers, AlliedSignal CEO Larry Bossidy instructed his management team to come up with a plan within two months that would establish them in the new world of the Internet—before they were outdone by the Dell equivalents in his industry. His team delivered and AlliedSignal continues to adapt successfully to market changes.

This is the kind of commitment and can-do spirit that is required for a company to establish a beachhead from which it can grow its own online presence. This is the kind of IT leadership that companies are seeking. Companies are looking for IT leaders who, besides bringing technology know-how to the mix, also have business savv strong communication skills, and—perhaps most important—the ability to wield IT a a competitive weapon.

Clearly, there is a need for e-business approaches that ensure a payback in th near-term. That in turn "throws down the gauntlet" to vendors, challenging them reduce time-to-solution, and to lower implementation risks. An innovative approac like Compaq NonStop e-business, blends services, adaptive architecture, and layere solutions to take the time, cost, and risk out of e-business deployments. A business th finds a reliable way to stay open and available 24/7 for its customers is going to ahead of the game.

# COLLABORATIVE E-COMMERCE

But this is just the beginning. A world much larger than today's e-business is on th horizon, and it promises to dwarf the already staggering growth in Internet applic tions. Newly emerging online marketplaces have forced The Gartner Group and ot ers to radically revise their estimates of the total dollar value of e-commerce in t near future. The Gartner Group's forecast of business-to-business (B2B) commerce more than $7 trillion in 2004 is based in part on what they call the new "e-market ma ers," the key catalysts who will drive nearly 40% of the total B2B e-commerce trar actions.

Who are these key catalysts? They are the new providers that are forming e-hu to serve business and consumers. They are establishing online marketplaces of end mous scale and adopting collaborative e-commerce practices. As Figure E.1 show many players are involved in the formation of this new trading environment:

- Consumer hubs (Amazon, eBay, Buy.com, Priceline)
- Value networks that provide Internet access, e-mail, knowledge sharing
- B2B hubs that create online exchanges (PlasticsNet.com, SciQuest.com, eSteel)
- Business service providers (banking, insurance, healthcare, transportation) that cater to outsourcing firms via the Internet
- IT service providers that guarantee end-to-end support for a company's applications, networks, or storage on a global basis.

On the B2B side of collaborative e-commerce, Ford, General Motors a DaimlerChrysler plan to build an e-marketplace for auto parts, raw materials, a components. The Big Three auto makers describe the company they are creating operate this B2B exchange as the "world's largest Internet-based virtual marketplac Other industries are moving at lightning speed to set up their own e-marketplaces. J

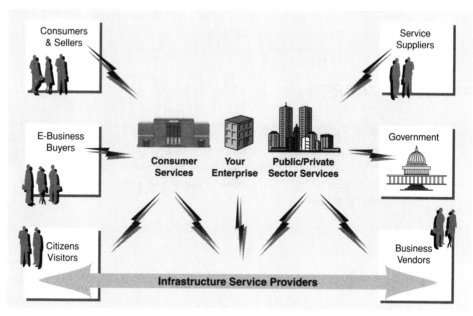

**Figure E.1**

Collaborative Commerce Scenario

a few of the industries to announce such collaboration in the first few weeks of 2000 include telecommunications, energy, trucking, chemicals, and pharmaceuticals.

B2B hubs represent the most powerful change agent on the Internet. They promote just-in-time pricing, services, and product-all at Internet speed. NonstopRx.com is one of the many examples of collaborative e-commerce launched in 2000. NonstopRx.com is an online marketplace for wholesalers and retailers in the pharmaceutical industry. The website is designed to allow wholesalers' and retailers' purchasing systems to interface directly with manufacturers. What makes NonstopRx.com different from other e-marketplaces is its focus on replenishment inventory, instead of goods that are used directly by consumers. NonstopRx.com officials say that their optimization software—which can help members determine the right number, mix, and price of products to maximize sales—will increase members' revenue.

The next generation of collaborative e-businesses will emerge from the innovation of aggressive business people, who will combine business-to-consumer (B2C) and B2B e-hubs based on a new business model and consumers needs. They will be the new pioneers in bringing together buyers and sellers in ever-expanding global communities—thus creating new value and offerings for customers. The explosion of collaborative e-commerce is now driving the need for 24/7 adaptive e-business infras-

tructures. It is also driving the need for innovative, flexible business models and a ne
generation of business thinking.

## A FINAL WORD

With the advance of Internet technology and its many applications, someone is alwa
ready to supplant your enterprise in the marketplace. Developing and seizing ne
opportunities, accessing the latest and most effective technologies, and integrati
your IT and business processes are keys—perhaps the only keys—to success in t
digital economy.

# Glossary

........................

**tiveAnswers**

An online knowledge center available from Compaq via the Internet that enables customers, VARs, and resellers to plan, deploy, and operate e-business systems on Compaq platforms thereby ensuring reduced risk and faster time to success.

**plication Service Provider (ASP)**

An organization that hosts software applications on its own servers within its own facilities. Customers access the application via private lines or the Internet. Also called a "commercial service provider." With the advent of the Web browser as the universal client interface, the ASP market is expected to grow rapidly.

**ray**

An ordered arrangement of data elements. A vector is a one-dimensional array; a matrix is a two-dimensional array. Most programming languages have the ability to store and manipulate arrays in one or more dimensions. Multi-dimensional arrays are used extensively in scientific simulation and mathematical processing; however, an array can be as simple as a pricing table held in memory for instant access by an order entry program.

**ailability**

The ability to continuously deliver accurate business services as measured by the customer of those services. It is important to note that availability is defined by the perception of the person interacting with a system as part of the business process. For example, an electronic storefront that cannot take orders during a database backup would not be available, despite the continued operations of the systems; one that could take orders, even if parts of the system are not functioning would be available.

**ckbone**

A centralized high-speed network that connects smaller, independent networks.

**ndwidth**

The capacity of a transmission medium. Stated in bits per second or as a frequency.

**olean Data**

Yes/no or true/false data.

**siness Intelligence (BI)**

The use of information produced by and captured within business processes to enhance the operations of the business process. BI describes the enterprise's ability to access and explore information (often contained in a data warehouse) and to analyze that information to develop insights and understanding, which leads to improved and informed decision-making.

**te**

Eight consecutive bits. Often interpreted as a character in the ASCII character code.

**che**

An intermediate storage location that keeps a copy of information from the Web that has already been seen. Caching prevents the Web browser from having to fetch frequently viewed data over the network repeatedly. Caching reduces network traffic and makes accessing pages faster.

**ll Center**

A company department that handles telephone sales and service. Call centers use automatic call distributors (ACDs) to route calls to the appropriate agent or operator.

**ient**

A system or process that requests a service from another system or process, called a server. Internet clients can be enabled on most workstations, terminals, and PCs.

**227**

Software includes Web browsers, Internet-enabled applications, Internet clie applications, utilities, and more.

**Collaboration**
The pooling of knowledge and resources to make better choices to achieve con mon goals and objectives. In a practical sense, collaboration can be described the ability of two or more people or groups to transfer data and information wi the capability of online interaction. The distinguishing feature is the ability f many-to-many interactions and information sharing, unlike e-mail where t interaction is one-to-one or one-to-many. Think of collaboration as a critical pie of infrastructure for enabling Knowledge Management.

**Connectivity**
Generally, connectivity refers to communications networks or the act of comm nicating between computers and terminals. Specifically, the term refers to devic such as bridges, routers, and gateways that link networks together.

**Continuous Operations**
The ability of a system or process to perform required tasks without interruptic Systems that have this capability can be said to be 24/7 or "always or Continuous in this context is defined by the requirements on the business proce that the system supports. It can apply to levels of service, not only time as the ter implies. For example, a business process may require that no data is ever lost corrupted while the system functions but does not necessarily need to be availab all the time. So, as long as the system does not lose data during its operations, t system is continuous.

**Customer Relationship Management (CRM)**
Customer Relationship Management comprises a set of business processes a enabling systems that support a business strategy to build long-term, profitab relationships with specific customers. The key objective of CRM is to expand t business by attracting new customers, retaining existing customers, and optimi ing the share of each customer's business. This growth objective is achieved profitably enhancing the customer value exchange through better understandi of individual needs and preferences.

**Daemon**
A program that is not invoked explicitly, but lies dormant, waiting for some co dition or conditions to occur. Daemons can perform various management task such as starting and stopping a client or server process, managing access to fi or printers, caching Web pages for later access, or serving as a firewall that allo internal users access to external Web pages. UNIX systems use daemons servers.

**Data Mart**
A store of relational data that usually supports a single business process (for exar ple, database marketing). This data is stored in a structure designed for analy (often a variant of a star structure).

**Data Mining**
Applying sophisticated algorithms to the data (data mart or warehouse) to iden fy patterns in the data.

**Data Warehouse**
A central repository of data that includes data from multiple source systems a supports multiple organizations. This data is stored in a structure designed analysis (often a variant of a star structure).

**Digital**
A device or method that uses discrete variations in voltage, frequency, amplitu and location to encode, process, or carry binary (zero or one) signals for sou video, computer data or other information. When analog signals are received a amplified at each repeater station, any noise is also amplified. Analog signals pic up noise from the equipment (thermal noise from an amplifier circuit) and wires.

|  | digital signal, however, is detected and regenerated (not amplified). Unlike amplification, any noise (less than a valid signal) is eliminated by digital regeneration. |

**E-Commerce**
The conducting of business communication and transactions over networks and through computers.

**Electronic Data Interchange (EDI)**
A service that enables multiple disparate business applications to work together to handle business transactions both within an enterprise and between enterprises.

**Encryption**
The process of scrambling a message so others cannot read it without a key. Encryption ensures users privacy when sending messages and enables users to verify the identity of a sender of a message.

**End User**
A person who uses products and services, such as a paying customer. Users are usually people, but can also be computers, objects, switches or other types of computer systems or communication equipment.

**Enterprise Applications (EA)**
Application software that is fundamental to the business, but not necessarily industry-specific. Enterprise applications are generally "horizontal" in nature; that is, they apply and are used by many different industries.

**Enterprise Resource Planning (ERP)**
An integrated information system that serves all departments within an enterprise. Evolving out of the manufacturing industry, ERP implies the use of packaged software rather than proprietary software written by or for one customer. ERP modules may be able to interface with an organization's own software with varying degrees of effort, and, depending on the software, ERP modules may be alterable via the vendor's proprietary tools as well as proprietary or standard programming languages.

**Extranet**
Extended intranets that connect not only internal personnel, but select customers, suppliers, and strategic partners. In both intranets and extranets, it is critical to be able to create high-quality interaction while ensuring confidentiality, security, and controlled access.

**Firewall**
A computer or router that protects private systems from encroachment. A firewall permits greater access from one side of a network link than from the other. Firewall technology is important for commercial operations that need to protect proprietary information while allowing internal users access to remote services outside the firewall. A firewall limits the number of gateways between the network and the outside world through which information packets can travel. These gateways restrict the types of accesses to a defined set of users or nodes.

**FTP**
File Transfer Protocol. A TCP/IP utility that lets users copy files from remote computers that support TCP/IP to their PC. If the user clicks on a hotspot whose URL specifies a file on an FTP server, the FTP server downloads that file to its PC. FTP does not handle data conversions. A very large amount of information is available through anonymous FTP, a variant of FTP where a set of files is made available for public access.

**Gateways**
A computer or router that forwards and routes data between two or more networks that have different protocols. For example, a mail gateway enables users who have only mail access to get files from the Web.

**Global Value Chain (GVC)**
Global Value Chain enables organizational capability and efficiency through automating business processes and linking suppliers, partners, and customers together.

**HTML**
Hypertext Markup Language. Refers both to the HTML document type and th markup language for representing instances of the HTML document type. HTM is the source code used to create pages for viewing in a Web browser's windov HTML allows for the creation of hyperlinks and specifies the formatting of th document (paragraphs, lists, titles, and so on). HTML source files have an .htr .html, .htl, or .hml file extension. HTML is based on the Standard Generic Marku Language (SGML) standard.

**HTTP**
Hypertext Transport Protocol. The principal protocol used to transfer documen and data on the Web. Also a search and retrieval protocol for use on the Worl Wide Web. HTTP is designed to operate in a client-server mode whereby th client submits a document request in the form of a line of ASCII characters. Th response is a message in HTML. HTTP is defined by an Internet request for con ments (RFC) that describes the interaction between the Web browser and th HTTP servers and daemons.

**Hyperlink**
A text or graphical pointer to information or to a service possibly located on anotl er computer. Clicking on a hyperlink with a mouse pointer lets you access th information or service where it is pointing. By default, hyperlinks usually appe highlighted in color, with recently used hyperlinks highlighted in a different colc

**Information Technology (IT)**
The organization within the enterprise responsible for its computer systems ope ation. (Also referred to as information systems or computer and programmir departments.)

**Infrastructure**
Entities, concepts, and processes that support and enhance the operation of a sy tem or subsystem. Infrastructure is almost always defined in a specific context, : the infrastructure for one system or subsystem may be the internal architecture a larger system. See Public Infrastructure and Private Infrastructure.

**Internet**
A worldwide collection of computers that communicate through a set of open sof ware protocols. World Wide Web software runs on the Internet and provides use with easy access to information and services through a Web browser. See al Intranet.

**Internet Service Provider (ISP)**
Internet Service Provider. A company that provides local connection services f users to the Internet. These services include a local phone number to call (or high-speed leased line) and an IP address to use. An ISP might also provide equi ment and services, such as electronic mail. ISPs use NSPs to access other ISF Also known as an Internet Access Provider (IAP).

**Intranet**
A private network inside a company or organization. The Intranet uses the san kinds of technologies used on the public Internet, but it is for internal use only. Th Intranet is usually protected from the Internet with a firewall.

**Java**
An object-oriented programming language created by Sun Microsystems th enables content providers to create application software that can run on a We browser.

**Knowledge Management**
A discipline that promotes an integrated approach to the creation, capture, orgai zation, access, and use of an enterprise's information assets. These informati assets may include databases, documents, policies and procedures, as well as t uncaptured tacit expertise and experience resident in individual workers.

| | |
|---|---|
| **LAN** | Local Area Network. A private data communications system that covers a limited geographical area, such as a section of a building, an entire building, or a group of buildings. |
| **Legacy System** | System used to run the mission-critical applications of the enterprise. |
| **Lynx** | A text-mode Web browser developed at the University of Kansas. It enables users to access the Web from character-cell terminals or from PCs that do not have SLIP access to the Internet. Lynx cannot display graphics and has only limited support for forms. |
| **Mainframe** | A very large and expensive computer capable of supporting hundreds, or even thousands, of users simultaneously. In the hierarchy that starts with a simple microprocessor (in watches, for example) at the bottom and moves to supercomputers at the top, mainframes are just below supercomputers. In some ways, mainframes are more powerful than supercomputers because they support more simultaneous programs. But supercomputers can execute a single program faster than a mainframe. The distinction between small mainframes and minicomputers is vague, depending really on how the manufacturer wants to market its machines. |
| **Manageability** | The ability to monitor operational metrics, such as performance, and proactively ensure continuous operations. To be manageable, a system must be capable of measuring that which occurs within it and have processes or tools to allow for the prevention or correction of situations that would lead to an interruption of service. |
| **Messaging** | Messaging is the electronic infrastructure upon which e-mail and other applications can reside. E-mail, along with scheduling, workflow, voice, and fax, uses the messaging infrastructure for delivery. Using a paper analogy, think of e-mail as the letter and messaging as the postal service that ensures it is delivered to the right person. |
| **Middleware** | See Processsware. |
| **Mirror Site** | A website that contains a complete copy of the contents of another website. You can use a mirror site to reduce load on a popular site, to enable access to a website that is otherwise restricted by a firewall, or to distribute sites geographically for better access. |
| **Mosaic** | A mouse-driven Web browser interface to the World Wide Web developed by the NCSA. Mosaic integrates the ability to retrieve, search, and store information using a wide variety of methods and protocols. Mosaic was developed by the National Center for Supercomputing Applications at the University of Illinois and is recognized for popularizing the use of the Web. |
| **MP3** | Motion Picture Experts, Group-1, Layer 3. |
| **Network** | Two or more computers linked together physically or via telecommunications for the purpose of electronically sharing resources such as computer files, programs, peripheral devices, and either centralized or distributed services. |
| **Network Service Provider (NSP)** | An NSP is a company that provides access to the Internet backbone and enables ISPs to connect to each other. |
| **NonStop™** | NonStop™ is a registered trademark of Compaq Computer Corporation. It is defined as the ability to be "always on." This ability encompasses availability, scalability, manageability, and security. |
| **NonStop™ Platform** | NonStop™ Platform is a Compaq Computer Corporation definition for the com- |

bination of hardware, hardware support utilities, operating system software, pr
cessware, application software, application support utilities, system support uti
ties, and services organized and integrated as a unit, such that the whole operat
in a Nonstop™ manner.

**Packet**  
A group of bytes sent from one Internet host to another host. Packets can conta
any kind of information.

**Platform**  
The underlying hardware or software for a system. The platform defines a sta
dard around which a system can be developed. Once the platform has be
defined, software developers can produce appropriate software and managers c
purchase appropriate hardware and applications. The term is often used as a sy
onym for operating system.

**Portal**  
A website or service that offers a broad array of resources and services, such as
mail, forums, search engines, and online shopping malls. The first Web port
were online services that provided access to the Web, but by now most of the t
ditional search engines have transformed themselves into Web portals to attr
and keep a larger audience.

**Private Infrastructure**  
The infrastructure internal and proprietary to the enterprise. LAN, WAN, and te
phone switching systems are examples of private infrastructure components.

**Processware**  
Software that provides cross-application business process functionality that co
plements underlying applications—essentially, the necessary business process
that get disparate applications to function as an integrated suite. Synonymous w
middleware.

**Protocol**  
Very specific rules/standards for information transmission. A formal set of cc
ventions governing the format and control of inputs and outputs between tv
communicating entities.

**Public Infrastructure**  
The infrastructure external to the enterprise and generally available to the pu
lic. The telephone system, utilities, and the Internet are part of the public inf
structure.

**Query**  
A search request on a database to locate one or more pieces of informati
(records) that meet selected criteria.

**Queuing**  
The act of "stacking" or holding calls to be answered by a specific person, tru
or trunk group.

**Realtime**  
Refers to use of a computer or device where responses to inputs return with
perceptible delay.

**Router**  
A dedicated computer, or other device, that determines the path that Internet tr
fic takes to reach its destination. A router can also filter network packets to rest
traffic in or out of its local network.

**Scalability**  
The ability to meet the dynamic capacity requirements of the business proc
without the interruption of services or operations. Thus, a system that is capa
of handling increased workloads (system performance being the measure) wi
out alteration of the business process would be considered scalable. Scalabi
encompasses both planned, linear growth and unplanned, explosive growth.

**Security**  
The ability to authorize and authenticate any individual or business system to c
duct business with any other individual or business system. Security encompa
es accountability and data integrity.

| | |
|---|---|
| Solution | An information system and its effective deployment into an operational environment to solve a business problem or address a business opportunity. The scope of a solution varies with the scope of the problem or opportunity. Solutions may themselves be a part of other solutions with "larger" scope. |
| Smart Cards | Plastic cards incorporating embedded microchips. Smart Cards allow the easy transportation and physical security of data and processing capability. Smart Cards may act as unique digital identification cards, electronic wallets for digital money, authentication key storage, and processing. |
| SMTP | Simple Mail Transport Protocol. An application-layer protocol that provides electronic mail services in an IP network. The Internet uses SMTP to transfer electronic mail. |
| SNMP | Simple Network Management Protocol. An application-layer protocol that provides network management control and monitoring services in an IP network. |
| System | A collection of components organized and integrated to accomplish a function or a specific set of functions. The scope of a system varies with the context in which it is placed. Systems may be subsystems within other systems of larger scope. The smallest piece of a system is a component. |
| TCP/IP | Transmission Control Protocol/Internet Protocol. A set of protocols developed to allow cooperating computers with different architectures and operating systems to share resources across a network. Any real application will use several of these protocols. Information is transferred in packets, which are sent through the network individually. |
| Throughput | The end result of data transmission (for a given period of time). It is a measure of the overall efficiency, quality and performance of a communications link and its software protocols. |
| URL | Uniform Resource Locator. A URL is a pointer to any resource accessible on the World Wide Web, such as another website, an image file, document, gopher object, or news archive. The URL allows a Web browser to find a resource across the network. The URL contains the access method (such as HTTP), the host name, and the path to the resource in the following format: access_method://host[:port]/-path/filename. |
| Value Added Networks (VAN) | A traditional network used for EDI or other electronic commerce. VAN access can be through a private line, closed line, leased line, or dial-up access. |
| VRML | Virtual Reality Modeling Language. |
| XML | Extensible Markup Language. The universal format for data on the Web. XML lets developers easily describe and deliver rich, structured data from any application in a standard, consistent way. XML does not replace HTML, but complements it. |
| Wallet | Bit of consumer software that contains enough information (usually in the form of certificates) to conduct commerce across the Internet. |
| WAN | Wide Area Network. A public or private data communications system that covers a wide geographical area and transmits data primarily over telephone lines. |
| Web | A client-server application that works over a wide area network (WAN) and is capable of tying together many different clients and servers from diverse loca- |

tions. The Web puts hypertext, multimedia, and wide area networking together
that the network is almost transparent.

**Web Browser**

Client software used to view the many kinds of information on the Web, such
HTML documents, Gopher pages, and FTP directories. The Web browser unde
stands how to interpret the hypertext links and makes the appropriate netwo
connections and requests to servers. The Web browser is responsible for navig
tion and may cache retrieved information so that subsequent retrievals of pag
are very quick. The Web browser also launches helper applications, where poss
ble, to interpret or display data types it cannot deal with directly. Netsca
Navigator is the most popular Web browser today, followed in popularity
NCSA Mosaic. Other browsers include Cello and Lynx. Also known as an HTM
browser or client.

**Website**

A collection of Web content or application(s), which are typically identified by
single home page and managed as a single entity.

**World Wide Web**

A distributed, multimedia network of hypertext documents. The World Wide W
consists of a series of hotspots that connect one piece of information or service
another across the Internet. Also known as WWW or W3.

**Zero-Latency**

Coined by the Gartner Group, zero latency is the immediate exchange of infc
mation across geographical, technical, and organizational boundaries so that
departments, customers, and related parties can work together in realtime.

# Bibliography

Adam, Nabil R., (ed.), et al., *Electronic Commerce: Technical, Business and Legal Issues*, Prentice Hall, 1998.

Bayne, Kim M., *Internet Marketing Plan*, John Wiley & Sons, 1999.

Bloomberg.com/News, Bloomberg Press, April 1999.

Brady, Regina, Forrest, Edward, and Mizerski, Richard, *CyberMarketing*, Ntc Business Books, 1997.

Cameron, Debra, *Electronic Commerce: The New Business Platform for the Internet*, Computer Technology Research Corporation, 1997.

Cashin, Jerry, *E-Commerce Success: Building a Global Business Architecture*, Computer Technology Research Corporation, 1999.

Cohen, Peter S., *Net Profit*, Jossey-Bass Publishers, 1999.

Davis, Stan, and Meyer, Christopher, *Blur: The Speed of Change in the Connected Economy*, Addison-Wesley, 1997.

Dell, Michael, *Direct from Dell*, Harperbusiness, 1999.

"The net imperative," economist.com, The Economist Newspaper Limited, June 26, 1999.

GartnerGroup Research Notes, "Outflank the Competition by Deploying IT to Build a Zero-Latency Enterprise," August 19, 1998.

Gates, Bill, *Business @ the Speed of Thought: Using a Digital Nervous System*, Warner Books, 1999.

Geilgun, Ron E., *One Business, Two Approaches: How to Succeed in Internet Business by Employing Real-World Strategies*, Actium Publishing, 1998.

Gibson, Rowan, (ed.), Brealey, Nicholas, *Rethinking the Future*, 1999.

Gillette, Frank E., with Ted Schadler, Ben Worthen, Amanda J. Clardelli, Stephenie Smith, "Building A Commerce API," *The Forrester Research Report*, Forrester Research, Inc., August 1999.

Grove, Andrew S., *Only the Paranoid Survive*, Bantam Books, 1999.

Hagel III, John, and Armstrong, Arthur G., *Net Gain: Expanding Markets Through Virtual Communities*, McGraw-Hill, 1997.

Hagel III, John, *Net Worth: Shaping Markets When Customers Make the Rules*, Harvard Business School Publishing, 1999.

Hamel, Gary, and Prahalad, C.K, *Competing for the Future*, Harvard Business School Press, 1996.

Hammer, Michael, *Beyond Reengineering*, HarperCollins, 1997.

Hammer, Michael, and Champy, James, *Reengineering the Corporatio* Harperbusiness, 1994.

Haylock, Christina Ford, et al., *Net Success: 24 Leaders in Web Commerce Show Y* *How to Put the Web to Work for Your Business*, Adams Media Corporation, 199

Hoskins, Jim, and Lupiano, Vincent, *Exploring IBM's Bold Internet Strateg* Maximum Press, 1997.

Judson, Bruce, and Kelly, Kate, *HyperWars: Eleven Rules for Survival in the Era of O* *Line Business*, Simon & Schuster Trade, 1999.

Kalakota, Ravi, and Whinston, Andrew B., (contributor), *Electronic Commerce:* *Manager's Guide*, Addison-Wesley, 1996.

Kelly, Kevin, *New Rules for the New Economy: 10 Radical Strategies for a Connect* *World*, Viking Press, 1998.

Komenar, Margo, *Electronic Marketing*, John Wiley & Sons, 1996.

Kosiur, David R., *Understanding Electronic Commerce* (Strategy Technology Serie* Microsoft Press, 1997.

Kurtzman, Joel, (ed.), *Thought Leaders...Insights on the Future of Business*, Jossey-Ba* Publishers, 1998.

Lanning, Michael J., *Delivering Profitable Value*, Perseus Books, 1998.

Maddox, Kate, and Blankenhorn, Dana, *Web Commerce: Building a Digital Busine* (Wiley/Upside Series), John Wiley & Sons, 1998.

Maklan, Stan, and Knox, Simon, *Competing on Value*, Financial Time Managemei* 1998.

Martin, Chuck, *The Digital Estate: Strategies for Competing, Surviving and Thriving* *an Internetworked World*, McGraw-Hill, 1997.

Martin, Chuck, *Net Future: The 7 Cybertrends That Will Drive Your Business, Crec* *New Wealth, and Define Your Future*, McGraw-Hill, 1998.

McClaren, Bruce J., and McClaren, Constance H., *E-Commerce: Business on* *Internet*, Southwestern Publishing, 1999.

Meyer, N. Dean, and Boone, Mary E., *The Information Edge*, NDMA Publishing, 199

Moad, Jeff, "Getting Down to e-Business," PC Week Online, zdnet.com/pcwee* November 15, 1999.

Moore, James F., *The Death of Competition*, Harperbusiness, 1997.

Mougayar, Walid, *Opening Digital Markets: Battle Plans for Internet Commer* McGraw-Hill, 1997.

Pappows, Jeff, and Moschella, David, *Enterprise.com*, Perseus Books Group, 1998.

Peppers, Don, and Rogers, Martha, *Enterprise One to One*, Doubleday, 1999.

Peppers, Don, and Rogers, Martha, PhD., *The One to One Future: Buildi* *Relationships One Customer at a Time,* Bantam Doubleday Dell Publishers, 199

Peters, Thomas J., and Waterman Jr., Robert H., *In Search of Excellence*, Warner Books, 1988.

Pine II, B. Joseph, *Mass Customization*, Harvard Business School Press, 1992.

Romm (ed.), Celia T., and Sudweeks (ed.), Fay, *Doing Business Electronically: A Global Perspective of Electronic Commerce*, Springer Verlag Publishing, 1998.

Schutzer, Dan, *Electronic Commerce: The Wired Corporation*, AP Professional Publishing, 1999.

Schwartz, Evan I., *Webonomics*, Broadway Books, 1997.

Seybold, Patricia B., *Customers.com: How to Create a Profitable Business Strategy for the Internet and Beyond*, Times Books, 1998.

Siebel, Thomas M., et al., *Cyber Rules: Strategies for Excelling at E-Business*, Doubleday, 1999.

Siebel, Thomas, and Malone, Michael, *Virtual Selling*, Free Press, 1996.

Silverstein, Barry, *Business-to-Business Internet Marketing: Five Proven Strategies for Increasing Profits through Internet Direct Marketing*, Maximum Press, 1998.

Szuprowicz, Bohdan O., *E-Commerce: Implementing Global Marketing Strategies*, Computer Technology Research Corporation, 1999.

Tapscott, Don, *The Digital Economy: Promise and Peril in the Age of Networked Intelligence*, McGraw-Hill, 1997.

Temkin, Bruce, "Insurers Wake Up to the Net," *The Forrester Research Report*, Forrester Research, Inc., October 1998.

Thurow, Lester, "Building Wealth," Harper Collins, 1999.

Treacy, Michael, and Wiersema, Frederik D., *The Discipline of Market Leaders*, Perseus Press, 1997.

Treese, G. Winfield, and Stewart, Lawrence C., *Designing Systems for Internet Commerce*, Addison-Wesley, 1998.

Washburn, Harry, and Wallace, Kim, *Why People Don't Buy Things*, Perseus Books, 1998.

# Index